Liberating Sanctuary

Liberating Sanctuary

100 Years of Women's Education at the College of St. Catherine

Edited by Jane Lamm Carroll, Joanne Cavallaro, and Sharon Doherty

LEXINGTON BOOKS
Lanham • Boulder • New York • Toronto • Plymouth, UK

Published by Lexington Books
A wholly owned subsidiary of The Rowman & Littlefield Publishing Group, Inc.
4501 Forbes Boulevard, Suite 200, Lanham, Maryland 20706
www.lexingtonbooks.com

Estover Road, Plymouth PL6 7PY, United Kingdom

British Library Cataloguing in Publication Information Available

Library of Congress Cataloging-in-Publication Data

Liberating sanctuary : 100 years of women's education at the College of St.
    Catherine / edited by Jane Lamm Carroll, Joanne Cavallaro, and Sharon
    Doherty.
        p. cm.
    Includes bibliographical references and index.
    ISBN 978-0-7391-7090-8 (cloth : alk. paper) — ISBN 978-0-7391-7091-5
(electronic)
    1. College of St. Catherine—History. 2. St. Catherine University—History.
I. Carroll, Jane Lamm. II. Cavallaro, Joanne, 1948– III. Doherty, Sharon.
LD7165.L53 2012
378.776′581—dc23

                                                              2011035352

Printed in the United States of America

For
Sister Antonia McHugh and
the Sisters of St. Joseph of Carondelet, St. Paul Province,
Founders and Leaders of the College

Contents

Acknowledgments

First and foremost, we thank Sister Andrea J. Lee, IHM, President of St. Catherine University, who conceived the idea of this book. Sister Andrea asked us to design and produce a book of essays on the College's history from feminist perspectives—this book is the result.

Our charge was to create a history of the College using a collaborative process. Our first step was to create a design committee consisting of faculty and staff from across the College; alumnae; and Sisters of St. Joseph. This committee designed the analytical framework for the book and the process for soliciting and selecting essays from various constituencies associated with the College (faculty, staff, students, alumnae, former faculty and staff, Sisters of St. Joseph, and others). Those who served on that committee contributed much time and talent to this project: Cecilia Konchar Farr, Melissa Flicek, Lynne Gildensoph, Karen Kennelly, CSJ, Catherine Lupori, William McDonough, Ann Ward Miller, Joan Mitchell, CSJ, Patricia Perell, and Lenore Ramsdell. The selected authors then formed the writing committee, which also worked collaboratively to design the structure of the book and produce these historical essays.

The contributions of both these committees were instrumental in bringing this volume to fruition. It was a pleasure to work with them, learn from them, and see this book evolve through their work. Thank you all!

We would like to thank the College of Saint Catherine Centennial Steering Committee, especially Kay Bendel, Kathleen Daniels, and Stacy Jacobson, for all their support and for generously funding our writers' retreat.

Sister Margery Smith, St. Catherine University archivist, opened the archives for our work, including extra hours in the summer when the archives would not normally be open. We thank her for her generosity of time and advice. We also thank Carol Johnson, Director of Libraries, Media Services, and Archives, for her help in pulling together the photos included here. And we thank Sia Vang for putting up with so many meetings in her space—her gracious generosity is greatly appreciated.

Finally, we are grateful to our editor, Toma Mulligan, who strengthened the book and boosted our spirits with his writing skill, deep engagement with both ideas and language, and enthusiasm for the project. Thank you, Toma.

Introduction: Taking Catholic Women Seriously

Joanne Cavallaro, Sharon Doherty, and Jane Lamm Carroll

"She respected us too much to accept from us a standard lower than the highest."[1]

On the day after Christmas in 1904, 27 Sisters of St. Joseph of Carondelet trudged through a Midwestern snowstorm, in full habit, walking a mile from the nearest streetcar stop to the corner of Cleveland and Randolph Avenues, to prepare the site of their new college in St. Paul, Minnesota. In September 1905, the Sisters began teaching college courses to seven young women students. A century later, the College of St. Catherine, now St. Catherine University, is the largest college for women in the United States.[2]

In 1968, at the peak of their growth, 130 Catholic women's colleges were educating some 100,000 students in the United States.[3] Although today only 18 of those colleges remain, their legacy is indisputable. Typically built by Sisters of various religious orders, these colleges were led by women religious who were early proponents of increased opportunities for women and who served as role models for women's leadership and autonomy. Given the important role these colleges have played in educating women, the lack of attention to them by historians is surprising. Textbooks examining the history of American higher education usually ignore the role played by Catholic higher education for women, at most touching upon it only briefly.

One finds a similar lack of attention to these colleges in feminist studies of higher education. Indeed, historians and women's studies scholars alike have generally dismissed Catholic women's lives, particularly Catholic Sisters' lives, as having been uniform and limited, and therefore not historically significant or interesting. As Tracy Schier and Cynthia Russett

1

College of St. Catherine 1915 postcard of Derham Hall and College Hall (later renamed Whitby Hall). Photo courtesy of St. Catherine University.

note, this neglect has left a large gap in our understanding of the history of U.S. women's education. In *Catholic Women's Colleges in America*, they call for further research into "histories of individual colleges ... . [to fill] in the blanks of our knowledge," adding that "we need to know a lot more about the cultures of these schools."[4]

This book fills in some of those blanks in our knowledge by examining one of the Catholic colleges for women that has survived—and prospered—during an era when other women's colleges have closed or become coeducational. The College of St. Catherine[5] has been educating women, both Catholic and non-Catholic, for over 100 years. Its history illuminates how one institution managed to flourish despite the contradictions, tensions, and inconsistencies that often characterize Catholic colleges for women.

Why should this matter to us today? Historically, women's colleges have been liberating sanctuaries in which women have always been regarded and treated as full human beings. Even when females were assumed to be intellectually and physically incapable of rigorous education and were defined almost exclusively as wives and mothers, women's colleges created spaces that enabled their students and faculties to develop their own intellectual and social identities as women. Today, according to Tidball et al., "taking women seriously" remains the essential element that differentiates women's colleges from other institutions of higher learning, and the essential element that explains their success, then and now, in cultivating women leaders and high achievers.[6]

Over the last few decades, studies have shown that women's colleges foster leadership, self-esteem, self-confidence, and high achievement in their students and alumnae at a significantly higher rate than coeducational institutions.[7] A 1993 U.S. study revealed that, although only 6 percent of undergraduate students had attended women's colleges, the alumnae of those colleges were disproportionately represented as leaders in business, government, medicine, and science. Graduates of women's colleges were also much more likely to pursue doctorate degrees.[8] According to a 2001 survey conducted by the Women's College Coalition, 53 percent of women's college graduates completed advanced degrees, while women graduates of both coeducational liberal arts colleges and public universities were much less likely to do so, 38 percent and 28 percent, respectively.[9]

Catholic women's colleges in particular have had a powerful impact on their students' subsequent lives and work. In 1980, Abigail Quigley McCarthy, author and alumna of the College of St. Catherine, noted in a speech to Catholic educators that over half of the women then serving in Congress were graduates of Catholic colleges for women. These colleges, she said, were influential in creating women leaders because the students "had been given a sense in their colleges that the sky was the limit, that there was nothing they couldn't do. . . . They had strong role models, but they also learned by precept that the goal of life was service to others. . . . The combination of self-confidence and desire to serve . . . brought them where they are."[10] A recent study of the alumnae of Catholic women's colleges confirms McCarthy's analysis. For the majority of graduates in the study, their college experience had been highly influential in developing strong self-definitions, as well as in affirming the belief that women could do anything and do it well. Alumnae remembered their college culture as supportive of them becoming "strong, independent and highly achieving women."[11]

HISTORICAL CONTEXT: COMPROMISE AND CONSENSUS

A Catholic college for women might seem an anachronism today or, even worse, an oxymoron—on the one hand, affiliated with a Church that limits women's opportunities within its own hierarchy; on the other, inspired by a feminist tradition that asserts that women can do anything men can do. This oxymoronic quality is not new, however. Since their inception, Catholic women's colleges have served contradictory aims and purposes.

In order to understand these contradictory purposes, we need to examine them in historical context. When the College of St. Catherine was founded in 1905, higher education in the U.S. had recently gone through a period of rapid growth.[12] The first institution to provide college-level academic experience for girls and women was Mount Holyoke Academy, established in 1837. As higher education slowly developed and expanded during the second half of the nineteenth century, many female academies became colleges, and new women's colleges, including Wellesley, Vassar, and Smith, were founded. By the turn of the century, there were 150 women's colleges in the United States, including a few new Catholic women's colleges.[13]

The first Catholic institution chartered to offer a baccalaureate degree to women was St. Mary of the Woods, founded in 1840 in Indiana by the Sisters of Providence.[14] Over the next 70 years, and especially during the period from 1890 to 1910, Catholic women religious rapidly transformed their female academies into colleges or established new women's colleges. The Sisters of St. Joseph of Carondelet were among those who led the way, founding the College of St. Catherine in St. Paul, one of the first Catholic women's colleges in the nation, and establishing St. Mary's School of Nursing across the Mississippi River in Minneapolis.

The Sisters founded these institutions at a time of great change for both American Catholicism and women's roles. During much of the nineteenth century and early twentieth century, the dominant forces of American society were often actively anti-Catholic. At the same time, the Catholic population of the country was growing, and Catholics were becoming increasingly middle class and assimilating to a society dominated by Protestant culture.

The increasing upward mobility of Catholics and the pressures to assimilate led to questions about the most appropriate type of higher education for Catholics. This question of appropriateness was seen as important for both women and men, but much more so for women, who were considered the carriers of religion and culture to the next generation.

In reality, the marked increase in Catholic women's attendance at both secular and Protestant institutions of higher education alarmed some Catholics but delighted others. Conservatives feared that Catholic women would succumb to the "pernicious influence of Protestantism and secularism." Progressives, on the other hand, worried that large numbers of Catholic women did not or could not attend higher education at all. They felt that "the lack of higher education for women reflected poorly on the church, confirming allegations that the church was against progress."[15]

As Kathleen Mahoney notes, Catholic colleges for women grew out of a consensus reached in the late nineteenth and early twentieth centuries within the Catholic Church. Opening Catholic colleges for women served the purposes both of conservatives, because Catholic women pursuing a higher education would be able to maintain their religious identity, and of progressives, because Catholic women would be able to share in the expanding social roles becoming available to all women. The success of this compromise is evident in the astounding growth in the number of Catholic colleges for women during the late 1800s and early to mid-1900s: in 1884, there were 60 Catholic colleges and one Catholic university for men in the U.S—there were none for women. By 1905, there were 10 Catholic colleges for women; by 1928, well over 40; and by 1968, 170 Catholic women's two- and four-year colleges were educating more women than all non-Catholic colleges for women combined.[16]

The growth in Catholic women's colleges parallels a similar growth in women's colleges in general, both secular and denominational. As Thomas Landy points out, "Americans [during this period] were deeply ambivalent about the role of women in society, and the woman's college was a social institution tailored to that ambivalence."[17] This ambivalence was exacerbated in Catholic circles, for it called into question some fundamental ideas about natural law that underlay much of Church teaching, particularly Thomist views about the natural and unique functions of humans. Although Thomist teachings view every person as having inherent dignity that must be preserved, they define as "natural law" the idea that a woman's proper role is as mother and wife and women's natural function is reproduction. Since what is natural is, per se, good, then this unique function of women is a good that should be preserved. Offering higher education to women placed this "special nature" into jeopardy, subverting "the divinely ordained plan for the sexes by undermining women's commitments."[18]

Still, many Catholic leaders of the time—notably Bishop John Spalding of Peoria, Illinois, and Archbishop John Ireland of St. Paul, Minnesota, an early supporter of the College of St. Catherine—championed higher education for women and the broader sphere of activity it would allow them. Bishop Spalding explicitly refused to limit women's proper sphere to the domestic, instead arguing that it "lies wherever she can live nobly and do useful work."[19] Perhaps many Catholic young women agreed, for they were increasingly attending the institutions of higher education that were open to them, regardless of whether the institutions were secular or Protestant. This increase in the number of Catholic women opting for higher education finally led to a consensus among progressives and conservatives that it was time to create Catholic colleges for women.

The opposing viewpoints brought together in this consensus were, in essence, conflicting concepts of what a woman should be, that is, conflicting "images of ideal womanhood."[20] These opposing images reflected an assumption that "ideal womanhood" was the province of white upper- and middle-class women, so questions about the "true nature" of woman were limited in terms of class and ethnicity. Were women ideally pure, pious, gentle, and obedient? Should their eventual destiny, as natural law conceived by Thomists argued, be within the domestic sphere, with marriage and motherhood? In that case, education should prepare them to "be fit mothers for the race," an enterprise best done in a place protective of women's "special nature"—an all-female environment. Or should women be encouraged to move beyond the domestic realm, as progressives argued, to engage in the world outside of home and children? In that case, education should offer them access to knowledge-based professions. For Catholic progressives, an all-female environment was, if not necessary, at least a compromise they were willing to make to ensure that Catholic women had opportunities for higher education and beyond.

Although both conservatives and progressives argued for such colleges, "viewed in the broader context of legacy, the decision to sponsor women's colleges appears primarily as a conservative endeavor."[21] Many women's colleges, Catholic and secular alike, worked, as Jill Ker Conway puts it, "to maximize women's intellectual potential but to direct it toward fulfillment in adulthood through family and through voluntary work on socially and culturally desirable causes," a compromise between giving women a space to engage in the life of the mind and promoting a primarily domestic role.[22] Landy notes the complexity of this compromise when he writes that, as a social institution, Catholic woman's colleges "proved paradoxically to be at the same time both a liberating and a conservative institution. . . . They could educate women in whatever ways were deemed important and prepare them for economic opportunity, yet shield them and teach them to value traditional notions of womanhood, whether in religious life or in marriage and motherhood."[23]

The proper role for women was being debated not only in Catholic circles but across the United States as well. With new opportunities for higher education and professional careers came renewed fears about what such an education might do to women and to families. Higher education came under special scrutiny as inherently detrimental to the spiritual, mental, and physical health of women. It "posed even more threat to women's health than sweatshop, cotton mill or canning plant" and would, according to an eminent physician of the time, "cause mental collapse, physical incapacity, infertility, and early death."[24]

It was within this context of fear and hostility that the Sisters of St. Joseph decided to open their college for women. In important ways, their decision was a continuation more than a transformation of their order's founding goals: zealous service to God and to the dear neighbor without distinction. The Sisters of St. Joseph, a community founded in 1650 in LePuy, France, followed the inspiration and teachings of Father Joseph Peter Medaille, who sought "the balance of love of God and love of neighbor."[25] They were called to be "entirely lost and absorbed in God and for God" and to be everything "for the dear neighbor," embracing "the service of hospitals, the direction of orphan homes, the visiting of the sick and poor, and also the instruction of girls in places where the religious already established do not care of this."[26]

Given these principles, the Sisters needed to be what we would now call "out on the street." Unlike nearly all other women religious orders at the time, the Daughters of St. Joseph, as they were originally called, were not a cloistered community, nor did they wear nuns' habits. Living outside of convents and wearing widow's garb, they followed the "Little Design" of Father Medaille in a "secret association of women living together in groups of three, all reduced to perfect unity by the renunciation of everything that they could own, all bound by secret vows, all dedicated to the advancement of God's glory and the sanctification of neighbor."[27] This sanctification involved "doing every good work 'of which woman is capable,'" most notably caring for the sick and orphaned and teaching "lace making to impoverished young women so they would have a way of supporting themselves other than prostitution."[28] This latter task of providing skills and a livelihood to young women is still talked about at the University and has become part of the shared historical lore at St. Catherine's, reflecting its mission of educating women and of serving the cause of social justice.

The Sisters' congregation grew in number, survived the French Revolution (during which several Sisters were beheaded), and eventually expanded beyond France to the United States in 1836. In this country, the Sisters set about doing good works for the "dear neighbor": opening hospitals, tending to the sick, and opening academies for girls. Almost immediately upon arriving in Saint Paul, Minnesota, in 1851, the Sisters founded St. Joseph's Academy, the first female academy in that city. One of the Academy's first graduates to join the Sisters of St. Joseph, Ellen Ireland (later Sister Seraphine), would go on to found the College of St. Catherine.[29]

CATHOLIC IDENTITY AND WOMEN'S MISSION

What did it mean for these early Sisters and those who came after them to create and develop a Catholic college for women? Certainly, the predominant aspects of the College's identity—women and Catholicism—were important. There was a paradox at the heart of this endeavor, for the College's goals were to liberate women, offering them opportunities, and to protect them, offering them sanctuary. Despite these contradictory aims, in its 100-year history, the College has promoted women's strength, well-being, and autonomy, sometimes by design, sometimes by accident, and sometimes despite its own intentions. How it managed to do so is the focus of this book.

Since its founding, St. Catherine's identity as a Catholic college has been central to its existence, but what that identity has meant to the College has changed over the century. The Sisters were, in their words, doing God's work by educating young Catholic women. But from very early on, St. Catherine's also welcomed non-Catholic students. A 1914 College *Bulletin* noted that "there is no interference with the religious convictions of non-Catholics," though it also notes that non-Catholics were required to attend Sunday chapel services.[30] While not seeking to convert its non-Catholic students, the College made the spiritual well-being and growth of all of its students a main focus of its educational efforts. Both the curriculum and co-curriculum included an explicit focus on the religious and spiritual aspects of the human experience, and all Catholic students were required to take courses in Catholic religion.

Attention to spiritual or religious development was not limited to religion classes or chapel attendance. In the early twentieth century, Catholic social teaching had a profound effect on the curriculum taught at Catholic women's colleges, including St. Catherine's. Pope Leo XIII's 1891 encyclical, *The Condition of Labor*, and Pope Pius XI's reaffirmation of the document in 1931, encouraged Catholics to actively work for social change and social justice. Teaching Catholic values at St. Catherine's meant, among other things, teaching students to be socially responsible. The 1944 College *Bulletin* notes one of the aims of a St. Catherine's education: "to graduate young women" who will live "responsible lives, aware not only of their privileges, but also of their duties as members of modern society, keenly conscious of the problems of that society, and prepared to assume positions of responsibility . . . within that society."[31] (See Cavallaro et al., in this volume for a discussion of the ways in which these values played out in the curriculum.)

St. Catherine's Catholic identity was always expressed within the context of its being a *woman's* college, just as its identity as a woman's college was always interwoven with its being a *Catholic* college. From its inception, St. Catherine's was dedicated to taking women seriously. The College expected women to engage in the same rigorous and far-ranging intellectual inquiry as men undertook. Indeed, the early Sisters explicitly rejected the idea of a curriculum designed specifically for women; instead, they modeled their curriculum on the best secular, coeducational universities—specifically, the University of Chicago—believing that women could achieve the same high academic standards as men.

At Catholic women's colleges, to an even greater extent than at secular or Protestant women's colleges, women's leadership in all aspects of institutional life was particularly evident.[32] Sisters established, staffed, and operated their institutions, subsidizing them with their own intellectual and physical labor. In her analysis of religious sisterhoods and Catholic higher education, Mary Oates notes that "in deliberately choosing to live in large female communities, nuns were radically challenging the social prescription that women belonged in the home."[33] In this challenge, the Sisters found important meaning through their work, at the same time serving as alternative role models for young women.

From its beginning, the College also defined itself as a liberal arts college, establishing a classic liberal arts and sciences curriculum as the core of students' educational experiences. Courses in philosophy, Latin, Greek, history, art, English, French, German, mathematics, physics, botany, and chemistry were all offered as early as 1906. Since then, the liberal arts curriculum has undergone many changes (see Cavallaro et al., this volume), but the core mission has remained the same: taking Catholic women seriously by recognizing their capacity to undertake rigorous intellectual inquiry in a setting comparable to the best secular institutions. Indeed, the Sisters thought it so important that all students be grounded in the liberal arts that, through much of the College's history, even students majoring in a professional field were required to have a liberal arts or science minor. In keeping with Catholic intellectual tradition, the Sisters asked all their students to engage in open intellectual inquiry, a hallmark of a liberal arts education. As Sister Eucharista Galvin, the College's second president, explained, "the duty of the Catholic college is to encourage students to search into and learn the facts about controversial questions."[34]

A BOTH/AND APPROACH

The authors of this book were inspired by our desire to examine the history of the College from specifically feminist perspectives. Through its focus on a particular institution during a particular historical era, this work has two aims: to illuminate how St. Catherine's has survived and flourished over the past 100 years, and to contribute to the scholarship on the history of women's education.

The process of creating this book was intentionally collaborative. All of the authors have been connected to the University; most are faculty there now. Insiders writing about their own institution bring with them certain dangers and dilemmas: how to ensure objectivity, if such is even possible; how to avoid self-interest, self-aggrandizement, or personal vendettas; and how to tell the truth as we know it, even if it creates an unflattering portrait of either the institution or specific individuals within it, individuals who may be our colleagues. Nevertheless, insiders often comprehend the nuances of a complex institutional history in important ways.

This is not a conventional, comprehensive, chronological history but a series of analytical essays exploring the full range of the College's history, including both its failures and its successes. We look at liberating as well as constraining pressures from the Church and society, and we examine continuing internal tensions that reflect the conflicting goals and aspirations present since the College's founding. Our perspectives are multiple and feminist. We do not emphasize stories of feminist *activism*, though such stories are present; instead, we engage in feminist *analysis*. As we define it, feminist analysis requires engagement with social contexts and attention to diverse women's lives, minds, talents, and leadership. In feminist analysis, considerations of power and questions of justice are paramount.

As collaborators, we have demanded of ourselves a critical perspective that aims to be "loyal to the truth, not disloyal to the past."[35] Since that critical perspective requires the passage of a certain amount of time, we have focused on the years from 1905 through the mid-1980s.

A recurring theme links the essays in this book: the complex and contradictory purposes that led to the formation of Catholic colleges for women exerted a profound influence on the type of college that St. Catherine's was to become. Never fully defining the true "nature of women" or "women's proper role," St. Catherine's promulgated a both/and approach: building on the work of Sisters who took vows of selfless obedience *and* carved out careers of personal and professional distinction; promoting intellectual and economic opportunities for women *and* settling for the few professional careers deemed suitable for them; teaching students the feminine graces that allowed them to be seen as ladies *and* the skills that would allow them to enter the male-dominated workplace; teaching students the middle-class manners of the dominant Protestant culture *and* encouraging them to remain true to their Catholic identity; creating a curriculum that valued women's issues, experiences, and concerns *and* did not challenge deeply entrenched male-centered epistemologies; and most of all, balancing institutional goals that sought to *both* liberate *and* constrain.

ORGANIZATION OF THE BOOK

Part I, "Liberating Visions, Remarkable Lives," introduces the historical context in which the founders and leaders of the College envisioned women's education, created the institution, developed its programs, and overcame challenges to its women's mission.

"Extravagantly Visionary Leadership: The Irelands and Sister Antonia McHugh" provides a historic overview of the founding and early development of the College from 1904 to 1940. The key figure in the College's rapid growth was Sister Antonia McHugh, dean and president from 1911 to 1937. From sending Sister faculty to the world's great secular universities for graduate degrees to personally soliciting and securing financial support from the Rockefeller and Carnegie foundations, Sister Antonia transcended the expectations and restrictions placed on the women of her time.

As "Portrait of a Daughter of St. Joseph: Sister Jeanne Marie Bonnett" illustrates, the College of St. Catherine owes its foundation and its founding character to the Sisters of St. Joseph of Carondelet. These pioneering women used their energy, determination, and creativity to build and refine a College that provided a community of caring and hospitality, that strove for excellence in all endeavors, and that responded to the needs of the surrounding community. Sister Jeanne Marie Bonnett was one of the many Sisters who worked for these goals. This biographical essay reveals key themes in the College's first 50 years through the life of one individual in community. As both a faculty member and administrator, Sister Jeanne Marie played a variety of significant roles in the development of women's education in the arts and sciences as well as in professional programs.

"Opening Doors: Sister AJ and the Minneapolis Campus" explores the history of St. Mary's Junior College and its founder, Sister Anne Joachim Moore. Created in 1963 as part of a movement to provide educational access to underserved populations, the coeducational junior college was the first in the nation to be devoted exclusively to health-care programs. Sister AJ's liberatory principles and commitment to working-class students deeply influenced the junior college's curriculum, pedagogy, and academic support strategies. In 1985, St. Mary's Junior College merged with the College of St. Catherine.

"Renewing the Meaning of a Women's College: Identity and Standpoint in the 1970s" traces the College's course through a turbulent decade in American higher education. In the face of economic, social, and political pressures, while numerous other women's colleges were closing or becoming coeducational, the College of St. Catherine chose to remain a college for women. This essay places that decision within the framework of emerging feminist theory that both supported and dismissed the College's work. Feminist standpoint theory is offered as an alternative to liberal feminism as a way to explore women's education in the context of an increasingly diverse student body.

Part II, "Intellectual Life: In and Out of the Classroom," focuses on the intellectual and curricular life of the College. From the beginning, the women's mission has engendered creative tensions that shaped the curriculum: seeking parity with men's and coeducational institutions while creating a women-centered education; developing and maintaining a strong liberal arts institution while offering specialized professional programs; and teaching women theology while remaining within the context of a patriarchal Church and society.

"What a Woman Should Know, What a Woman Can Be: Curriculum as Prism" explores the heart of the College: its curriculum. This historical survey analyzes how the curriculum has both challenged and reinforced expectations and stereotypes of women's roles in society. Like all women's colleges, in its first decades St. Catherine's had to assure the public that the intellectual development it demanded of its students would not undermine their femininity. At the same time, the College challenged feminine stereotypes by offering a rigorous liberal arts education modeled on such institutions as the University of Chicago. Recognizing the social location and economic realities of its students, the College also offered professional studies that would allow alumnae to support themselves in a world of limited opportunities for women.

"Theology Fit for Women: Religious Wisdom, St. Catherine's Style" examines how religion has been taught at the College and focuses on curricular changes leading to a theology by and for women, including changes in who has been allowed—or not allowed—to teach theology. In describing how the teaching of religion has responded to changes in women's lives, this essay illuminates important questions of identity and mission that the College of St. Catherine, as a Catholic women's college, has faced throughout the past century.

"Communion with Books: The Double Life of Literature" describes the confluence of forces that made St. Catherine's an exceptional environment for nurturing a distinctive and significant sort of literary work. While aspiring to the highest intellectual rigor of liberal education in the United States, the College embraced a distinctly democratic approach to literature and authors, one that emphasized community and claimed both the disciplined space of the classroom and the domestic space of the women's club.

Part III, "Unique Legacy: Faculty and Student Experiences," traces the experiences of students and faculty, which were shaped not only by women-centered scholarship and learning, but also by their own diverse lives as women, both within and beyond the campus.

"Learning and Earning: The Work-Study Experience" examines the history of financial support offered to students at the College from its early years to the 1980s. This essay describes the experiences, both negative and positive, of students for whom this aid made a St. Catherine's education possible. The broad availability of this support reflected the commitment of the Sisters of St. Joseph to the education of women, regardless of class. Through the College's early informal work-study programs and later governmental programs, work-study allowed hundreds of less affluent women to attend the College.

"Possumus: Sisters' Education in Feminism" considers the experiences of the Sisters of St. Joseph who taught at the College during the second-wave feminist movement. At that time, the percentage of St. Catherine's Sister faculty with Ph.D.s far surpassed the percentage of both male and female faculty with doctorates at four-year colleges across the country. Through retrospective interviews with 20 Sister faculty who taught from 1974 to 1976, the authors explore the Sisters' graduate education and their education in feminism. While the perspectives of these Sisters reflect continuity with earlier generations of Sister faculty, they also reveal a changed consciousness in the context of movements for justice.

The last essay, "Postscript: Questions for the Twenty-First Century," revisits themes from the introduction, putting them into a present-day context. It examines how the University's educational mission continues to thrive in a very different world from that of its founding, a world in which new and different ideas of women's roles and identities can both challenge and enrich that mission.

NOTES

1. Jane Lamm Carroll, "The College of St. Catherine: Taking Women Seriously for 100 Years," (Unpublished Manuscript) College of St. Catherine (CSC) Archives, St. Paul, Minnesota, p. 28.

2. The College of St. Catherine Marketing and Communications Office, "Becoming a University," *The College of St. Catherine Alumnae News*, Vol. 83, #2, May 2008, p. 3.

3. Thomas Landy, "The Colleges in Context," in Tracy Schier and Cynthia Russett, eds., *Catholic Women's Colleges in America* (Baltimore: Johns Hopkins University Press, 2002), p. 66.

4. Tracy Schier and Cynthia Russett, eds., *Catholic Women's Colleges in America* (Baltimore: Johns Hopkins University Press, 2002), p. 24.

5. Throughout this book, we use the term, the College of St. Catherine, when referring to events before the transition to university status in 2009. In discussions of current issues, we use the institution's new name since 2009, St. Catherine University.

6. M. Elizabeth Tidball, Daryl G. Smith, Charles S. Tidball, and Lisa E. Wolf-Wendel, eds., *Taking Women Seriously: Lessons and Legacies for Educating the Majority* (Phoenix: American Council on Education and the Oryx Press, 1999); Nancy Woloch, *Women and the American Experience* (Boston: McGraw Hill, 2000).

7. Jane Redmont, "Live Minds and Yearning Spirits," in Schier and Russett, eds., *Catholic Women's Colleges in America*, p. 203.

8. Tidball, Smith, Tidball, and Wolf-Wendel, eds., *Taking Women Seriously*, pp. 20, 25, 34–53.

9. Hardwik Day, Inc., *What Matters in College After College: A Comparative Alumnae Research Study* (Commissioned by the Women's College Coalition, March 2008), p. 99 (posted on Women'sColleges.org).

10. Dorothy M. Brown and Carol Hurd Green, "Making It: Stories of Persistence and Success," in Schier and Russett, eds., *Catholic Women's Colleges in America*, p. 274; Rosalie Ryan, CSJ and John Christine Wolkerstorfer, CSJ, *More Than a Dream* (St. Paul: College of St. Catherine, 1992), p. 131.

11. Redmont, p. 203.

12. Woloch, p. 282.

13. Tidball et al., pp. 5–7.

14. *Ibid.*

15. Kathleen Mahoney, "American Catholic Colleges for Women: Historical Origins," in Schier and Russett, *Catholic Women's Colleges in America*, pp. 25–54, at pp. 49–51.

16. Mahoney, p. 26.

17. Landy, pp. 55–97, at p. 63.

18. Mahoney, p. 43.

19. Mahoney, p. 46.

20. Mahoney, p. 27.

21. Mahoney, p. 52.

22. Jill Ker Conway, "Faith, Knowledge and Gender," in Schier and Russett, *Catholic Women's Colleges in America*, pp. 11–16, at pp. 11–12.

23. Landy, p. 63.

24. Woloch, p. 283.

25. Sisters of St. Joseph of Carondelet, St. Paul Province, *Eyes Open on a World* (St. Cloud, MN: North Star Press, 2001), p. 7.

26. Sisters of St. Joseph of Carondelet, *The Sisters of St. Joseph of Carondelet* (St. Louis: B. Herder Book Co., 1966), pp. 20–21, 27–28.

27. *Ibid.*, p. 19.

28. Sisters of St. Joseph of Carondelet, St. Paul Province, *Eyes Open on a World*, p. 6.

29. *Ibid.*, pp. 8–13.

30. College of St. Catherine *Bulletin*, 1914, CSC Archives, St. Paul, Minnesota, p. 18.

31. College of St. Catherine *Bulletin*, 1944, CSC Archives, p. 7.

32. Mary Oates, "Sisterhoods and Catholic Higher Education, 1890–1960," in Schier and Russett, eds., *Catholic Women's Colleges in America*, pp. 161–194, at pp. 168–174.

33. *Ibid.*, p. 164.

34. College of St. Catherine, *Presidents of the College of St. Catherine*, 1998, CSC Archives.

35. Sisters of the Immaculate Heart of Mary, *Building Sisterhood: A Feminist History of the Sisters, Servants of the Immaculate Heart of Mary* (Detroit: Sisters of the IHM, 1997), p. 365.

I

LIBERATING VISIONS,
REMARKABLE LIVES

1

Extravagantly Visionary Leadership

The Irelands and Sister Antonia McHugh

Jane Lamm Carroll

"It is the aim of those in charge to make this college the best and highest of its kind in the Northwest."[1]

"When I think of Mother Antonia, I think of strength and firmness, and the authority of her presence. I think she invented vigor. She held up to us an example of invincibility—that is if you really made up your mind to do it, you could conquer—you could win."[2]

"The College is unwilling to grant her degrees to mere bridge-players or mere bookworms—both of whom may be spendthrifts of their inheritance; she would keep her reward for what she aims to ensure, the development of the happy, energetic, richly educated and therefore resourceful girls—ready, capable, glad to serve, with the strength and beauty of Catholic womanhood."[3]

Many Catholic women religious in the United States have long histories of educating girls and young women, and their experience in running female academies for generations in the nineteenth century laid the intellectual and practical foundations for the later successful conduct of their women's colleges.[4] According to Karen Kennelly:

> Virtually every congregation that established colleges during the pioneer period from 1890 to 1920 had by that time one—and often two or three—generations of members who had taught in academies. The academy curricula offered by sister-faculty had expanded during the late nineteenth-century as sisters recognized changing expectations for women and adapted classical structures many had brought with them from European convent schools. Such experience was antecedent to the scholarly seriousness necessary for the development of a collegiate atmosphere.[5]

The Sisters of St. Joseph (CSJ) illustrate this pattern in the history of Catholic women's colleges. They founded St. Joseph's Academy, the first female academy in St. Paul, almost immediately upon their arrival in 1851. One of the first graduates of St. Joseph's Academy to enter the Sisters of St. Joseph, Ellen Ireland (Sister Seraphine), would later found the College of St. Catherine.[6] Just a few years prior to the 1905 opening of the College of St. Catherine, the first graduates of St. Mary's School of Nursing received diplomas. The Sisters of St. Joseph had been operating St. Mary's Hospital in Minneapolis since 1887. As the hospital expanded and nursing became increasingly technical and professional, the Sisters themselves could not meet St. Mary's demand for nurses. Hence, they established a school of nursing at the hospital in the early 1900s. After a decade of collaborating with St. Mary's in developing nursing education, the College of St. Catherine established a full nursing degree program on its campus in the early 1940s, leaving St. Mary's providing only the clinical aspects of nursing education for students. In 1958 the two institutions separated again, and in 1963 the Sisters replaced the Nursing School with St. Mary's Junior College. St. Catherine's and St. Mary's eventually merged in 1986.

SISTERS: EDUCATORS AND LEADERS

Women's colleges created spaces that allowed their students and faculty to develop their own intellectual and social identities as women, becoming islands of liberty in which women were, first and foremost, human beings.[7] However, when the first women's colleges were founded in the late nineteenth and early twentieth centuries, they were faced with multiple missions and placed in a rather defensive position *vis-à-vis* social expectations and fears about female education. Not only did women's colleges have to prove to society that women were capable of undertaking a rigorously intellectual education, but they also had to show that such an education did not impair women's health, make them less feminine, encourage sexual impropriety, or discourage women from becoming wives and mothers.[8]

The women religious who founded and operated Catholic women's colleges have historically offered a "counter social model" of life for young women in a way that non-Catholic women's colleges could not. Catholic women's colleges, earlier than their secular counterparts, recognized that women could have vocations in life other than marriage and motherhood and that many women needed an education in order to become self-supporting. Moreover, unlike some prominent non-Catholic women's colleges, in Catholic institutions, the presidents, administrators, and faculty were almost entirely, if not exclusively, women.[9]

Earlier in the twentieth century, the Sisters in particular were exemplars of women living lives that were alternatives to the social roles of marriage and motherhood and that challenged the social assumption that women were or should be dependent upon men.[10] To establish, expand, fund, and maintain their institutions, the Sisters operated successfully in a male-dominated world. Indeed, their religious sisterhood empowered them to act in ways that were highly unusual for laywomen of their own times. Thus, the Sisters were inspiring examples of what women could be and do.

At Catholic women's colleges, to an even greater extent than at secular women's colleges, women's leadership in all aspects of institutional life was particularly evident. At Catholic women's colleges, Sisters established, operated, and staffed the institutions, subsidizing them with their own intellectual and physical labor.[11] In her analysis of religious sisterhoods and Catholic higher education, Mary Oates claims that, "in deliberately choosing to live in large female communities, nuns were radically challenging the social prescription that women belonged in the home."[12]

At the College of St. Catherine, St. Mary's Hospital, and St. Mary's School of Nursing, the Sisters of St. Joseph who served as administrators, faculty, and staff were influential role models for their students. They functioned in positions of power over men or in collaboration with them, including professionals (doctors, interns, and chaplains) and staff (orderlies, maintenance men), positions rare for women during the first half, and even later decades, of the twentieth century. Hospital and Nursing School administrators, like Presidents of the College, also had to be skilled at raising funds in the wider community, which meant seeking financial support from male business owners and philanthropists.[13]

ROOTS AND FOUNDERS:
THE SISTERS OF ST. JOSEPH AND THE IRELANDS

The Sisters of St. Joseph began their charitable and educational work in 1650 in LePuy, France. Dedicating themselves to combating poverty and ignorance, they established orphanages, hospitals, free and tuition schools, and hospices for the aged. By the time of the French Revolution, the Sisters had developed over 150 communities across France. The Revolution (1789–1794) brought the virtual dissolution of the congregation, as the zeal of the revolutionaries to create a completely secular state led to the widespread oppression of the clergy and Catholic religious communities. During the Revolution, the Sisters were scattered and persecuted. French authorities imprisoned many and executed five of the Sisters. One Sister who narrowly escaped the guillotine, Mother St. John Fontbonne, lived to rebuild the congregation based in Lyons. By the time of her death in 1843, the Sisters of St. Joseph had 244 houses and 3,000 members.[14]

In 1836, under Mother St. John Fontbonne's leadership, the congregation's first mission outside France was sent to North America, to a French settlement, Carondelet, on the Mississippi River near St. Louis. In 1851, Bishop Joseph Cretin of Minnesota Territory invited the Sisters of St. Joseph to journey up the Mississippi to teach immigrant and American Indian children in St. Paul. Four Sisters arrived that same year and settled in a small shanty on the riverbank. In a nearby log cabin that was the frontier town's first and only Catholic church, the Sisters immediately established St. Joseph's Academy for girls, the first female academy in the region. The log cabin church also served as a hospital where the Sisters treated victims of the 1853 cholera epidemic.[15]

By 1901, when the Sisters of St. Joseph of Carondelet celebrated their 50th Jubilee, they had founded and were operating two hospitals, two nursing schools, two girls' academies, a conservatory for art and music, several orphanages, and numerous parish schools in the Twin Cities of Minneapolis and St. Paul, as well as in rural areas of Minnesota and the Dakotas.[16] The first graduates of St. Mary's School of Nursing in Minneapolis matriculated in 1903.[17] Archbishop John Ireland and his sister, Sister Seraphine Ireland, the Provincial Superior of the Sisters of St. Joseph since 1884, worked closely together on all of the Sisters' endeavors.[18]

John Ireland was one of the influential leaders of a movement among American Catholics in the late nineteenth century seeking to "Americanize" the Church in order to remove the stigma attached to Catholics as immigrants and second-class citizens in a predominantly Protestant nation. One important aspect of the Americanization movement was the effort to make all levels of the Catholic educational system the equal of secular and Protestant institutions.[19]

Archbishop Ireland was particularly anxious that Catholic women have access to the higher education they needed to answer the new demands of American womanhood that were apparent by 1900. He saw his own sister, Mother Seraphine, and her Sisters of St. Joseph of St. Paul as the valuable vanguard who would realize his goals for the higher education of Catholic women in the Northwest.[20] In his 1901 address to the Sisters of St. Joseph on the occasion of their 50th Jubilee, Ireland expressed his desire to see Catholic women educated to become effective and capable American citizens:

> Your special province is the training of womanhood. In this new world of ours, there is in a true and honorable sense of the word, the new woman. Beyond a doubt, the sphere of woman's activities has widened; women's influence reaches much farther than ever before: and for such new conditions she must be prepared by an intellectual training higher and more thorough than has heretofore been necessary. . . . I am a firm believer in the higher education of women: I covet for the daughters of the people, . . . the opportunities of receiving under the protecting hand of religion the fullest intellectual equipment of which woman is capable.[21]

Archbishop John Ireland, early advocate for women's education and sponsor of the College. Photo courtesy of St. Catherine University.

The Sisters of St. Joseph had planned to open their college in the 1890s, but the severe financial panic of 1893 and the subsequent recession created financial difficulties that delayed their plans. Eventually the economic situation improved, and in 1900 the Archbishop spurred a renewal of the effort by giving the Sisters the royalties from his newest book, which they peddled on the streets to raise $60,000. In addition, Archbishop Ireland persuaded a local Catholic farmer, Hugh Derham, to donate $25,000 to the Sisters' college fund. In 1903 the Sisters broke ground for the College of St. Catherine's first building, Derham Hall. The first students came in January 1905, just weeks after the first Sisters arrived in a snowstorm to prepare the new building for occupants.[22]

Sister Seraphine Ireland, founder of the College of St. Catherine. Photo courtesy of St. Catherine University.

The Irelands were extravagantly visionary in establishing the College of St. Catherine in 1905, for at the time none of the Sisters of St. Joseph had a bachelor of arts degree.[23] Among the 27 Sisters who transferred from St. Joseph's Academy to Derham Hall, however, there was a cadre of exceptional and experienced teachers who would form the nucleus of the College's first faculty.[24] Although they lacked the requisite credentials for college teaching, according to Sister Teresa Toomey, "they were well equipped in learning, in appreciation of art and music, in enthusiasm for literature, classical and modern, and in an understanding of the demands of scholarship."[25]

Moreover, the Sisters acted quickly to educate themselves further and to earn their degrees. The College developed and prospered in direct proportion to the cultivation of the Sisters of St. Joseph who served as its faculty. In the year before the College opened, Mother Seraphine sent Sister Hyacinth Werden, a German teacher and the first superior of the College, and Sister Bridget Bohan, the music teacher, on a wide-ranging tour of Europe to study its systems of higher education and to visit its great cultural and historic sites.[26] Most of the Sisters took correspondence courses and attended summer school courses to work toward degrees. In the summer of 1905 the Sisters who taught history, English, math, and science left to obtain bachelor's degrees, two at Harvard University and two at the University of Chicago.[27] Sister Antonia McHugh, the history teacher, was allowed several leaves of absence from teaching to complete two bachelor's degrees by 1908 in education and philosophy, and by 1909 a master's degree in philosophy. By 1913, two Sisters teaching at the College had bachelor's degrees and three had master's degrees.[28] After 1913, the challenge of continuing to build a qualified faculty from the ranks of the Sisters would fall to Sister Antonia as Dean, and later President, of the College. In later years, Sister Antonia would argue successfully, as she sought accreditation and a chapter of Phi Beta Kappa for St. Catherine's, that her faculty of Sisters was the College's endowment.[29]

The Sisters operated a preparatory program and the early college program side-by-side in Derham Hall. In 1905–1906, its first year, the College of St. Catherine had seven students and attracted between five and nine students each year between 1906 and 1910. Until 1911, the Sisters offered no courses for juniors and seniors, so students who wanted to finish their degrees went on to the University of Minnesota. In 1909, the first student enrolled who would complete all four years of the bachelor's degree at St. Catherine's. The College found it very difficult to retain students in the years before 1911; in its first six years, only seven of 43 students stayed to begin their sophomore year and none of those seven returned as juniors.[30] The tide turned in 1911–1912, when an unprecedented 19 students enrolled, starting a dramatic upward trend that was not reversed. By 1914–1915, the College had 51 students, by 1916–1917 it had 116, and by 1919–1920 there were 238 enrolled. A decade later, 404 women attended the College and throughout the 1930s, despite the Depression, enrollment continued to rise; by 1934–1935 there were 573 students.[31]

The Irelands, Mother Seraphine and Archbishop John, were 62 and 66 years of age, respectively, when the College of St. Catherine opened its doors. They were the founders of an institution that they saw as the crowning and appropriate achievement of over a half-century of work by the Sisters of St. Joseph of St. Paul. However, it would be the next generation of Sisters, under the remarkable acumen and leadership of Sister Antonia McHugh, who would actually create the College that the Irelands had first envisioned in the 1880s. Indeed, perhaps the Archbishop's greatest legacy to the College, having provided it with the necessary financial foundation, was to single out Sister Antonia McHugh as especially talented and to recommend her to Mother Seraphine as the Sister he thought most capable of leading St. Catherine's into the new century.

Students with Dolly, the campus horse, 1914. Photo courtesy of St. Catherine University.

SISTER ANTONIA: CONVERTING VISION INTO REALITY

It may be impossible to overstate the significance of Sister Antonia McHugh's vision, leadership, and influence upon the development of the College of St. Catherine. Among the Sisters of St. Joseph, it was Sister Antonia who determined what the College should be and how to make that vision a reality. It was Sister Antonia, in turn, who chose and cultivated other Sisters who shared her vision and subscribed to the College ethos she created, and who in subsequent generations would carry the work forward. Many Sisters made essential and lasting contributions to the College of St. Catherine in the first decades of its existence. However, it was Sister Antonia McHugh, more than any other person, who was responsible for establishing a sound financial base for the College, building its community of scholars, refining and expanding its curriculum, and constructing most of its buildings, all of which were essential to the creation of a nationally recognized liberal arts institution. In 1937, her remarkable achievements culminated in the endowment for the College of a chapter of the nation's oldest and most prestigious honor society, Phi Beta Kappa.[32] Notably, the College of St. Catherine was the first Catholic college in the United States deemed worthy of this honor by the Phi Beta Kappa Society. Key to gaining the Gamma Chapter of Phi Beta Kappa was the Society's assessment of the College's faculty, which it described as:

Sister Antonia McHugh, Dean and President of the College, 1913–1937. Photo courtesy of St. Catherine University.

Young, capable and well qualified. It is the committee's strong conviction that the College of St. Catherine has an alert, well trained, scholarly, interested and deeply intellectual group of administrators and teachers.[33]

It should not be forgotten, however, that Sister Antonia's leadership and vision, to the extent that they changed the lives of her sister religious, also created tensions within the Sisters of St. Joseph community. Committed to building a faculty and college on the model of the University of Chicago, Sister Antonia sent Sisters off to earn degrees at prestigious secular and even Protestant universities all over the world. She also required Sisters to travel to Europe and New York City as part of their educations.[34] When Sister Antonia became Dean of the College in 1914, only three of the Sisters teaching at the College had master's degrees. Under her leadership as dean, and later president, the Sisters obtained master's and doctorate degrees at a break-neck pace: by 1936, an additional 25 advanced degrees had been earned. In addition, at least 13 Sisters had had the opportunity to travel abroad.[35]

Education and cultural activities beyond the convent walls, especially travel and study far from St. Paul, did not sit well with all the Sisters, especially those of the older generation. As Sister Helen Angela Hurley explained in her history of the Sisters of St. Joseph of St. Paul:

> Going outside the convent for higher education was a distinct departure from custom. Yet each of the sisters thus developed a stronger individuality and assurance about the proper way to conduct activities in her field. Sister Antonia was regarded as aggressive and domineering, but she differed from her companions in degree rather than kind. None of them contemplated any departure from either the letter or spirit of their religious profession. They felt that they were merely carrying out the prescriptions of the Third Plenary council of Baltimore, which insisted that Catholic schools should be at least as good as public schools of a similar grade. The pronouncements and the ideas of Pope Leo XIII on the subject they had heard many times from Archbishop Ireland.[36]

Sister Teresa Toomey, a historian who began teaching at St. Catherine's in 1918, says Sister Antonia's superiors in the community often got in her way as she acted to implement her vision as Dean of the College. Significantly, Sister Antonia would not be named President of the College until 1929 and never held any office in the Sisters of St. Joseph community higher than superior to the Sisters of the College (1931 to 1937).[37] Thus, during most of the years she labored to build the College, Sister Antonia contended with authority figures in the community who were not always supportive of her plans. In 1958, Toomey, in reflecting upon the College's early years, provided the following assessment of the situation:

> Sister Antonia's labors were made the heavier, but unintentionally so, by some who were above her office in the community, and who withheld from her that degree of authority within her assigned area of action which she deemed indispensable for success. In her mind, since she had been given a work to do for God, it could not have been intended that she fail therein, and fail she certainly would not. She took a broad interpretation of the powers inherent in the mandate given her to run the college, and with unflinching courage returned again and again to the charge in behalf of all the demands she kept making for the progress of St. Catherine's. Often it seemed that it was easier for her to go to New York and secure a substantial grant of money for the college than to win a point concerning the study or travel of the sisters.[38]

Even Mother Seraphine, Provincial Superior until 1921 and founder of the College, was at times taken aback by the changes in the lives of the Sisters wrought by Sister Antonia's leadership. According to Hurley, "Mother Seraphine gasped at some of the developments under Sister Antonia, not in disapproval, but as a sort of reminder to the community that all of them were not acts of God and the letter of the law was still in force."[39] Sister Antonia was apparently too progressive and liberal for some in the community; it was she whom Sisters sought out for support in undertaking unusual opportunities that required waivers from "religious restrictions."[40] Always convinced that her way was the best way, and apparently frequently dismissive of those who dared to disagree, she made "more than a few enemies" during her years as dean and president.[41] According to Hurley, if a Sister questioned Sister Antonia's plan to send her to a secular institution to earn an advanced degree, "she was apt to have a new address by the fall."[42] Those who challenged her ideas or did not meet with her approval in some way were dismissed as "jackasses" or "babies," and told their claims were "nonsense."[43]

In her unwavering determination and effort to build a community of scholars of the highest caliber, Sister Antonia McHugh was seen by some as ruthless and insensitive to the personal needs of some Sisters. Driven by a desire for excellence as well as a virtual obsession with achieving the best possible credentials for the College, and disappointed that she herself had been unable to earn a doctorate degree, Sister Antonia drove her Sisters to quickly obtain advanced degrees with little reference to individual needs or wishes.[44] Sacrificed for the greater good of the College, some bore scars.

What enabled Sister Antonia to be as successful as she was, despite obstacles within the CSJ community, was the support of Archbishop Ireland. Sister Antonia was his protégé. It was he who had singled her out as one of a small group of young teachers who should be sent to Harvard and the University of Chicago for bachelor's degrees. It was the Archbishop who had "insisted" to his sister, Mother Seraphine, that Sister Antonia be named Dean of the College. Sister Antonia's intelligence, frankness, and self-confidence had brought her to the Archbishop's attention. Later in her life, Sister Antonia would recall: "The Archbishop liked me. I would talk to him. He knew I wasn't afraid of him."[45] Until his death in 1918, the Archbishop, a frequent visitor to the College, offered unflagging support for Sister Antonia's efforts on behalf of the College. According to Sister Helen Angela Hurley, "publicly and privately he encouraged Sister Antonia, and he kept his eyes open to see that she was not being hampered in her plans."[46] Thus, the Archbishop exercised his considerable influence with Mother Seraphine and the Sisters of St. Joseph on her behalf.[47]

Anna McHugh first encountered the Sisters of St. Joseph in 1885 at the age of 12, when she traveled from her home in North Dakota to attend St. Joseph's Academy for girls in St. Paul. Anna spent only a year in St. Paul and then, because it was closer to her home, transferred to St. Mary's Academy in Winnipeg, Canada, run by the Sisters of the Holy Name, also known as the Gray Nuns. Unexpectedly and to the particular dismay of her father, Anna decided after her academy education that she wanted to become a Gray Nun herself. Her father insisted she delay entering the convent for a year, during which time he presumably hoped Anna would reconsider. However, Anna remained determined. Upon learning that the Gray Nuns

required a steep dowry to enter their order, she entered the Sisters of St. Joseph novitiate instead in 1890, at 17 years of age. Anna was better educated
than most of the other young women who entered the novitiate in St. Paul
that year, and was quickly put to work teaching both the other novices and
the St. Joseph academy students. She took the name Antonia and made her
permanent vows in 1898.[48]

In addition to her convent education, Anna's parents and her experiences
growing up on the North Dakota frontier were significant in forming her
character and vision. Her father, Patrick McHugh, was a prominent busi-
nessman and politician who took Anna with him to political conventions
and on business trips in between her terms at boarding school. In the year
before Anna entered the novitiate, Patrick and Anna traveled through Yel-
lowstone Park and attended the North Dakota constitutional convention.
As Karen Kennelly explains:

> Childhood experiences in the Dakotas, in the 1870s and 1880s taught Anna
> to confront all manner of people and situations with curiosity rather than fear
> and to associate the idea of education with people, travel, and events, as much
> as with book learning and schools. She came also to conceive of women's work
> in an expansive way, not just in the religious precepts taught by her grand-
> mother and mother but in their personal examples of courage and generosity.[49]

In 1904 Sister Antonia McHugh was among the first group of Sisters who
left St. Joseph's Academy and moved to Derham Hall, the nucleus of the
College of St. Catherine. There she met a demanding routine of teaching,
cleaning, housekeeping, supervising resident students, and attending daily
prayers. As a teacher of history, Sister Antonia was both loved and feared,
but always respected. An alumna from the earliest years at the College remembered that Sister Antonia

> knew everything about us, every thought, every idle dream, every latent possibil-
> ity. . . . It was plain that she would tolerate no indirectness, superficiality, bad
> manners, slovenly thinking, sham or nonsense in any shape or form. . . . She
> respected us too much to accept from us a standard lower than the highest.[50]

Sister Helen Angela Hurley describes Sister Antonia's significant impact
on her students as a teacher in the years before she became Dean of the
College in 1914:

> She was just a teacher, not an official for the first ten years after Derham Hall
> opened, but no girl ever took her lightly. "Energize yourself," she would pro-
> nounce and they moved. There was an endless calendar of her oft-repeated dicta.
> . . . "It's terrible to have a stagnant mind," "self-pity is a destructive force," "fill
> your minds with great things and there will be no trivialities," and "she who
> would be a woman must avoid mediocrity." . . . Room 12 was Sister Antonia's

classroom and the place whence apples and advice were dealt out with an impartial hand to the starved and the maladjusted. . . . It was always the hub of the universe to the students, even though not officially so designated.[51]

As dean, Sister Antonia commanded even more respect from students and novices. Sister Marie Philip Haley recalled that when she first arrived at the College in 1917, Sister Antonia loomed very large:

> I knew from the minute I set my foot here that she was the most important one on campus. She was the one I loved most, feared most, respected most, and she certainly was running things. There was no doubt about who was running the students.[52]

Just as Sister Antonia took her students seriously as scholars, she devoted her free time to furthering her own scholarship, attending summer school and taking correspondence courses during the school year from the University of Chicago. Finally allowed a leave of absence to attend the University during regular sessions, she completed a bachelor's degree in philosophy and education by 1908 and a master's degree in history by 1909.[53]

The University of Chicago provided Sister Antonia not only with an education, but also with important friends and mentors from among its faculty and administrators. One of these, Dr. George Edgar Vincent, the Dean of the Faculty, would prove to be a useful and influential ally as she struggled to build St. Catherine's. Vincent became president of the University of Minnesota in 1911 and was close enough for the next five years to act as a frequent consultant.[54] Sister Antonia later recalled:

> During his administration, from 1911 to 1916, St. Catherine's was in the hazardous days of its beginnings, and it was Dr. Vincent, more than anyone else, who helped make it secure. With his characteristic generosity and splendid spirit of service, he made clear to me what to do, how to organize, and how to bring about the improvements that made the accrediting of the college possible.[55]

Dr. Vincent left the University of Minnesota in 1917 and, serendipitously for Sister Antonia, became the head of the Rockefeller Foundation's General Education Fund. She applied to the Foundation in 1918 for funds and largely credited Vincent for the $100,000 grant she obtained for the College.[56]

At Chicago, Sister Antonia also developed close ties with Dr. James Angell, her professor of psychology, and Dr. William Rainey Harper, the president of the University. Attending Harper's convocations at Chicago, Sister Antonia said, gave her a "burning desire to have some part, however small, in the work in education in the Northwest."[57] Sister Antonia adopted Harper's idea that a university should be a community of scholars and, after becoming dean in 1914, she was determined to implement his model at St. Catherine's. Angell would prove an essential ally; when he later served as a board member of both the Carnegie and Rockefeller Foundations, Sister Antonia applied to both for funding for the College. In 1926, under Angell's auspices, the Carnegie Foundation gave the College a five-year grant totaling $40,000. In the late 1920s, the Rockefeller Foundation granted St. Catherine's an additional $400,000 to build a science building and health center (Mendel and Fontbonne Halls).[58] Another former teacher and friend from the University of Chicago, Professor Charles Judd, helped Sister Antonia present a successful case for accreditation of the College. At the meeting of the North Central Association of Colleges and Universities in 1916, their novel argument was that the Sisters, as faculty, constituted the equivalent of a cash endowment.[59]

Sister Antonia concerned herself with all facets of the College's development; in addition to ordering the curriculum and raising funds, she oversaw construction of six buildings, the landscaping of the campus, the recruiting of students, advertising, and obtaining accreditation. Most importantly, she knew that the development of her faculty was key to creating the fine liberal arts college she envisioned. Consequently, Sister Antonia set her sights on building a community of scholars on the Chicago model and achieving accreditation for the College as quickly as possible. These dual goals meant the continued, swift cultivation of her faculty of Sisters. St. Catherine's was not unusual in its drive to rapidly develop its faculty; this was the norm for all Catholic women's colleges in the first half of the twentieth century. According to Karen Kennelly, because congregations wanted to teach students themselves rather than hire lay faculty, women religious "were soon greatly exceeding the rate of earning of advanced degrees by lay women in the United States and Europe."[60]

Sister Agnes Rita Lingl, who earned a doctorate in German from the University of Munich in 1933, remembered that Sister Antonia's insistence that the Sisters obtain degrees from the most prominent universities was controversial among Catholics:

> To the horror of some people, sometimes bishops, she sent the sisters out to many non-Catholic or rather secular universities. . . . She saw to it that the sisters got to Chicago, Columbia, to other secular institutions. . . . When we went to the secular institutions at that time, the sisters from other communities were all being sent to the Catholic University or Notre Dame.[61]

Despite Sister Rita's recollection, other Catholic women's colleges in the United States did send their sisters for graduate educations at non-Catholic universities, mainly because few Catholic universities offered advanced degrees in the fields needed by the women religious running colleges.[62] Moreover, Sister Antonia shared Archbishop Ireland's insistence that the credentials of faculty teaching at all levels of Catholic education be comparable to that of faculty at secular and Protestant institutions.[63]

Derham Hall, 1910, the College's first building. Photo courtesy of St. Catherine University.

Sister Antonia's grueling program of faculty development required that Sisters obtain doctorates before the age of 35. Sisters teaching in the preparatory program who did not have bachelor's degrees were required to take college courses on Saturdays and during the summer. These younger sisters were sent on trips to learn how to travel and attended local cultural events and institutions as part of their educations as well. Once a Sister obtained her bachelor's degree, she was immediately sent off to earn a master's degree or doctorate at a prestigious institution in the United States or Europe.[64] Sister Helen Angela Hurley described the swift pace of faculty development under Sister Antonia's leadership:

> With factory-like speed Sisters were hurried through college and shipped away for graduate work. College and high school graduates began entering the novitiate. The instant they were released from the religious training required of them by Canon Law, Sister Antonia insisted on taking them over. . . . The young sisters grasped the intellectual challenge and pleasure which foot-loose travel and study, the necessary concomitants of Sister Antonia's ideas in education, brought them. Not a few scars must be attributed to the reckless distribution of opportunities.[65]

Sister Antonia's plans for faculty improvement suffered a temporary setback in 1920–1921, when five of the Sisters who had earned advanced degrees, apparently rankled by her leadership, requested and obtained assignments at other institutions. Sister Maris Stella Smith, who was a student at the time, recalled her impression of why the five Sisters left the College:

> I was here for a year with Sister Clara as principal of Derham Hall High School. Sister Clara wasn't here when I was a Senior. I think she went to St. Margaret's or some place; I suppose she got a mission. I think perhaps there was an element of Sister Clara and Sister Antonia not seeing eye-to-eye. . . . Sister Clara was more conventional. Sister Mary John and Sister Eva were also more of the conventional school, and they dropped out somewhere when I was in the novitiate. They were, I think you might call them casualties.[66]

Sister Antonia's response to the loss was to immediately enact an even more ambitious plan to prepare faculty for the College. She quickly selected the most promising young Sisters from the novitiate, including Sisters Maris Stella Smith, Teresa Joseph Griswold, Helen Margaret Peck, Antonius Kennelly, Agnes Rita Lingl, Jeanne D'Arc Hurley, and Cecilia Manion, to pursue advanced studies. Sister Antonia also acted to free some of the College's faculty for a term, summer, or year to pursue further graduate studies. She made it possible for several of the Sisters to travel and study abroad over the next 10 years. Finally, to ensure the College would not lose ground, she employed highly competent instructors from nearby institutions, including the University of Minnesota, as substitutes for these Sisters.[67]

Under Sister Antonia's program of faculty development, the Sisters of St. Joseph at the College of St. Catherine rapidly accumulated advanced degrees at prestigious institutions, including the University of Munich, Columbia University, and the University of Louvain in Belgium, as well as the universities of Chicago, Minnesota, Michigan, and Catholic University. Two other Sisters received master's degrees from Oxford University.[68] Other Sisters spent several years traveling and studying in Europe. In the early 1920s, Sister Anna Goulet and Sister Cecilia Manion went to Paris to study music under the composer Marcel Dupre. Sister Eleanor Michel studied art history at the University of Madrid for a year and continued her studies in Florence, Paris, and Havana, Cuba.[69] By 1933, the College's faculty included 47 Sisters of St. Joseph and 19 laywomen. About two-thirds of the Sisters held advanced degrees from a variety of American and European universities. In contrast, most of the lay female faculty held degrees from regional institutions.[70]

In addition to cultivating the faculty, Sister Antonia's objectives for the College included building a financial endowment, raising the funds necessary to erect new buildings, maintaining an adequate library, and achieving national recognition for the scholastic achievements of the College.[71] During her tenure as dean and then president, she successfully solicited funds from both the Carnegie and Rockefeller Foundations that totaled $540,000. In addition, the Archdiocese of St. Paul gave the College a grant of $200,000 out of the Archbishop Ireland Educational Fund in 1921; it was the last time in the College's history that the Archdiocese would provide St. Catherine's with financial support. In response to a stipulation of the Rockefeller grant, Sister Antonia also organized the College's first Board of Trustees in 1920.[72]

Successful fundraising allowed Sister Antonia to pursue an ambitious plan for constructing new buildings and landscaping the College campus. As the newly appointed dean in 1914, she oversaw the construction already under way of Whitby Hall. Between 1921 and 1932 she built Caecilian, Mendel, and Fontbonne Halls and Our Lady of Victory Chapel. Funding from the Carnegie Foundation allowed Sister Antonia to expand the library's holdings from 12,000 books in 1916 to 50,000 volumes by 1937.[73]

Library in Derham Hall, 1914. Photo courtesy of St. Catherine University.

National recognition of the College of St. Catherine resulted from Sister Antonia's leadership and the scholarly achievements of her faculty Sisters. Having achieved regional accreditation in 1916, Sister Antonia immediately turned to the National Association of American Universities, receiving its stamp of approval in 1917. By 1924, she had successfully won for the College membership in the Association of American University Women.[74] Sister Antonia herself served as president of the Minnesota Association of Colleges and as chair of the National Catholic Educational Association Conference of Colleges for Women; she also held executive positions in the American Association of Colleges and participated in a White House conference on Child Health and Protection in 1930. Sister Antonia received papal honors in 1931, an honorary degree from the University of Minnesota in 1936, and a Distinguished Alumni award from the University of Chicago in 1937.[75] However, her greatest triumph and the crowning achievement of her administrative career was securing a chapter of the nation's oldest and most prestigious academic honor society, Phi Beta Kappa, for the College.

Sister Antonia had been dogged in her pursuit of Phi Beta Kappa membership. She first applied for a chapter of the Society in 1921, but was forced to abandon the effort due to a lack of support from administrators of liberal arts institutions that were already members of Phi Beta Kappa.[76] According to Sister Rosalie Ryan, there were subsequent unsuccessful attempts to secure a chapter as well. At one point, Sister Antonia was told that the College's library holdings were insufficient and the French Department was too weak. Sister Antonia's response to such rejections was to right whatever the review committee found wrong with the College and to try again.[77] Despite persistent obstacles, Sister Antonia was resolute in her determination to gain Phi Beta Kappa's imprimatur for the College. As Charles Buzicky explains, "The achievement of a Phi Beta Kappa chapter became an obsession with her; it was the measuring stick of her success as an educator."[78]

The final application to the Society began in 1933, when Sister Antonia asked Sister Jeanne Marie Bonnett, who had earned a doctorate in psychology from the University of Louvain, to steer the College through the review process. Sister Jeanne Marie wrote a 138-page report highlighting the College's qualifications as a liberal arts institution with a highly accomplished, committed faculty. To ensure that St. Catherine's would receive a site visit, Sister Jeanne Marie traveled to New York to meet with the Society's president, "to refute rumors that Catholic colleges curtailed academic freedom or suffered from 'in-breeding' of faculty." The Society conducted a site visit of St. Catherine's in December 1936. Early in 1937, the Society voted to grant the College membership.[79] For many years, St. Catherine's would remain the only Catholic college in the nation with a Phi Beta Kappa chapter, a stunning achievement for a young, small, Catholic women's college in the Upper Midwest.

It is difficult to exaggerate the import of Sister Antonia McHugh's influence and leadership in the history of the College of St. Catherine. Sister Antonia's expansive vision, heroic efforts, remarkable achievements, and devotion to mission constitute her continuing legacy to the College. Indeed, she is still with us at the College in many symbolic ways, such as the Antonian Scholars Program and the Mother Antonia McHugh Award. Moreover, Antonia lore (some of which, as with all legends, is not accurate) still abounds. Certainly the essential matter of her legacy remains: the conviction that the liberal arts and sciences should be the core, if not the entire substance, of a woman's college education. But she was not a saint, nor was her leadership always easy for others to bear: "her yoke was not always sweet or her burden light."[80] Sister Antonia's relentless pursuit of excellence brought change, wrought "gasps" from her superiors, and flung some of her Sisters aside, yet it also created a Catholic college for women of the highest caliber, one on par with the best secular institutions of its time. The genius behind her leadership was her ability to envision the future and to act as if it were already accomplished, which somehow, in the end, made it so. Like the Irelands before her, she too was extravagantly visionary. In 1936, the College's student fine arts publication, *Ariston*, explained Sister Antonia's talent for effecting change:

> But always to her St. Catherine's had been a great college, even when it was only a dream. Never just a building on a hill, it was a growing family of buildings: Caecilian, Mendel, the Health Center, the Chapel. All these she planned, built and peopled in her mind long before the architects were ever summoned. The pews of Our Lady of Victory Chapel were filled with girls in caps and gowns when the old chapel on Fourth Derham was still adequate to the College needs. It is that vision for the future, that aspiration for excellence and the creative power to convert vision into reality that has distinguished Mother Antonia's work in the entire field of education.[81]

NOTES

1. 1904 Announcement of Opening of the College of St. Catherine, St. Paul, Minnesota, College of St. Catherine (CSC) Archives.

2. Helena Caven Murray, CSC Alumna, Class of 1937, Alumnae Reminiscences of Mother Antonia McHugh, 1973, McHugh Papers, CSC Archives, Box 8.

3. Mother Antonia McHugh, "Address to the National Catholic Council of Women," undated, McHugh Papers, CSC Archives, Box 8.

4. Karen Kennelly, "Faculties and What They Taught," in Tracy Schier and Cynthia Russett, *Catholic Women's Colleges in America* (Baltimore: Johns Hopkins University Press, 2002), pp. 98–121.

5. *Ibid*, p. 98.

6. Sister Helen Angela Hurley, *On Good Ground: The Sisters of St. Joseph of Caron-delet* (Minneapolis: University of Minnesota Press, 1957), p. 86.

7. Nancy Woloch, *Women and the American Experience* (Boston: McGraw Hill, 2000), 3rd edition, chapters 4, 6, 8, 10, 12; M. Elizabeth Tidball, Daryl Smith, Charles Tidball, and Lisa Wolf-Wendel, *Taking Women Seriously* (Phoenix: American Council on Education, 1999), pp. 69–70.

8. Woloch, pp. 281–292.

9. Jill Ker Conway, "Faith, Knowledge and Gender," in *Catholic Women's Colleges in America*, pp. 11–16, at pp. 13–15; Kennelly, pp. 99–100; Woloch, p. 284. Welles-ley was the only prominent non-Catholic women's college with the tradition of a female president and all-female faculty in the late nineteenth century.

10. Woloch, chapters 14, 16, 18, 20.

11. Mary Oates, "Sisterhoods and Catholic Higher Education," in *Catholic Wom-en's Colleges in America*, p. 164.

12. *Ibid.*, p. 171.

13. Sister Anne Thomasine Sampson, *Care With a Prayer* (Minneapolis: St. Mary's Hospital, 1987); Sister Rosalie Ryan and Sr. John Christine Wolkerstorfer, *More Than A Dream* (St. Paul: College of St. Catherine, 1992); Charles Buzicky, "Mother Antonia's Impossible Dream: The College of St. Catherine," *Scan* (Fall 1973), pp. 5–12; Woloch, *Women and the American Experience*, chapters 10, 12, 14, 18.

14. Hurley, pp. 1–8.

15. Hurley, pp. 5–20.

16. Hurley, pp. 113–193.

17. Sampson, p. 11.

18. Hurley, pp. 164, 197–227. The Archbishop's cousin, Sister Celestine Howard, and another of his sisters, Sister St. John Ireland, were also prominent leaders in the order.

19. Hurley, pp. 200–210; William Watts Folwell, *A History of Minnesota* (St. Paul: Minnesota Historical Society, 1926), Volume IV, pp. 180–182; Reverend John Ire-land, *The Church and Modern Society* (St. Paul: Pioneer Press, 1904).

20. Hurley, p. 225; Karen Kennelly, "The Dynamic Sister Antonia and the College of St. Catherine," *Ramsey County History* (Fall/Winter 1978), pp. 3–18 at p. 7.

21. As quoted in Buzicky, p. 7; Ireland, *The Church and Modern Society*, pp. 300–301.

22. Hurley, pp. 228–229; Kennelly, "The Dynamic Sister Antonia," p. 7. Derham donated $20,000 for the building and $5,000 for a scholarship fund.

23. Sister Teresa Toomey, "The Best and Highest of Its Kind," *Scan* (Spring 1958), p. 10.

24. Toomey, p. 11.

25. Toomey, p. 10.

26. Toomey, p. 11; Sister Helen Margaret Peck, "An Academic History of the Col-lege of St. Catherine," (unpublished manuscript, 1982), Volume II, College of St. Catherine Archives, p. 29.

27. Peck, pp. 28–29. They were Sister Antonia, Sister De Sales Kilty, Sister Mary Joseph Kelly, and Sister Clara Graham.

28. Toomey, p. 12.

29. Kennelly, "The Dynamic Sister Antonia," p. 13.

30. Peck, "Academic History," pp. 1–2.

31. Sister Helen Margaret Peck, "The Growth and Expansion of the College of St. Catherine to the End of the Presidency of Sister Antonia McHugh," (unpublished manuscript, 1982), CSC Archives, pp. 3–4.

32. Buzicky, pp. 11–13; Kennelly, "The Dynamic Sister Antonia," pp. 11–12.

33. "PBK Investigative Report," 1937, as quoted in Buzicky, p. 12.

34. Toomey, pp. 13–14; Kennelly, "The Dynamic Sister Antonia," pp. 13–14.

35. Kennelly, "The Dynamic Sister Antonia," p. 13; Toomey, p. 14.

36. Hurley, pp. 236–237.

37. Hurley, p. 254, p. 264.

38. Toomey, p. 13.

39. Hurley, p. 229.

40. Hurley, p. 254.

41. Kennelly, "The Dynamic Sister Antonia," p. 16; Hurley, p. 245.

42. Hurley, p. 245.

43. Hurley, p. 245; Kennelly, "The Dynamic Sister Antonia," p. 16.

44. Buzicky, p. 12.

45. Kennelly, "The Dynamic Sister Antonia," p. 11; Hurley, p. 236.

46. Hurley, p. 248.

47. Hurley, p. 247.

48. Kennelly, "The Dynamic Sister Antonia," pp. 8–9; Ryan and Wolkerstorfer, p. 8.

49. Kennelly, "The Dynamic Sister Antonia," p. 8.

50. As quoted in Buzicky, p. 9.

51. Hurley, pp. 240–241.

52. Sister Marie Philip Haley, Oral History Interview, June 16, 1975, as quoted in Ryan manuscript for *More Than A Dream*, CSC Archives, p. 12a.

53. Sister Rosalie Ryan, Manuscript for *More Than a Dream*, CSC Archives, pp. 9–10.

54. Buzicky, p. 8.

55. Sister Antonia McHugh, "Recollections," Box 9, CSC Archives, as quoted in Ryan manuscript, p. 10.

56. Ryan manuscript, p. 10; Hurley, p. 248.

57. Sister Antonia, as quoted in Ryan manuscript, p. 10; Hurley, p. 235; Buzicky, pp. 8–10.

58. Hurley, p. 249.

59. Kennelly, "The Dynamic Sister Antonia," p. 13; Toomey, p. 20; Hurley, p. 244.

60. Kennelly, "Faculties and What They Taught," p. 105.

61. Sister Agnes Rita Lingl, Oral History, p. 13, as quoted in Ryan manuscript, p. 22a.

62. Kennelly, "Faculties and What They Taught," pp. 105–108.

63. Hurley, p. 245.

64. Toomey, p. 14.

65. Hurley, p. 245.

66. Sister Maris Stella Smith Oral Interview, January 14, 1975, CSC Archives, as quoted in Ryan manuscript, CSC Archives.

67. Peck, "Growth and Expansion," p. 47.

68. Kennelly, "The Dynamic Sister Antonia," p. 13.

69. Ryan manuscript, pp. 23, 25b.

70. Kennelly, "Faculties and What They Taught," p. 105.

71. Toomey, Material Collected on Sister Antonia McHugh, Box 8, CSC Archives, as quoted in Ryan manuscript, p. 19.

72. Toomey, p. 20.

73. *Ibid.*

74. *Ibid.*

75. Kennelly, "The Dynamic Sister Antonia," p. 16.

76. Kennelly, "The Dynamic Sister Antonia," p. 15.

77. Ryan and Wolkerstorfer, *More than a Dream*, pp. 31–32.

78. Buzicky, p. 12.

79. Buzicky, p. 12.

80. Buzicky, p. 12.

81. *Ariston*, 1936, as quoted in Peck, "Growth and Expansion," p. 118.

2

Portrait of a Daughter of Saint Joseph

Sister Jeanne Marie Bonnett

John Fleming

"Eyes open, ears attentive, and spirit alert, sleeves rolled up for ministry, without excluding the more humble, the less pleasing, the less noticeable."[1]

On first glance, "Portrait of a Daughter of Saint Joseph" by Father Marius Nepper, SJ, presents a commonly held view of women religious: the self-effacing, unassuming, naïve, and sheltered Sister. But a closer examination of women's religious orders in the middle of the twentieth century, especially Catholic religious orders, reveals a more richly nuanced portrait of their lives and works.

In their book, *Spirited Lives*, Carol Coburn and Martha Smith argue that communities of women religious, such as the Sisters of St. Joseph of Carondelet, embody four characteristics: an ethnic and cultural diversity, lifelong education and work, perpetual vows, and a distinctive environment and tradition. Drawing on these strengths, the Sisters created a female power base that enabled independent activity, limited patriarchal interference, and helped shape American Catholic culture and public life.[2]

With their European origins, the Sisters of St. Joseph remained culturally distinct, though they became just "Americanized" enough in order to successfully perform their ministries of service within the broader Protestant culture. The Sisters also devoted themselves to a lifelong commitment to education, which found expression in their various educational missions, including their founding of the College of St. Catherine. Moreover, their perpetual vows of poverty, obedience, and chastity helped the Sisters in their work with the heavily immigrant populations of their ministries and allowed them to maintain a distinct identity and perspective as they interacted with secular individuals and institutions. Their vow of obedience to the female superior of the order also served as a useful tool to limit or resist patriarchal influence. Finally, the closeness and inclusiveness of the religious community allowed the Sisters to live and work in a familial, sheltered setting that embraced multiple generations of Sisters. This woman-focused environment—established outside of the traditional roles of marriage and motherhood—allowed the construction of a collective power base that validated the significance of each Sister's life.[3]

This essay focuses on the life and contributions of one Sister of St. Joseph, Sister Jeanne Marie Bonnett, as a way of illuminating the early motivations and achievements of all the Sisters of St. Joseph as they founded and developed the College of St. Catherine. As historian Susan Geiger notes, life history research is a useful method to explore the relationship between experience and consciousness.[4] Among other feminist research methods, the holistic approach of interpreting a life story provides "new insights into social reality."[5]

Sister Jeanne Marie's life is, first and foremost, an American story of an individual living in community. Though the dominant forces of society were characterized by individualism, Sister Jeanne Marie lived and worked in relationship to others. Her entire adult life was framed by the Sisters of St. Joseph of Carondelet, St. Paul Province (CSJ). That community created common purposes in work, religion, and daily life. To be a member of the community required a vowed commitment, and life in that context involved both support and restrictions. After Jeanne Marie entered the congregation at age 18, like all Sisters she was assigned specific fields of study, professional roles to assume, and places to live. Within this system, however, Sister Jeanne Marie was anything but passive or powerless. As an individual living within a community, she negotiated with leaders, adapted to new contexts, formed alliances, and developed strategies to achieve her own goals on behalf of the congregation and College. Her relational approach to life and work, grounded in the Sisters' community and its religious convictions, was evident in her scholarship and teaching, as well as in her leadership roles within the College and in higher education nationally.

Arriving at the College of St. Catherine in its tenth year, Sister Jeanne Marie was a central figure in the institution's work over the next four decades. Her contributions reflected personal effort as well as the collective character of the Sisters of St. Joseph. As Geiger argues, it is misleading to create arguments of "representativeness" regarding a story of one individual.[6] Sister Jeanne Marie was not representative of the Sisters' community at St. Catherine's; the array of personalities and points of view defied the idea of a typical Sister. Nonetheless, her individual life story illuminates trends and key developments in the College's history. The challenges Sister Jeanne Marie faced and the contributions she made were expressions of the CSJ community.

Individual Sisters created unique lives even as they interacted to form their community. Sister Antonia provided the guidance and leadership in the early years of the College, but all members of the order were involved in discerning the needs of the broader community of neighbors. In that context, Sister Jeanne Marie made significant and lasting contributions to the development and daily business of the College. Active first as a student, then as a faculty member, and later as an administrator, Sister Jeanne Marie was affiliated with the College from 1915 until her death in 1958. Her life at St. Catherine's reflected how the skills and abilities of the Sisters were able to grow and adapt in order to meet "the needs of the good neighbor"—and how the Sisters' faith in God grounded all their works. Sister Jeanne Marie's career at St. Catherine's reflected the Sisters' mission to create a place where women could find meaningful lives for themselves and contribute richly to the wider society.

GROWING UP

Sister Jeanne Marie (Ruth Marguerite) Bonnett was born on January 17, 1897, to Anna and Abraham Bonnett of Magnolia, Minnesota. The family—which included Ruth Marguerite's two older brothers, Leonard and John, and a younger sister, Thelma—eventually settled in Grand Forks, North Dakota, where Abraham was involved in the grocery store business.[7]

Family letters indicate that the Bonnetts were close as a family, with Anna a strong influence in the lives of both her daughters. Education was of paramount importance to Anna Bonnett, and she pushed both girls to become students of high achievement. They were "students first, from day one."[8] Both girls graduated from Central High School in Grand Forks, and Thelma would later obtain a Ph.D. in English and psychology from the University of North Dakota.

Sister Jeanne Marie expressed her early interest in a life of religious devotion by wanting to join the Sisters of St. Joseph at age 16. Anna convinced her instead to enter college, so Sister Jeanne Marie attended the University of North Dakota from 1913 to 1915.[9] However, she did not lose her interest in the Sisters of St. Joseph and was received into the order in 1915, when she was 18. She then attended the College of St. Catherine as a student from 1915 to 1917, graduating with a B.A. in Latin, German, and English. She took her final vows two days after Christmas in 1920.

SISTER ANTONIA MCHUGH

While Anna Bonnett was a central figure in Sister Jeanne Marie's young life, a significant role model in her adult life was Sister Antonia McHugh. With her powerful personality and strong vision for the College of St. Catherine, Sister Antonia made a forceful impression on everyone around her, students and

Sisters alike. As Mary Ellen Chase recalls in *A Goodly Fellowship*, Sister Antonia "went at the realization of St. Catherine's College with everything she had in her, and she had literally everything. . . . She had a positive genius for detail, and she was a perfectionist in every sense of the word."[10]

Such intense dedication resonated with Sister Jeanne Marie. Individuals who knew Sister Jeanne Marie from her years at St. Catherine's describe her as determined, never standing still, and consumed to do the best job possible with whatever she set out to accomplish.[11] Speaking of Sister Jeanne Marie, former St. Catherine's president Sister Mary William Brady noted, "She was a driven women and she drove everybody. . . . I think she was deeply interested in Saint Catherine's. I think she wanted to see it as perfect a college as she could. . . . Her part was to make this area [her work] absolutely perfect."[12]

No doubt sensing Sister Jeanne Marie's talents and potential, Sister Antonia sent her to the University of Minnesota for further study. In 1919, Sister Jeanne Marie earned a master's degree in psychology and in educational psychology, after which she was appointed as a faculty member of the Psychology and Education Department at St. Catherine's. Teaching, though, was only part of her duties. Along with Sister Antonia and Sister Ste. Helene Guthrie, Sister Jeanne Marie now became part of a powerful and dynamic trio that would guide the development of the College during the 1920s and 1930s.

STUDY ABROAD

Fulfilling Sister Antonia's dreams and expectations for the growing College would require a core faculty of first-rate scholars who were well-traveled and culturally aware, who were recognized experts in their fields, and who held Ph.D.s from major world universities. To forge such a faculty, Sister Antonia charged a vanguard of Sisters to undertake extensive travel and study in both the United States and Europe. (See Carroll, this volume, for further discussion.) Sister Jeanne Marie had studied at the University of Chicago in 1920 and at Columbia University in 1922. In 1924, she and Sister Ste. Helene were selected by Sister Antonia to study in Oxford, England. The two embarked on the *Paquebot Paris* for the trip across the Atlantic on August 20, 1924, landing in England on August 25.

Although Sister Jeanne Marie and Sister Ste. Helene were originally directed to study at Oxford and tour English public schools, Sister Jeanne Marie's penchant for taking initiative and making connections created another option, one that opened her "assignment" to negotiation with her superior. A letter to Sister Antonia written on September 5 contained some "startling" news:

I am so excited that I can not begin to think of anything until I have written about it to you. At the suggestion of Mr. Simpson of the American Union of Universities, I wrote to the American Institute in Berlin for information about Munich and Freiburg, and to the Foundation Universitare in Brussels for the same about Louvain. . . . The letter from Father Van von Essen, the Secretary of Louvain overcame me with assurance that a Ph.D. could be obtained at Louvain with one year's residence (at least), the transfer of my credits, and the completion of my thesis (if its subject wins approval) under the direction of an assigned professor. I am fool enough, Sister, to be willing to try, should you desire me so. Of course I shall await your direction before making any final decision. . . . All of this would mean giving up Oxford and being with Sister (Ste. Helene) but if she gets England and I Louvain and Munich or Berlin, we can exchange experiences and, so profit doubly. Sister is very anxious for me to do Louvain. If I could only transfer her confidence to myself. I should be less timorous than I am. I wish you were here to give me a little push—but you just look sweetly down from the mantle as if to say "Do what you think best and all will be well." I need the push though really.[13]

The approval must have arrived because her credits were transferred and her master's thesis was sent, allowing Sister Jeanne Marie to start at Louvain in October of 1924. The Catholic University of Louvain in Louvain, Belgium, was founded in 1425 by a papal bull issued by Pope Martin V. It is the oldest Catholic University in the world and included the American College at Louvain. Founded in 1857 to train European priests for American missions, the American College had become by 1924 a center for the training of American priests. Both the University and the American College had fine reputations as centers of advanced thinking on the ecclesiastical issues of the day.[14]

Although it was an exciting time for Sister Jeanne Marie, the experience of traveling to Louvain and settling in was not without new revelations and adjustments. Much of Belgium, including the University itself, was still recovering from the destruction of World War I, as Sister Jeanne Marie noted in a letter to Sister Ste. Helene:

Buildings, narrow and small, alternated with broken spaces. The latter mark the places where the Germans destroyed the town; their concrete dugouts still line the shore, and become harder and more impossible to remove each year; they cannot be used for anything.[15]

More challenges awaited Sister Jeanne Marie when she began her studies in the Pedagogy Department, which had only been in existence for a year. The Doctorat en Pedagogie was an arduous program, and Sister Jeanne Marie now found herself a woman in an overwhelmingly male-dominated academic environment. In that unfamiliar environment that did not necessarily welcome her interests, she wrote to Sister Antonia, "I think it is diplomacy

I am trying to practice, is it? If I can find out what is wanted here, I shall not spare any effort to satisfy their wants. It seems safer to work on their interests here, rather than mine."[16]

Her studies, moreover, were a challenge because they were in French, which Sister Jeanne Marie only barely spoke when she arrived. To improve her French and to keep up with the subject matter in her lessons, she obtained complete notes from other students, copied them, and then memorized them. During her first semester, she wrote to Sister Ste. Helene that "I have now gone from the 'copying' stage to the 'verifying' stage." At this "verifying" stage, she was able to understand most of the French words in her notes. As she wrote to Sister Ste. Helene, "It is a queer way to study; don't you think?"[17]

Loneliness was another struggle for Sister Jeanne Marie, as it was for Sister Ste. Helene, the two friends now studying hundreds of miles apart. Yet Sister Jeanne Marie did make new friends at Louvain. One American priest she met there, Father (later Bishop) Fulton Sheen, was to become a lifelong friend of both Sister Jeanne Marie and her family.

In her doctoral studies, Sister Jeanne Marie strove to create "a distinct piece of work here at Louvain." In her thesis, entitled "The Teaching of Religion," she examined how religion was being taught at the College of St. Catherine and at several schools in Belgium. This work would prove to be foundational to further work she undertook on women's pedagogy and her continued interest in teaching religion. As Sister Jeanne Marie described in a letter to Sister Antonia, her final exams and dissertation defense were a combination of nerve-wracking and exhilarating: "After each of them [her final exams] I felt as though some electrical instrument had been passed over my whole body. . . . Thank God they are all over and never to be taken again."[18] She completed all her work successfully and was awarded a Doctorat en Pedagogie—the first woman to earn such a degree at Louvain, a fact that must have contributed to the status of the College. Her degree was also granted with *plus grande distinction*. ("Why they gave me plus grande distinction the angels alone know,"[19] she wrote to Sister Antonia.) Her work at Louvain now finished, Sister Jeanne Marie returned to St. Paul with Sister Ste. Helene in August of 1925.

WOMEN'S EDUCATION

During the 1930s and 1940s, decades before the second-wave women's movement, the Sisters of St. Joseph of Carondelet were actively involved in writing and speaking about the education of women. Sister Jeanne Marie played a leading role in these efforts, writing and speaking publicly about education, especially as it pertained to religion and the development of character. In "The Religious Development of Women at the College of St. Catherine" and "The Education of Christian Character," both published in 1933, Sister Jeanne Marie explored the goals of women's education when set within a religious context.[20] She sought to move students toward "sincere holiness in life, toward religious maturity," with Christ being the model. The developmental ideal was "a woman of demonstrated power to think, speak, and act in a unique way on an elevated plane of wholesome integration because of guided religious development."[21] According to Sister Jeanne Marie, the curriculum at St. Catherine's was designed to guide students toward that ideal during the four years of their college education.

The question of a curriculum specific to women was, of course, of great interest to her. She was, in many ways, a pioneer in grappling with questions of gender in the early to mid-twentieth century, and her contributions, which challenged some of the conventional notions of her day, laid the groundwork for later studies of gender. In 1932, she spoke on "The Problems of a Differentiated Curriculum for Women" at the Conference of the National Association of Deans of Women in Washington, D.C. Specifically addressing how women's college curricula might differ from those of men, she asked whether there should be any difference at all and went on to connect this question to whether curricular changes should be related to the social and economic conditions of the time. She argued that certain principles of "universal and permanent value" may be found in the "unexcelled statements of the natural law"; these principles, she said, remain the same from one era to the next and thus should be the same for women's and men's curriculum. Within different contexts, however, she advocated changes relating to "the particular aspects of those adjustments called for in the occupations of individuals . . . thought of as social and economic." Colleges, in her view, should adapt "the program of studies to the newer demands made on individuals by society today." In this, she hints at movement away from a strict adherence to the same standards and curriculum for women as for men that Mother Antonia advocated. Sister Jeanne Marie seems to have recognized that the same "universal truths" should be taught to both women and men, and like Mother Antonia, strongly believed in women's intellectual abilities to reach the same high educational standards as men in learning these truths. Yet she also seems to have recognized that what might today be called social locations—social, economic, gender locations—can and should be taken into account when devising a curriculum.[22]

In her writing, Sister Jeanne Marie discussed St. Catherine's curriculum and noted Mother Antonia's aims "to enable the young women of the northwest to do their share of the world's work in a generous, gracious, beneficent manner." Sister Jeanne Marie also identified the occupations for which she was preparing young women: "To teach, to heal, to make a home, to know the law and to participate in government, to rehabilitate the handicapped, to guide the reading of the community, and to continue to study." Faculty and administrators must possess "respect for the intelligence of women and an attitude of reasonable adaptability . . . and sincere and earnest scholarship." To Sister Jeanne Marie, all these educational objectives on behalf of women must be addressed simultaneously: "let us avoid . . . the fallacy of 'either or' or of 'not this, but that' . . . any partial objective will miss the target of wholesome personality development . . . our difference must be only in emphasis . . . we must move the whole ahead."[23]

In addition to her writing, Sister Jeanne Marie often spoke to audiences outside the College on topics related to education and religion. Though many of these lectures have been lost, one of her presentations that still remains was delivered to the American Association of University Women on May 10, 1937. In her talk, entitled "Reviews and Previews of College Life,"[24] she reflects on college life in terms of experiential "lenses," which for her included architecture (the buildings and physical makeup of a campus), fine arts, reading, science, philosophy, scholarship, and companionship. All of these are important to the student experience, she emphasized, though she particularly identified the company of women and women teachers as an advantage to the prospective college student. "To live and learn with women who are scholars in their own right is no small advantage. Admittedly some of the best teachers of women are women. At least at first, and in certain colleges now, the intellectual life of women is better respected and better fostered in colleges for women alone."[25]

Within the strong thread of faith and devotion in her works, Sister Jeanne Marie argued for women making the most of themselves and contributing to society in a meaningful way. For example, in a 1946 speech entitled "Women in Medical Science," she stated that a woman who is interested in a medical science career should consider becoming a physician as her first option. If a woman "in her mind and her heart" cannot see herself as a doctor, she remarked, then other medical fields offered suitable professional options.[26]

RECRUITMENT DUTIES

Finding talented students to attend St. Catherine's occupied many Sisters throughout its early history. One of the most consistently excellent recruiters on campus was Sister Jeanne Marie, who, during the 1930s and early 1940s, would often spend an entire quarter away from the College on recruiting trips.[27] To find prospective students, parish priests, alumnae, and high school officials were all contacted on a regular basis. Class valedictorians were especially prized and were given scholarships to St. Catherine's.

Chemistry lab, Mendel Hall, 1940. Photo courtesy of St. Catherine University.

Sister Jeanne Marie often wrote the dean, Sister Ste. Helene, on her recruiting trips, reporting about the girls she was visiting and their qualifications and raising questions about how the College might support their enrollment. Competition among colleges for these girls could be fierce at times, and persuasive negotiation was critical if the College was to successfully attract a particularly talented student. The following example is typical of Sister Jeanne Marie's correspondence:

[She] has an average for four years of high school of 97.3 and has given a public piano recital. St. Teresa nuns had come in April and interviewed her. The Franciscan College at Joliet offered her a $350 scholarship and have been sending urgent letters regularly once a week. My argument: A class "A" mind deserves a class "A" college and vice versa finally won and we secured her reservation—as a graduation gift (from her parents). I hope you approve of the several conditions I had to arrange. I almost called you long distance, but the payment is so secure and the girl so really wonderful that I counted on your approval. It is very likely that one or two other girls will come with her. They are definitely and seriously considering it. I called on six.[28]

The student described here is Alberta Huber, who joined the Sisters of St. Joseph and later became President of the College from 1964 to 1979.

PHI BETA KAPPA

Perhaps the crowning achievement of Sister Antonia's tenure as president of St. Catherine's was its acceptance into Phi Beta Kappa. Jeanne Marie played a central role in this accomplishment as well, having authored the report to the Qualifications Committee in the College's 1936 application to the Honor Society. (See Carroll, this volume.) Included in this report was a statement of the College's purposes: "to develop in students dependable power through genuine experience of what is true and fine in the present and the past; to challenge them in both thought and will; to sensitize students to many kinds of excellence; to cultivate in them universal sympathies and truly liberal taste; and leadership and group responsibilities."[29]

Sister Jeanne Marie, who had become a Phi Beta Kappa member in 1917 while attending the University of Minnesota, was inducted into St. Catherine's Gamma chapter as an alumnae member and then named its first secretary-treasurer. Although the College now had a chapter, not all Phi Beta Kappa members were happy with its induction into the Honor Society. In 1939, Dr. William Shimer, the secretary of Phi Beta Kappa, asked Sister Jeanne Marie to respond to members who were protesting the awarding of a Phi Beta Kappa chapter to a Roman Catholic school. According to the protesters, following the Pope and the Church was "antagonistic" to the religious, philosophical, and political principles of the United States and Phi Beta Kappa, which valued intellectual freedom.[30]

Jeanne Marie, after consulting with Sister Antonia, wrote a detailed reply to their arguments. While pointing out the commonalities of all Christendom to divine knowledge and the separation of the Church from the affairs of government and science, "provided that they do not violate the rights of God and man," Sister Jeanne Marie commented on the level of prejudice and misunderstanding reflected in the protests:

> At first thought, one might wonder why anyone would raise the question of Church affiliation when a purely academic matter is under consideration. But on second thought, one realizes that, of course the persons entrusted with the academic distinction are also persons who live according to the precepts of their churches. Would that we could dissolve prejudice with truth more whole seen, and allay fear by more frequent good example. Perhaps in admitting Catholics to membership in their Society, Phi Beta Kappa will increase its burden somewhat, but if we are not already all the present members think we should be, even academically, ought they not be willing to regard us as brothers and be our keepers, lifting us to their level, so that we may do our work better in this nation of ours?[31]

Eventually, the protests subsided and Phi Beta Kappa became part of the College's academic life. A lifelong dream of Sister Antonia's had now been reached, one that was a College-wide effort and source of pride, and Sister Jeanne Marie's contributions to these efforts were particularly noted. As Sister Mona Riley stated, "I think much of the work that was done to get Phi Beta Kappa was under the hard work and contribution of Sister Jeanne Marie. Sister Antonia wanted it, but it was Sister Jeanne Marie who maneuvered it. They were a great team."[32]

NEW CAREER DIRECTIONS

By the late 1930s, Sister Jeanne Marie had achieved a position at St. Catherine's that was fulfilling and deeply integrated into its intellectual life. However, beginning in 1937, a series of events changed the direction of her career, with the result that she no longer commanded the same influence within the College.

In 1936, Sister Antonia suffered several strokes that caused her to resign as College president in 1937. Although she would continue to receive awards and dispense advice when asked, Sister Antonia now led a quieter life outside the mainstream of College business. During the following years, Sister Jeanne Marie accompanied Sister Antonia on professional business trips, providing support to her.[33] With Sister Antonia's retirement, however, Sister Jeanne Marie had lost her most important ally and mentor.

Another blow fell to Sister Jeanne Marie on May 2, 1939, when Anna Bonnett—another confidant and mentor—died from a brain tumor and bronchopneumonia.[34] After her mother's death, Sister Jeanne Marie assumed an even greater role as the primary caretaker of her family, which now included providing financial support to her brother Leonard and his children.

Changes were also taking place in the Psychology and Education Department, which Sister Jeanne Marie had chaired since 1924. In 1941, Sister Annette Walters became the new head of department, a position she would hold until 1961. A former student of Sister Jeanne Marie, Sister Annette had attended St. Catherine's in the 1930s and started teaching in the Psychology and Education Department in 1938. In 1941, she completed a Ph.D. in Experimental Psychology at the University of Minnesota. Although there is no direct record of a conflict between the two, Sister Annette evidently brought significantly new viewpoints to the department. In addition to being replaced as department chair, Sister Jeanne Marie's course load was also being reduced. By the 1942–1943 academic year, she was only teaching four courses.

Being marginalized in both her teaching and leadership roles must have frustrated Sister Jeanne Marie, a woman who was always more intently focused on the intellectual life of the College than on its social aspects and relationships.[35] In a letter to her sister Thelma some years later, Sister Jeanne Marie acknowledged some of her own social shortcomings: "I am not

attractive to anyone, as you know, because work and study and prayer fill
every hour and I have never 'socialized.' . . . I am certainly not popular."[36]

Without her chief ally, Sister Antonia, the enforced changes in her relationships and work left Sister Jeanne Marie without a clear path and
purpose. Someone who was not a Sister and so deeply committed to her
community and work might well have been temped to move to a different educational institution; Sister Jeanne Marie, of course, remained at St.
Catherine's, in her community. Her career might then have drifted indefi-
nitely or faded slowly into obscurity, but a new and unexpected challenge
presented itself to her, leading her to make some of her best known contributions to the College of St. Catherine.

STUDYING OCCUPATIONAL THERAPY

During World War II, the College experienced new demands from students
and the community. Many advocated for an expansion of majors in medical
and professional fields that would be helpful to the nation during wartime.
Led by Sister Eucharista Galvin, President of the College from 1937 to 1943,
and Sister Antonius Kennelly, President from 1943 to 1949, the College demonstrated its patriotic support through several war drives, Red Cross projects,
and prayer campaigns. As the need for trained health care workers became
evident, the College responded by starting a nursing program in 1942, with
a Cadet Nursing program being offered from 1943 to 1948.

The relatively new field of Occupational Therapy (OT) also experienced
growth across the country during and after the war. In April of 1944, Roxa
Henderson, an occupational therapist from the Veterans Administration
Hospital in Minneapolis, made an influential presentation on campus that
galvanized interest in starting an OT program at St. Catherine's.[37] Some of
the faculty also agreed that an OT curriculum would be worthwhile. Sister
Antonius, who was College president at the time, stated, "We did start the occupational therapy department. . . . I had some doubts about it because they
[nursing and occupational therapy] were both non-liberal . . . and I was supposed to be standing up for a liberal arts college. But I felt it was patriotic to do
it to help out the war effort and also take care of the increased enrollment."[38]

Some of this push undoubtedly came from trends outside the College
in the field of occupational therapy itself. The profession had begun a process of academic formalization in the 1930s by emphasizing educational
standards and increased professionalism through an association with the
American Medical Association. World War II accelerated this process and
created pressure to develop qualified graduates within a shorter training
period. The American Occupational Therapy Association then started working with the United States Army, which culminated in the development of
shorter "War Emergency Courses."

Somewhat surprisingly, St. Catherine's now found itself a latecomer to a growing national trend to start and expand academic programs in occupational therapy.[39] To rectify this situation, Sister Antonius appointed Sister Jeanne Marie to develop and administer an OT program. One might ask why Sister Jeanne Marie was selected for this position. Several factors may explain Sister Antonius's choice. As noted earlier, Sister Jeanne Marie had experienced major shifts in her duties that left her much less busy on campus. Moreover, Sister Jeanne Marie was greatly respected for her intellect and was viewed as someone who could meet the enormous demands of changing her career direction in a short period of time. And although OT used arts and crafts rather extensively—not exactly areas of expertise for Sister Jeanne Marie—occupational therapy also integrated such disciplines as psychology and social services, while holding to a holistic view of physical and mental health. These areas were deeply related to much of what Sister Jeanne Marie had taught in the Psychology and Education Department.

By July of 1944—less than four months after Roxa Henderson's speech at St. Catherine's—Sister Jeanne Marie was taking courses at the Boston School of Occupational Therapy (now part of Tufts University). Although learning crafts posed a challenge for her, it also brought her pleasure. "I love woodwork. St. Joseph seems very near when I use the chisel, plane, and saw."

During her studies, Sister Jeanne Marie also worked with the Boston faculty and with the OT school at New York University to develop an OT program for St. Catherine's—an interesting challenge for her as OT curricula varied greatly. She was also enriched by her own clinical experiences: "It is good to have patients as assignments; mine have numbered ten so far and I have learned much from trying to help each one of them." In September 1945, she finished her clinical fieldwork in Boston and New York; she then returned to St. Paul to start the OT program.

DEVELOPING AN OT PROGRAM

Courses and lectures now had to be developed, students recruited and enrolled, and fieldwork affiliations established. Two issues were particularly challenging: developing lectures around medical issues and landing clinical affiliations for students. Adding to these early difficulties was the fact that there was no medical school affiliated with the College of St. Catherine. For medical lectures, Sister Jeanne Marie proved her resourcefulness by organizing them in conjunction with the nursing students at five Twin Cities hospitals. She also called upon Sisters from the College's Art Department to teach classes in crafts.[40] As part of her own teaching contribution to the new department, Sister Jeanne Marie taught a printing class as well as theory courses in occupational therapy.

Thirteen students enrolled in the OT program's initial classes. The first student to graduate from the program, Dolores Zumwalde, completed her studies in 1946 and went on to become the director of Minnesota's Tuberculosis Sanitarium. Within a year of graduating its first student, the OT program received a vote of encouragement from the Educational Committee of the American Occupational Therapy Association, which granted its final accreditation in 1947—the first OT program to be accredited in the state of Minnesota.

Sister Jeanne Marie worked tirelessly to expand the OT program and to develop new agreements with clinical sites for affiliations. When necessary, she even started her own clinical experiences with students. Frequently, the pilot projects she began turned into full occupational therapy departments, often with a St. Catherine's graduate serving as department head. OT programs were begun in this fashion at St. Mary's Hospital, Anoka State Hospital, and St. Joseph's Hospital in Saint Paul.[41] St. Catherine's OT alumnae soon became an important regional presence in occupational therapy practice; a number of them would become faculty members in St. Catherine's OT Department, with several rising to become department chairs.

Another challenge facing Sister Jeanne Marie and the OT program was the integration of professional education with the liberal arts. While some on campus viewed the OT program's creation as a patriotic duty, others believed that all professional departments compromised the liberal arts character of the College. To Sister Jeanne Marie, the connection between the liberal arts and occupational therapy was obvious, but within the College she felt that the connection had to be repeatedly emphasized in department reports and activities.

In one such department report of 1957, "An Interpretation of Departmental Responsibility to Liberal Arts Education," Sister Jeanne Marie pointed out that occupational therapy contained liberal arts at its core. She wrote:

> In a democracy it is preferable to begin liberal and professional education together—in college—and to continue them together after college, rather than to have "a plus-plus arrangement" of general education followed by professional education within a program of liberal arts.[42]

She further pointed out the variety and depth of study required of OT students, noting that two of them had been admitted to Phi Beta Kappa. She disagreed with occupational therapy being classified in the College's Division of Community Services, stating that its rightful place was "interdepartmental and interdivisional." The report also advocates the continuation of the Occupational Therapy program—her response, perhaps, to those at the College who questioned the program or wanted to eliminate it. Many OT students agreed that the program's emphasis on the liberal arts gave the St. Catherine's graduate a distinctive, possibly unique perspective on occupational therapy practice.

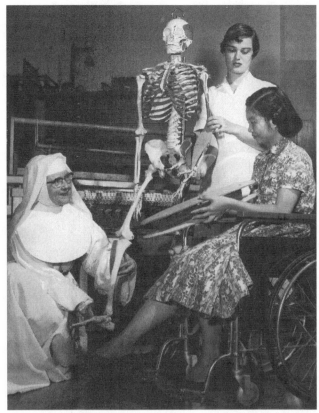

Sister Jeanne Marie Bonnett with students in occupational therapy lab, 1956. Photo courtesy of St. Catherine University.

BEARING GOOD FRUIT

Through her study on the East Coast and her development of St. Catherine's OT program, Sister Jeanne Marie built an extensive network of professional associates in the field of occupational therapy. She was actively involved in the American Occupational Therapy Association, which elected her to its governing Board of Management in 1948; she would serve on the Board for 10 years. As chair of the Committee on Graduate Study, Sister Jeanne Marie researched national trends in occupational therapy and examined the educational requirements for graduate study within the field. She also proposed a master's degree program for the College of St. Catherine. (Her proposal was not accepted, however; a graduate program in Occupational Therapy would have to wait until 1994.)

By 1958, Sister Jeanne Marie's work was "bearing good fruit," and occupational therapy had grown into a strong department at the College of
St. Catherine. In April 1958, though, Sister Jeanne Marie suddenly became
ill, a problem later diagnosed as heart fibrillation. After an initial hospital
stay, Sister Jeanne Marie returned to campus with strict orders to rest and
take care of herself. She was too driven, however, to remain inactive. She
would wait until the campus quieted down and then run back to her office
to continue her work.[43] Eventually, she had to return to the hospital, where
she passed away on May 10, 1958, at the age of 61.

Tributes to Sister Jeanne Marie flowed in to the College from individuals,
government agencies, and academic programs in occupational therapy. A
common theme in this correspondence was the quality of energy and excellence that Sister Jeanne Marie exhibited in all matters related to education.
As one OT colleague said of her, "there are few of us in this world who
combine her gentle spirit with such dedicated strength."[44]

NOTES

1. Marius Nepper, S.J., "Portrait of a Daughter of Saint Joseph," in Ann Thomasine Sampson, CSJ, *Seeds on Good Ground* (St. Paul: Sisters of Saint Joseph of Carondelet, 2000), p. 369.

2. Carol K. Coburn and Martha Smith, *Spirited Lives: How Nuns Shaped Catholic
Culture and American Life, 1836–1920* (Chapel Hill: University of North Carolina
Press, 1999), pp. 3–9.

3. *Ibid.*, pp. 9–11.

4. Susan Geiger, "Women's Life Histories: Method and Content," *Signs, Journal
of Women in Culture and Society* 11 (2) (1986): pp. 334–351.

5. Sharlene Nagy Hesse-Biber, Patricia Leavy, and Michelle Yaiser, "Feminist Approaches to Research as a Process: Reconceptualizing Epistemology, Methodology,
and Method," in S. N. Hesse-Biber and M. L. Yaiser, eds., *Feminist Perspectives on
Social Research* (New York: Oxford University Press, 2004), pp. 3–26.

6. Susan Geiger, "What's so Feminist About Women's Oral History?" *Journal of
Woman's History* 2 (1) (1990): pp. 169–182.

7. Oral History interview with Rozanne Ebersole, grand niece of Sister Jeanne
Marie Bonnett, (December 15, 2004), College of Saint Catherine Occupational
Therapy Department Archives (CSC OT Archives).

8. Oral history interview, Rozanne Ebersole, CSC OT Archives.

9. *Ibid.*; Educational records of Sister Jeanne Marie Bonnett, Sisters of Saint Joseph of Carondelet (CSJ) Archives.

10. Mary Ellen Chase, *A Goodly Fellowship* (New York: MacMillan Company,
1959), p. 233 (originally published in 1939).

11. Oral History interviews, Rozanne Ebersole, Mary Virginia Micka, Sister Alberta Huber, December 3, 2004; Sister Mary William Brady, December 1, 2004,
CSC OT Archives.

12. Oral history interview, Mary William Brady, CSJ, CSC OT Archives.

13. Sister Jeanne Marie Bonnett to Sister Antonia McHugh, September 5, 1924, CSJ Archives.

14. "University of Louvain," *New Catholic Encyclopedia*, 1967, pp. 1033–1038.

15. Sister Jeanne Marie Bonnett to Sister Ste. Helene Guthrie, October 10, 1925, CSJ Archives.

16. Sister Jeanne Marie Bonnett to Sister Antonia McHugh, Feast of Saint Catherine, 1925, CSJ Archives.

17. Sister Jeanne Marie Bonnett to Sister Ste. Helene Guthrie, Feast of Saint Catherine, 1925, CSJ Archives.

18. Sister Jeanne Marie Bonnett to Sister Antonia McHugh, July 28, 1925, CSJ Archives.

19. *Ibid.*

20. Jeanne Marie Bonnett, CSJ, "The Religious Development of Women at the College of St. Catherine," *Journal of Religious Instruction* (June 1933): pp. 868–885; "The Education of Christian Character," *Catholic Education Review* (June 1933): pp. 345–357.

21. Bonnett, "Religious Development," pp. 870, 871.

22. Jeanne Marie Bonnett, CSJ, "Problems of a Differentiated Curriculum for Women," *Catholic Education Review* (May and June 1932): pp. 273–281, 359–366.

23. *Ibid.*

24. Jeanne Marie Bonnett, CSJ, " Reviews and Previews of College Life," (May 10, 1937), CSJ Archives.

25. *Ibid.*

26. Jeanne Marie Bonnett, CSJ, "Women in Medical Science" (1946), CSJ Archives.

27. Oral History Interviews of Mona Riley, CSJ, September 22, 1982, and Helen Peck, CSJ, July 8, 1974, College of St. Catherine (CSC) Archives.

28. Sister Jeanne Marie Bonnett to Sister Ste. Helene Guthrie, May 26, 1933, CSJ Archives.

29. Jeanne Marie Bonnett, CSJ, "The General Report of the College of Saint Catherine to the Phi Beta Kappa Committee on Qualifications," (1935), CSJ Archives.

30. Jeanne Marie Bonnett, CSJ, "Factors which Operate to Disqualify Roman Catholic Educational Institutions for Fellowship with Phi Beta Kappa," Attached to a letter from William A. Shimer, July 24, 1939, Phi Beta Kappa File, CSC Archives.

31. Sister Jeanne Marie Bonnett to William A. Shimer, August 7, 1939, Phi Beta Kappa File, CSC Archives.

32. Mona Riley interview, September 22, 1982, CSC Archives.

33. Antonius Kennelly, CSJ, Oral History Interview, December 14, 1973, CSC Archives.

34. Autopsy Report, May 2, 1939, University of Minnesota Hospitals and letters from Sister Jeanne Marie to Anna Bonnett, 1925–1939, CSJ Archives.

35. Mary William Brady, CSJ, Alberta Huber, CSJ, Virginia Micka, CSJ, interviews, CSC Archives.

36. Sister Jeanne Marie Bonnett to Thelma Fitzgerald, November 28, 1953, Family letter collection of Rozanne Ebersole.

37. *St Catherine Wheel*, October 14, 1944, CSC Archives. There is also a comment in a letter from Sister Jeanne Marie to Sister Antonius, January 11, 1945, that two students have written her in Boston specifically inquiring about OT courses, Letters to CSC Presidents, CSJ Archives.

38. Antonius Kennelly, CSJ, Oral history interview (December 14, 1973), CSC Archives.

39. Wendy Colman, "Evolving Practices in Occupational Therapy: The War Emergency Courses, 1936–1954," *American Journal of Occupational Therapy* 44 (1) (1990): pp. 1028–1036.

40. Jeanne Marie Bonnett, CSJ, "Occupational Therapy Department Report, 1945–1946," CSC OT Archives.

41. *Ibid.*

42. Sister Jeanne Bonnett, "An Interpretation of Departmental Responsibility to Liberal Arts Education," March 25, 1957, CSC OT Archives.

43. Mary William Brady, interview, CSC Archives.

44. Elizabeth Fuchs to CSC President Mary William Brady, CSJ, May 18, 1958, Obituary correspondence, CSJ Archives.

3

Opening Doors

Sister AJ and the Minneapolis Campus

Deborah Churchill and Thelma Obah

After more than 60 years as a school of nursing at St. Mary's Hospital, what is now the Minneapolis campus of St. Catherine University became a coeducational junior college in 1963. The first junior college in the nation devoted exclusively to health care programs, St. Mary's was part of a movement to provide educational access to underserved populations. The campus's liberatory principles, commitment to working-class students, and insistence on providing academic support to all students reflect the influence of its founder, Sister Anne Joachim Moore (1916-2010), whose visionary leadership continues to infuse and motivate the campus today. The story of St. Mary's is inseparable from her story.

BEGINNINGS

In 1887, the Sisters of St. Joseph of Carondelet took over the operation of a hospital founded 20 years earlier by the Sisters of Mercy. During a cholera epidemic, the Sisters of St. Joseph were having difficulties meeting the hospital's staffing needs, so they started their own school of nursing, graduating a first class of three students in 1903. The school later received national accreditation and, by 1928, a "Class A" rating from the American College of Surgeons.[1]

It was to this hospital-based School of Nursing that Catherine Mary Moore (later Sister Anne Joachim) came in 1934 upon her graduation from Derham Hall, a high school sponsored by the Sisters of St. Joseph. Moore graduated with a three-year diploma in nursing in 1937. She then moved to Connecticut and worked as a staff nurse and Industrial First Aid Specialist for five

St. Mary's Junior College, 1960s. Photo courtesy of St. Catherine University.

years. When she joined the Army Nurse Corps in 1943, she might well have thought that her connection to nursing education in Minneapolis was over.

In 1945, after serving in World War II in England, Moore returned to Minnesota and enrolled at the College of St. Catherine as one of 24 female veterans who "unexpectedly . . . decided to return to college" with benefits from the GI Bill.[2] She received her baccalaureate in nursing in 1946, when she was almost 30 years old. Moore was a self-described "late bloomer." After later enrolling at the St. Paul College of Law, she became interested in becoming a nun. However, the novice mistress explained to Moore that "it's either this year or never," as novices could be no more than 35 years old when entering the convent.[3] Moore immediately dropped out of law school, joined the Sisters of St. Joseph in 1949, and then finished her law degree in 1950.

As Sister Anne Joachim Moore (or Sister AJ, as she was affectionately known), her first assignment was in Fargo, North Dakota, as the associate director of the Sisters of St. Joseph School of Nursing. She served there until 1957, when she was called back to Minneapolis to become the director of the St. Mary's Hospital School of Nursing, the school that had granted her a nursing diploma 20 years earlier.[4] From 1942 until 1957, the College of St. Catherine had operated the School of Nursing, which would now establish itself as an independent entity with Sister AJ's arrival.

CHALLENGING TIMES

In nursing education, this was a time of significant disagreement and up-heaval as nurses and nursing educators struggled to define the role of the "professional nurse" and determine the best way to educate her. Across the United States, a movement emerged to move three-year diploma nursing programs, which were based in hospitals, into independent educational institutions. Many nursing educators, however, were concerned that only baccalaureate nurses, and not nurses trained in the three-year diploma pro-grams, would be considered as professional nurses. Sister AJ's background as both a diploma-trained and baccalaureate-educated nurse, as well as her experience as director of a hospital-based diploma nursing program, gave her a unique perspective on this debate.

Sister AJ was enrolled in the University of Minnesota's Master of Educa-tion program at this time, so she was deeply immersed in these questions as part of her coursework. At the University of Minnesota, she established con-nections with faculty in nursing, education, and other departments; years later, she would still be collaborating with many of these same scholars.

Sister AJ earned her master's degree in 1958. In 1959, she and her faculty implemented significant curriculum changes at the newly independent St. Mary's School of Nursing. To shift the curriculum away from the apprentice-type training of the hospitals and toward a broader education for nurses, the entire program was modified and intensified. Sister AJ did not shy away from change. According to Sister Karen Hilgers, one of the Sisters with whom she lived and worked, Sister AJ believed that "when everything is up in the air it inspired a person's creativity to guide things back to earth in a new order."[5]

RESPONDING TO THE CALL

In November 1962, Sister AJ read the report of a junior college task force commissioned by President O. Meredith Wilson of the University of Min-nesota. This report cited a population expansion of 29 percent in the Minne-apolis-St. Paul area and stated that the baby boom generation would begin entering college in 1964. The task force predicted that even if the University of Minnesota and all of the four-year private colleges in the Twin Cities ex-panded to their maximum capacity, the projected increase in students could not be accommodated. The report specifically recommended that two-year junior and community colleges be developed to help meet this need.[6] When reflecting on this 1962 report in later years, Sister AJ said, "It struck me that the state was practically asking for St. Mary's Junior College."[7]

Immediately, Sister AJ began exploring the idea of a "single purpose" junior college for nursing education. She was interested in nursing educator Mildred

Montag's two-year plan for nursing education, and she knew that California had already instituted such programs. However, after visiting several community colleges and consulting with colleagues in higher education and nursing, Sister AJ expanded her original plan to include programs granting an associate's degree for a variety of health-care disciplines. Hospitals were expanding and had an increasing number of openings for X-ray technicians, inhalation therapists, medical records clerks, and other allied positions, but there were no solid educational programs to prepare individuals for these fields. So Sister AJ began formulating her plan for a junior college that would meet those educational needs.

STREAMS OF INFLUENCE

As she conceptualized this new junior college, which would become the first in the nation devoted exclusively to health-care programs,[8] Sister AJ kept the goals of the growing community-college movement in mind. Called "open door colleges" by the Carnegie Commission on Higher Education, these two-year colleges were to provide an access point for students who could not attend four-year colleges, whether because of inadequate academic preparation, cost, or geographic distance. In 1960, 600,000 students were enrolled in two-year institutions of higher education; by 1969, that number had grown to almost 2,000,000 students, or 30 percent of all U.S. undergraduates.[9]

Among the reasons for this extraordinary growth was the nation's growing commitment to equality of opportunity, including access to higher education. President Johnson's War on Poverty, the Great Society, the Civil Rights movement, and the second wave of the women's movement all contributed to a rising demand for higher education as a way of participating fully in American society.

Sister AJ, liberated by the changes brought about by Vatican II and shaped by the Catholic social teaching of her day, embraced these goals. Vatican II (see Connors et al. this volume for further discussion of Vatican II) allowed Sisters to become more actively involved in their communities, and Catholic social teaching, informed by liberation theology, emphasized that a just society should be judged on how well the poorest 20 percent of its population was doing, not the wealthiest 20 percent.[10] As a Sister of St. Joseph, Sister AJ was well aware of her congregation's historical commitment to caring for society's outcasts and those without power—the "dear neighbor." Moreover, through her extensive community connections with organizations such as the National Association for the Advancement of Colored People, the Bridge for Runaway Youth, and the West Bank Process, Sister AJ knew the people who would benefit most from a degree and a good job in health care. "I believe . . . that the essential way out of misery . . . for the oppressed and downtrodden citizens of the world is education—education for work."[11]

In January 1963, when Sister AJ asked the St. Paul Province of the Sisters of St. Joseph for their support in starting a coeducational junior college, she was careful in how she described the purpose of the junior college—to educate "technical level workers in health care"—and the types of students she hoped to attract: those "disadvantaged by poverty, racial prejudice, physical, psychological, and educational handicaps."[12] She emphasized that the mission and educational offerings of the junior college would be distinct from those at the College of St. Catherine, as would its student population. By creating an "open door" junior college focused on education for health care, Sister AJ hoped to institutionalize the values of social justice and equal opportunity long championed by the Sisters of St. Joseph. When the St. Paul Province gave its approval in 1963, Sister AJ plunged into planning for the new junior college.

THE ST. MARY'S PLAN AND ACADEMIC SUPPORT

At the very beginning of St. Mary's Junior College, considerable thought and collaboration went into developing a document that would define its mission and goals. The result was "The St. Mary's Plan," which was written by Sister AJ and Dr. Grace Carlson, one of the early psychology professors at the School of Nursing. Ten years after development of the St. Mary's Plan, Sister AJ reflected on its centrality to the junior college: "The single most important thing was time and effort spent at the beginning on a statement clearly defining (a) the purpose of the college, (b) technical education, (c) the kind of student body anticipated and (d) the responsibilities of faculty to students."[13]

This early document also set the stage for how students would receive academic support at the junior college. The intended rigor of the programs, along with the characteristics of the students that the school hoped to attract, demanded careful consideration of how these learners would be taught and supported. Sister AJ insisted that

> technical education *is* education, not training. Technical education approaches the student as a learner, not as a worker. [It] considers how a student changes, not how skills develop. [It] is concerned with theory and skills, not with skills alone. Students in technical education programs are urged to develop a sense of social responsibility.[14]

An unusual feature of the nursing and allied health programs at the junior college was the balance of coursework: half of the credits were in the liberal arts and sciences, and half were in the technical portion of the program. Even though the associate of applied science degree was intended to be "terminal," St. Mary's emphasized lifelong learning and cultivating interests in the arts and civic engagement. The emphasis was not only on *what* needed to be learned, but also on *how* to learn. The junior college promoted a holistic, well-rounded education for its students, who were understood to be more than "workers." (Dr. Grace Carlson, an active member of the Socialist Workers Party, often insisted, "There is nothing too good for the workers!"[15])As expressed in the college's first catalogue, "each program . . . is designed to educate the student as a person as well as a worker in today's society. General and technical education are correlated to develop a socially responsible practitioner."[16]

St. Mary's Junior College was resolute in its mission to open the doors of health-care education to students who had not been well served by colleges in the past:

> Students are admitted to the college who do not fit, or at least are not measured by, the usual college health career entrance requirements which tend to feed practitioners into the field who look like those who already populate it. Rather we attempt to determine what each student needs in the program at SMJC in order to develop the necessary competence to enter the field at graduation.[17]

Many first-generation students were recruited and admitted to the junior college, as well as students of color and those from backgrounds of poverty. Also admitted were students who had significant weaknesses or gaps in their educational preparation. The ACT mean score of enrolled students was the 51st percentile, and the high school rank mean was the 64th percentile.[18] In 1975, Sister AJ described the students and their aspirations:

> The majority of these students have been job-oriented individuals who never lost faith in the value of upward mobility and in the power of higher education to move them up the vocational ladder. An ever-growing number of these have come from the ranks of those disadvantaged by poverty, racial prejudice, physical, psychological and educational handicaps.[19]

FUNCTIONAL LITERACY

The St. Mary's Plan acknowledged that this practice of admitting disadvantaged students required "quite different performance and viewpoints on the part of faculty."[20] Sister AJ frequently emphasized that faculty at the junior college were *professional educators* and that the students' learning, rather than the curriculum or content, was the central focus of their college education. In her view, the curriculum and content could—and should—be regularly modified, repackaged, and shifted to meet the needs of the students. In particular, she emphasized to her faculty the theory of functional literacy, which stated that students would become proficient in the necessary literacy skills (such as reading, writing, oral presentations, critical thinking) if the teaching of those skills was embedded into the health sciences curriculum. It wasn't literacy for its own sake, but rather literacy for the purpose of becoming educated as a nurse or occupational therapy assistant or other allied health technician.[21]

If a student struggled, each faculty member was charged with assessing the reasons for the difficulty, modifying her teaching to better address the student's needs, and providing the type of academic support that could transform previously unsuccessful students into successful ones. This emphasis on the faculty's role in academic support was unusual in its time. In an address to new faculty, Sister AJ acknowledged both the burdens and benefits of this approach:

> It is precisely these attempts [to figure out why a student is having difficulty learning] which have yielded clues for the faculty member about better ways to organize and present material to the benefit of all students. Do not be too quick to send the student for tutoring or other counselor help. My message is for you first to make serious efforts at helping the students as a serious professional educator. . . . I have a very high interest in pushing faculty members to try all sorts of ways to help bring about learning. You are encouraged to use a variety of different ways to attack the problem of the student who does not learn, who may seem that he or she can't learn. You are held accountable for trying to help students learn. Trying a new approach which, it turns out, does not work is no disaster, but what is no good is the failure to try different approaches.[22]

Clearly, faculty had the primary responsibility of providing academic support to students, but there were also systems in place to assist faculty in this role. In February 1965, professional counselors were hired to work with students, and in the fall of 1966 a Student Personnel Office (SPO) opened. SPO faculty and staff responded to the many types of problems that could interfere with a student's educational progress: housing issues, financial concerns, interpersonal difficulties, career questions, and so on. At St. Mary's Junior College, the psychologists who worked in Student Personnel were considered part of the General Education faculty. They were available to work with students and faculty in all departments to help determine what might be causing a particular student's academic difficulties. They met with students individually to assess and intervene; they also sat in on classes and provided suggestions and feedback to faculty peers about ways to improve or vary the presentation of information.

But Sister AJ didn't want faculty making referrals to SPO too quickly. She felt there was much to be gained by individual teachers struggling to understand a particular student's difficulty. As she said to new faculty:

> That means hard work for the faculty—hard work with the student to try to figure out not only what the learning problem is, but also what to do about it. It means actively working at identifying as early as possible the student who may be going to have academic trouble, actively approaching that student to diagnose and treat the problem. It means that the SMJC faculty member cannot be passive, waiting for the student to come to him/her. It means being available to students through faithfully kept office hours and also being available outside of office hours. It means being interrupted by and responding to the student.[23]

RESOURCES

From St. Mary's beginning in 1964 until the mid-1970s, each faculty member was considered the primary resource to identify and address individual student learning needs. In the mid-1970s this situation changed with the influx of federal grant dollars directed at a variety of academic support projects, such as Title III. According to Mary Broderick, academic dean from 1980 to 1994, St. Mary's actively sought these grants; at one time, approximately one-third of the college's budget came from these federal grants.[24] Doctoral students from the University of Minnesota were hired to direct these projects, bringing with them the latest thinking in cognitive and educational psychology. Many of the projects targeted nontraditional students and provided for an extensive array of out-of-classroom supports, such as tutoring, writing and study skills workshops, as well as specialized services for students with physical and learning disabilities. While some of these projects were short-lived, others continued at the junior college for many years, creating in their wake systemic changes in how student learning was supported.

Sister AJ was particularly proud of one federal grant project that addressed the learning needs of blind and visually impaired students who wanted to become physical or occupational therapy assistants (PTAs or OTAs). During this 10-year project, approximately 90 blind students graduated from the junior college. It was clear that faculty did not have the background or experience to address the specialized learning needs of blind students. However, through this grant, staff with the required skills and training were hired to work with the faculty to help the students succeed. The staff did not take over the faculty's role as teacher, but rather assisted with providing the strategies and equipment necessary for the learning to take place. In this way, the project established a strong new partnership model between faculty and staff for supporting students.

By 1980, according to Dr. Broderick, this new faculty-staff partnership had transformed into a "creative tension" about how best to support the increasingly complex learning needs of the student body. Many faculty felt that embedding the instruction of basic or developmental skills into the regular curriculum was becoming untenable. Yet the range and depth of special learning needs of the student body were expanding, even as the curricular demands of nursing and allied health fields were becoming increasingly complex and technical. By the early 1980s, faculty were pushing the administration for increased out-of-classroom support for students.

During the early 1980s, Sister AJ's role as the president of St. Mary's was also changing. She became less involved in the day-to-day operations of the college and more involved in external affairs, including raising funds and exploring potential linkages with other institutions. Decision-making about academic concerns fell more to the academic dean, program directors, and faculty committees. In addition, a 1980 North Central accreditation report suggested a new direction for academic support at the campus:

> There is a need for a college-wide program to provide a systematic method of identifying and supporting high risk students. . . . The general education program has a great need for the development of a well-staffed learning center to augment the individual student support. The counseling and advising presently occurring is informal, people-centered, and appears to be quite adequate for the general college program. However, with a recognized 20% of "high risk" students, the general education department needs the support of a basic learning center.[25]

THE LEARNING CENTER

St. Mary's responded to this report by gathering the scattered resources for peer tutoring, professional writing and study skills assistance, English as a Second Language support, and services for students with disabilities into a centralized Learning Center in the mid-1980s. This move paralleled a trend in higher education at the time, as colleges and universities throughout the country institutionalized the various support programs that had been started with federal grants. At St. Mary's Junior College, an emphasis on embedding academic literacy skills into the curriculum continued, though individual faculty were no longer solely responsible for helping students to develop these skills.

For example, faculty in the Occupational Therapy Assistant program had developed a strategy called "Learning Through Discussion" to improve their students' ability to learn from expository texts. The LTD format is a structured tool designed to help students learn the vocabulary of the discipline, pull meaning from assigned readings, connect it to other sources of information, and respond effectively. The format is used in all OTA courses at St. Mary's, from Physical Disabilities to Mental Health.[26] But if OTA students continued to struggle with reading skills, even after using the technique integrated into the curriculum, the faculty could refer those students to a reading specialist in the Learning Center for further work. This model of pairing a centralized learning-assistance center with an intentionally developmental curriculum remains a key element of what St. Mary's Junior College became, the Minneapolis campus of St. Catherine University.

THE MERGER

In 1985, the boards of directors of the College of St. Catherine and St. Mary's Junior College voted to merge the two institutions. Sister AJ stepped down as president. In her last address to the junior college faculty, she said:

> How could anyone be other than amazed to see the dream of such a college as ours come to the lively, dynamic, indeed holy, reality that St. Mary's Junior College is.[27]

The junior college was renamed the St. Mary's Campus of the College of St. Catherine; its mission of providing access for underserved students to associate-degree education in health care has remained. The model of pairing a centralized learning-assistance center with a developmental curriculum that encourages the acquisition of academic literacy skills has also remained.

Sister Ann Joachim Moore signing the documents to merge St. Mary's Junior College with the College of St. Catherine, September 1, 1986, with Sister Karen Kennelly, Sister Mary Hasbrouck, and President Anita Pampusch. Photo courtesy of St. Catherine University.

Sister AJ's legacy of service was acknowledged publicly when she resigned as St. Mary's president. At the College's last faculty meeting, Dr. Broderick described Sister AJ's "aversion to stagnation, complacency, and the conventional."[28] Citing the College's array of programs in the health sciences, robust enrollments, and thousands of graduates, she said, "What we see showed the power of an idea, and of one person's human energy engaging, synergizing, catalyzing the energies of many others."[29]

Numerous citations and awards acknowledged Sister AJ as a "national leader in the education of allied health personnel; and a strong supporter of programs to recruit and retain minority and disadvantaged students."[30] The American Medical Association noted that "Sister is considered a pioneer in raising allied health professions to their current status as integral components of quality health care systems."[31] The governor of Minnesota and mayors of Minneapolis and St. Paul declared a day in her honor. Yet the accolade that Sister AJ seemed to enjoy most was delivered by Sue Torgrimson, a two-time graduate of St. Mary's Junior College (OTA 1967, Nursing 1973). As a young student, Sue said that she had found much to admire and emulate in Sister AJ:

> She was a nurse, lawyer, college president. As a young woman with limited life experience I hadn't considered the broad possibilities for a woman. Here was a woman who didn't seem to place limitations on her life or allow them to be placed on her. Where others saw problems in the health fields she saw opportunities for innovation and entrepreneurship; not just for herself but for those around her as well. She didn't follow what others were doing but showed courage in going in a new direction. That attitude permeated the school and I, like many others began to think opportunities without limitations, realizing that where there was risk there was also excitement."[32]

NOTES

1. Jane Lamm Carroll, *Taking Women Seriously for 100 Years* (St. Paul, MN: The College of St. Catherine, 2005), p. 15.

2. Rosalie Ryan, CSJ and John Christine Wolkerstorfer, CSJ, *More than a Dream: 85 Years at the College of St. Catherine* (St. Paul, MN: The College of St. Catherine, 1992), p. 69.

3. Sister Joanne Emmer, CSJ, Interview with Deborah Churchill, October 27, 2004.

4. Sister Anne Joachim Moore, CSJ, Sisters of St. Joseph of Carondelet, St. Paul Provincial Archives, St. Paul (CSJ Archives).

5. Sister Karen Hilgers, CSJ, interview with Deborah Churchill, October 12, 2004.

6. "Report of the University of Minnesota Faculty Senate Junior College Task Force," November 1962, CSJ Archives.

7. Anne Joachim Moore, CSJ, "Remembering Grace Holmes Carlson," Eulogy delivered November 25, 1992, CSJ Archives.

8. "Proclamation from State of Minnesota: Sister Anne Joachim Moore Day," 1974, CSJ Archives.

9. Carnegie Commission on Higher Education, *The Open Door Colleges: Policies for Community Colleges* (New York: McGraw Hill: 1970).

10. Sister Catherine Michaud, CSJ, and Thomas H. West, "The Catholic Tradition and Social Justice," in *The Reflective Woman*, 6th ed. (Acton, MA: Copley Custom Publishing Group, 2004), pp. 386–399 at 394.

11. SAJM notes for May 7, 1986, faculty meeting, CSJ Archives.

12. "St. Mary's Plan" (1975 version), St. Mary's Junior College box, College of St. Catherine Archives, St. Paul, Minnesota.

13. Anne Joachim Moore, "Technical Level Education for the Health Fields," *Journal of Allied Health* 3 (3) (1974): 100–103.

14. "The Plan Itself" in 1964–65, St. Mary's Junior College Catalog, p. 4, CSC Archives.

15. Moore, "Remembering Grace Carlson."

16. St Mary's Junior College Catalog, 1964–65, p. 9.

17. Moore, "Technical Level Education."

18. 1965 Progress Report of St. Mary's Junior College, CSC Archives.

19. SAJM comments about the St Mary's Plan in 1975, CSJ Archives.

20. "The Plan Itself," p. 4.

21. Hilgers Interview.

22. Sister Anne Joachim Moore, CSJ, Address to new faculty August 1977, CSJ Archives.

23. *Ibid.*

24. Mary Broderick, interview with Deborah Churchill, November 11, 2004.

25. "North Central Accreditation Report" (1980), p. 17, CSJ Archives.

26. Tone Blechert, interview with Deborah Churchill, September 29, 2004.

27. Anne Joachim Moore, CSJ, Address at last faculty meeting of St. Mary's Junior College, May 7, 1984, CSJ Archives.

28. Mary Broderick, Address to faculty, May 7, 1984, CSJ Archives.

29. *Ibid.*

30. University of Minnesota Outstanding Achievement Award, 1982, SAJM box in CSJ Archives.

31. American Medical Association Citation, 1974, SAJM box in CSJ Archives.

32. Sue Torgrimson, remarks at event honoring Sister Anne Joachim Moore, May 1984, CSJ Archives.

4

Renewing the Meaning of a Women's College

Identity and Standpoint in the 1970s

Sharon Doherty and Catherine Lupori

Paradox can be a powerful force. Sometimes the most profound action is to hold still. In 1976, the College of St. Catherine appeared to be holding still. No major initiatives were introduced. The curriculum as a whole was not transformed. Student activism was similar to the activism of the year before. Continuing Education built its programs for older women students as it had for the past two years. A Sister of St. Joseph of Carondelet, Alberta Huber, continued her tenure as president. From the outside, nothing at all extraordinary seemed to be occurring at the College.

What was extraordinary at St. Catherine's in 1976 was a decision to maintain the status quo, to resist a new path that to some seemed inevitable. In the face of national pressures, opposing ideologies, financial risk, and a daunting move by a brother institution, the College of St. Catherine decided to remain a college for women.

In October of that year, neighboring St. Thomas College announced a plan to open its doors to women students, joining the many private men's colleges in the United States that produced this late chapter in the story of coeducation. Fifty-four formerly men's colleges began admitting women between 1970 and 1990. During that same era, often in the face of declining resources, 132 women's colleges across the country chose either to become coeducational or to close their doors.[1] The College of St. Catherine stood in the midst of this storm, remaining open and maintaining its identity as a college for women. This maintenance of the status quo was deliberate. By 1976, groups on campus had been debating the question of "going coed" for two years. When the time came to make a decision, the faculty voted almost unanimously in favor of remaining a women's college; alumnae supported the idea by a two-to-one margin; and the College trustees decided not to make a change.[2]

By this time, coeducation at the college level had existed in the United States for 140 years. In 1837, Oberlin (founded in 1833) became the first college to enroll both men and women, with the first woman graduating in 1841. Locally, when the College of St. Catherine was founded in 1905, six of the nine private colleges in Minnesota were open to both men and women, as was the University of Minnesota.[3] (The University of Minnesota began admitting women in 1869, during the great expansion of opportunities for women in higher education after the Civil War.) Among American Catholic colleges, even though the Vatican at the time viewed coeducation unfavorably, some options became available in the early twentieth century; DePaul University was the first coeducational Catholic college, opening in 1914.[4]

In the late 1960s, more than a century after coeducation had first emerged in United States higher education, discussions of the issue intensified at private men's and women's colleges. Men's institutions going coed in the 1970s included Ivy League schools and many Catholic men's colleges. For many, business considerations played a larger part in the decision than did discussions of promoting equal opportunity. The post–World War II baby boom was drawing to a close and enrollments of traditional-age college students were projected to decline. As former St. Catherine's President Anita Pampusch notes,

> [A] 1970 study of the declining birthrate suggested that college aged students would be significantly fewer by 1988. Everyone was motivated to keep enrollments up.[5]

To increase total student numbers, many boards of trustees of men's colleges decided it was time for greater inclusivity. Sister Alberta, who as St. Catherine's president held "meeting after meeting" with St. Thomas President Monsignor Terrence Murphy, trying to develop a workable course of action for both institutions, remembers that the big question was not if St. Thomas would go coed, but when. St. Thomas enrollments already had begun to decline. By 1973, undergraduate enrollment was at its lowest point in seven years.

> With less than 2,000 undergraduates, there was concern throughout the whole campus about the student population. Responding to this, Msgr. Murphy decided to bring the question of becoming a co-educational institution back to the table for discussion.[6]

The St. Thomas trustees voted in the fall of 1976 to begin admitting women, effective the next year. Rumors circulated for years regarding why St. Catherine's and St. Thomas did not proceed collaboratively on the question of coeducation in 1976. Some, like St. Catherine's history professor James Cunningham, suggested that the St. Thomas leadership was hostile and St. Catherine's was passive. In a memo to faculty and administrative colleagues the next academic year, Cunningham cited an unnamed friend on the St. Thomas faculty as saying "there was no escaping the realization that the STC Administration intends to 'grind St. Catherine's into the dust.'"[7]

Sister Alberta didn't consider the St. Thomas president's motivation to be that ill-intentioned. "Monsignor Murphy and I were good friends," she recalled. "He wanted us to go coed at the same time." In their discussions, Sister Alberta learned that St. Thomas, in interviewing students, had found that young men were becoming less interested in attending a men's-only institution: "they wanted some girls around."[8] In a 1975 report, a committee established by St. Thomas had argued that

> [the] available evidence . . . indicates strongly that enrollment would increase as a result of coeducation. The increase might result in as much as $150,000 the first year. It should eventually reach five times that.[9]

Sister Alberta did not spend her energy trying to stop St. Thomas from its plans, nor did she follow the men's institution in opting for coeducation. She turned her attention to what she and the College would do next, in day-to-day work and in strategic changes. The two institutions continued to work together in such areas as speech/theater and social work, but the College of St. Catherine remained an independent college for women. Looking back on the decision 30 years later, Sister Alberta said, "I was then and I am still strongly interested in the education of women."[10]

RAPID DISAPPEARANCE OF WOMEN'S COLLEGES

From a distance, most feminists would assume that, regardless of the institutional motivation, opening men's institutions to women was the right thing to do in the interest of a more just society. But change is never that simple. In many cases, the move to greater inclusivity had the practical effect of damaging women's colleges, particularly those that had been in "brother-sister" relationships with the private men's colleges. In an unequal world, money and prestige tend to follow society's dominant groups. If a high school girl was accepted to, for example, both Harvard and Radcliffe—after Harvard began accepting women and while Radcliffe still existed as a college—the attraction of Harvard's prestige and power could be irresistible. Enrollments at women's colleges dropped, and in the last third of the twentieth century dozens of them closed. Among

Catholic women's colleges in particular the numbers are dramatic. At their peak—1968—"there were more than 170 two- and four-year Catholic women's colleges" in the U.S.[11] By 2002, only 18 of those colleges remained.[12]

The opening of the men's colleges, however, was not the sole reason for this plunge. Rapid social changes were upending the realities of both coeducational and single-sex small colleges across the country. As M. Elizabeth Tidball and her colleagues write in *Taking Women Seriously,*

> Student demands for change in virtually everything, along with disruptive and costly campus demonstrations and an emphasis on personal and sexual freedom, not only brought about a new era of redefinition but led also to the dissolution of many small, private, liberal arts colleges with limited resources—women's, men's, and coeducational, especially those closely church-related. After 1960, the number of women's colleges declined. An even greater loss befell coeducational colleges of similar size and control. . . . Clearly, for the young, the place to be was large, coeducational, open, and pulsating with excitement—a kind of four-year Woodstock.[13]

But Catholic women's colleges had thrived during other eras of disruption and competition. Something quite different was happening during the last third of the twentieth century, and that historic phenomenon was related to, but larger than, either the opening of men's colleges or students' demands for greater personal freedom. The larger societal context was shaped by profound challenges to traditional institutions and traditional social structures in the wider society. "The sixties" and the decades following witnessed new currents in thinking, debate, and action dedicated to human freedom. At St. Catherine's that time of questioning and change affected people's sense of purpose and direction, as well as the institution's economic position.

WOMEN'S FREEDOM AND THE BOTTOM LINE

One center of massive change during the last third of the twentieth century was the Roman Catholic Church. Among other groups with other questions, women religious within the Church—as individuals and as congregations of sisters—began to question long-standing expectations and restrictions regarding women's roles and status. Many Sisters also reconsidered how to best use their talents and energy to help create a better world, as social movements for peace, civil rights, and other goals consistent with their values grew.

Two results of this questioning are particularly important to the College of St. Catherine in the mid-1970s: (1) the decline in the number of women religious in the United States, and (2) a change in focus among many Sisters of St. Joseph, from institutional work in education and health care to grassroots social change and other less institutionally focused careers.[14] A third consequence would not fully affect St. Catherine's until the 1980s: decisions by congregations of Sisters to request financial compensation for their labor.

The decline in the number of Sisters directly affected the resource bases of Catholic women's colleges. The colleges were made possible not only by the vision of the Sisters in their founding congregations, but also by their intellectual, physical, and managerial labor over many decades. At the College of St. Catherine, the faculty and staff in the early years consisted almost entirely of Sisters of St. Joseph. This amounted to the subsidizing of every student's education by the unpaid labor of Sisters, some of whom worked as many as 18 hours a day. (Sister-faculty, for example, often also served as prefects in dormitories.) After "the great and unexpected exodus from the convent in the 1960s and 1970s,"[15] fewer Sisters were available to do this work. As Jane Carroll notes, the number of women religious in the United States peaked in the mid-1960s at approximately 180,000; "by 1976 that number was already reduced to 131,500 and continued to decline in subsequent years."[16]

Because St. Catherine's had begun hiring significant numbers of lay faculty early in its history, it was better situated than most Catholic colleges to respond to the precipitous drop in the number of sisters. (See Carroll in this volume for a discussion of the hiring of lay faculty in earlier decades.[17])

In addition to reducing the number of Sister faculty, the drop in the number of Sisters nationally also affected student numbers at Catholic women's colleges. The Sister Formation movement, developed in the 1950s, had led to increased numbers of Sisters across the United States who were pursuing college-level education. Other religious communities across the country often sent student Sisters to the College of St. Catherine for their degrees in education and other fields. As fewer young women became Sisters, fewer came to the College.

Another change was that more Sisters of St. Joseph began to express their professional talents and passions for justice in grassroots and entrepreneurial settings. This transformation, related to greater individual freedom and to strategies for social change emerging at that time, resulted in fewer Sisters being available to work in large institutions such as the College. Sisters of St. Joseph have made important contributions in settings from the Twin Cities to Jonestown, Mississippi, to Chimbote, Peru, in work on a range of issues from housing to literacy to peace activism. Their desire for less restrictive, more fluid work settings, as well as their dedication to community work, meant that fewer Sisters were working in schools at all levels.

The decline in the number of Sisters occurred as more specialized staff positions were being added at colleges across the United States, including at St. Catherine's. The student affairs area was becoming increasingly formalized; new positions were dedicated to holistic engagement with students in leadership development, support, and social activities. Fundraising, college communications, and other administrative areas also grew, and without Sisters to fill the new roles, many more lay staff needed to be hired and paid.

While the local Catholic community continued to be interested in St. Catherine's, the Sisters of St. Joseph, as the College's sponsors, were responsible for its financial well-being. Unlike St. Thomas, which was and continues to be substantially funded by Archdiocesan resources, the College of St. Catherine has always been considered the Sisters' school, not an Archdiocesan institution. It therefore is not funded in the annual Archdiocesan budget.

QUESTIONS OF PURPOSE:
FEMINIST THOUGHT AND THE WOMEN'S COLLEGE

While debates during the 1970s about coeducation versus single-gender education occurred in the context of economic pressures and projected declines in overall college enrollments, questions of justice for women in an unequal world inevitably became part of the conversation. The second-wave feminist movement was gaining momentum at the time, with new ideas and new strategies for change. On the federal level, Title IX of the U.S. Education Amendments became law in 1972. The Title IX antidiscrimination message was clear:

> No person in the United States shall, on the basis of sex, be excluded from participation in, be denied the benefits of, or be subjected to discrimination under any education program or activity receiving Federal financial assistance.[18]

At that same historical moment in the U.S., women's studies as an academic field was gaining momentum (the first women's studies program began at San Diego State University in 1970), and scholars were developing theoretical approaches to feminism. Since that time, many ideas have emerged about what it will take to create a just world for women and men, girls and boys. Feminist theory today offers discussions of liberal feminism, radical feminism, socialist feminism, psychoanalytic feminism, postmodern feminism, multicultural feminism, ecofeminism, and a host of other approaches. The change to coeducation at exclusive men's colleges is usually analyzed in the context of liberal feminism.

Equal access, a key principle of liberal feminism, is grounded in the idea that to be whole people, women and men should not be contained in separate spheres based on stereotypes about their capabilities. Instead, both women and men should have opportunities for similar experiences, equal challenges, comparable nurturing of talent, and fair compensation for work. In the public world, according to this line of thought, equal access will result in a society in which a girl with the talent and desire to become a chemist or poet or government leader will have just as much support for her dreams as will her equally talented and ambitious brother.

Coeducation has the potential to be an exemplar of liberal feminism, but historically this generally has not been the case. As Karen Kennelly points out, simply having a policy that women *could* be admitted did not mean that many women *were* admitted in the early decades of coeducation.

> On the average only a little more than five women each year had earned degrees from the University of Minnesota in the 1870s and 1880s. Of the six private colleges [in Minnesota] enrolling women, only two (Hamline and Carleton) were attracting them in significant numbers.[19]

Even as women were admitted in greater numbers throughout the twentieth century, institutions often did not provide equal opportunities. As microcosms of the wider society, coed colleges tended to exhibit in both curriculum and campus life the biases and inequalities of the wider society. Many coed colleges, through formal policies or informal practice, had regularly tracked women and men into separate, gender-based majors and courses of study. Directing women disproportionately toward female-dominated fields also occurred in women's colleges, but "freedom to pursue studies of any sort was evident for both women and men in women's colleges and men's colleges."[20] A 1956 study, for example, found that

> [the number of] women in coeducational institutions majoring in the sciences was 10 percent compared with 19 percent in women's colleges; and men in coeducational institutions majoring in the arts and humanities was 7 percent compared with 19 percent in men's colleges.[21]

By mid-century, coeducational colleges were far from being liberal feminist exemplars of resisting gender stereotypes.

But the analytical limitations of liberal feminism itself become clear when we consider why a college like St. Catherine's would choose not to become coeducational in the late twentieth century. Because the focus of liberal feminism was on breaking down stereotypes and avoiding separate

Students in physics lab, Mendel Hall, 1940s. Photo courtesy of St. Catherine University.

spheres, its conceptual framework during the 1960s and '70s did not work when analyzing women's colleges, especially Catholic women's colleges. From a distance, these institutions could be seen as anachronisms in a time of women's liberation. Operating within a patriarchal church, separating women from the wider society—in the context of liberal feminism, such practices would seem oppressive, backward-looking.

How is it, then, that separating women educationally, in the context of a church that saw women and men in terms of complementarity rather than equality, could be a force for women's strength, well-being, and ultimately equality in the wider society? Why did the faculty and the alumnae at St. Catherine's believe that remaining a women's college was the right thing to do? Educational outcomes research provides some insight into these questions. As Tidball and her coauthors argue, three generations of research on women's colleges, producing more than 200 research papers and surveys about students' educational outcomes, lead to the following conclusion:

"[T]he overriding characteristic of institutions that are highly productive of achieving women is their focus on women."[22]

This simple statement contains many complex truths. The centrality of the colleges' focus on women is an expression of historian Sara Evans's idea of "free social spaces," contexts where groups not in power in society congregate, acting together and talking with each other. In their research of the nineteenth-century United States, Evans and her coauthor, Harry Boyte, found that ostensibly apolitical women's clubs became grassroots forces for women's suffrage, and that church services among African American slaves became settings for resistance to slavery. When people of similar circumstances gather, they have opportunities to analyze their situations together, to build knowledge, creativity, strength, and strategies as a group.[23]

It is crucial to understand the role of power in this phenomenon. Evans and Boyte focus in particular on how oppressed groups—disenfranchised women, slaves, and others—have used free social spaces to work for democratic change in the United States. When members of dominant groups get together, the dynamic is different and the outcomes have tended to be less democratic for society. Because of the power differences in the wider society, exclusive men's colleges generally concentrate power further, while women's colleges can contribute to a more balanced society.

A college designed for women, run by women, can be an especially powerful social space, as its explicit purpose is to help women develop their abilities together and prepare together to contribute to the world and to the well-being of themselves and their families. St. Catherine's, like other Catholic women's colleges, was developed with Catholic women as its focus. St. Catherine's was *for them*; they were not merely being allowed to enter into an institution developed with other students in mind (in the coed colleges, the students at the center of attention were usually men, usually white Anglo-Saxon Protestants, usually middle class).[24]

In contrast to liberal feminist theory, standpoint theory provides a conceptual approach to explore these complexities. Standpoint feminism helps us to understand how a person's position in society shapes what she knows and allows her access to information different from that available to people in other societal positions. The differences are not neutral. According to standpoint theory, people in lower power positions in a society have the potential for a more accurate understanding of the whole society than do the people at the top. Patricia Hill Collins explains this in her discussion of "outsiders within."[25] Women who clean other people's houses, Hill Collins argues, can know more about their society than can most of the people whose houses they clean. They know their own houses and what happens there, and they know the houses and activities of the more affluent people who employ and have power over them.

Standpoint feminism is not essentialist; that is, the approach does not operate from an idea of biological or religious determinism. People can develop different standpoints because they have different experiences, grounded in their socialization and position in society. Those different experiences influence people's ideas, values, and contributions to society. Because it was designed and administered by highly educated Sisters of St. Joseph, with a majority of women faculty, the College of St. Catherine offered something different to its students than did most other colleges. (Even Smith, a great leader among American women's colleges, did not have a woman president until 1974. Every president of the College of St. Catherine has been a woman.)

At St. Catherine's, second-wave feminism interacted with a long history of women-centered education, and with the experiences and perspectives of Sisters, laywomen, and men among the faculty, students, trustees, staff, and alumnae. People remember the 1970s not only as an economically stressful time, but also as a time that seemed filled with the potential for creating a more just world. Within the College, new ideas created an array of strategies for change. As in the wider women's movement, individuals of differing backgrounds brought their experiences and intellectual frameworks to the task of thinking about what a women's college could contribute to a changing society and what niche it should fill. While this theorizing was not intellectually monolithic or even consistent (see Cavallaro et al., for a discussion of this in the curriculum), the College's actions reflected an increasing consciousness that a women's college had important contributions to make to a more just world. Standpoint theory helps us to understand not just the decision to remain a women's college, but also the prevailing ideas and institutional strategies of that era. Standpoint, as Sandra Harding argues, is not a position "that oppressed groups can claim automatically. Rather, a standpoint is an achievement, something for which oppressed groups must struggle, something that requires both [analysis] and politics."[26]

The College itself struggled to articulate its place in the world, to reaffirm its strengths even as its leaders began to recognize both limitations and new possibilities in the context of the women's movement. Few would have considered Catholic Sisters to be leaders of the liberal feminism that dominated the early second wave. By becoming Sisters, they had accepted separate spheres based on gender; Catholicism maintained (and maintains) its long-standing restrictions regarding what roles were (and are) open to men and to women moved by religious vocation. But the paradox of free social spaces leads us to consider the standpoints operating within the Sisters' sphere and the contributions emerging from it. How, for example, did the influence of the Sisters of St. Joseph within their women-led institution support students' achievements as new opportunities opened in the wider society?

Sister Mary Thompson, a 1953 alumna who earned her Ph.D. in chemistry at the University of California, Berkeley, and who taught in St. Catherine's chemistry department, remembers the paradoxes regarding opportunity for women in the 1970s. In the context of the second-wave movement, many traditionally male fields were becoming more open to women. Sister Mary and other faculty advisors intensified their efforts to encourage students to enter graduate and professional programs in such fields as chemistry and medicine. While coeducational institutions generally had greater financial resources, the College of St. Catherine provided something different to students eager to break through traditional barriers. One student of Sister Mary's, who took a chemistry course at the University of Minnesota, came back to the College and said, "St. Catherine's is interested in helping women succeed."[27]

That help was rare at many schools, Sister Mary recalled. "They didn't know how to teach women because they didn't want to—even if [a woman was] the top student in a class."[28] While the idea that "they didn't want to" support women's achievement may seem extreme, it is nevertheless consistent with events in the University of Minnesota's chemistry department at that time. In 1975 a lawsuit filed two years earlier by Dr. Shyamala Rajender was expanded to become a class action sex-discrimination suit on behalf of all women academic employees at the University. Dr. Rajender, a temporary faculty member in the chemistry department, filed the original suit on the basis of sex and national origin. As part of a 1980 settlement of the suit, the University agreed to sweeping changes intended to increase the number of women on the faculty and in administrative positions. The "Rajender Consent Decree" is nationally known as one of the largest class action sex-discrimination settlements in U.S. higher education history.[29]

Sister Mary remembers the St. Catherine's chemistry students she encouraged during that era who went on to earn doctorates from such institutions as MIT and Berkeley. While her work was influenced by the liberal promise of breaking down stereotypes, Sister Mary's approach to encouraging women was grounded in the institution's history of being "interested in helping women succeed" and in her own standpoint as a woman scientist and a Sister.

WHICH WOMEN?
STANDPOINT AND INTERSECTING DIFFERENCES

But St. Catherine's itself needed to face issues of unequal access, marginalization, and differential power among women. While those setting the College's agenda were in relatively low-power societal positions because they were women and the institution was Catholic, they had to address power issues related to other elements of the institution's identity, demographics, and guiding ideas. Throughout the 1970s, many innovations and struggles emerged in response to women's different identities and circumstances. The national context for this included an increasingly multifaceted second-wave women's movement. While liberal feminism dominated discussions and guided most strategies at the beginning of the second wave, other ideas rapidly emerged. If we take standpoint theory seriously, we recognize that the life experiences, worldviews, and societal power of those involved in the movement shaped what people thought and did. It is not surprising that middle class and affluent white women stepped into power within the feminist movement in its early years. But because the movement itself was about justice, and because its own roots were in the civil rights movement,[30] it was not long before African American women and other groups began to successfully challenge the newly constructed feminist status quo and offer different ideas and strategies.

This is important to understand in order to analyze a women's college that survived the era. The optimism and moral power of liberal feminism deeply influenced St. Catherine's and other women's colleges during the second wave: people should not discriminate against others; we are all equal. As former president Anita Pampusch recalled, the debate about going coed prompted many women's colleges to examine their views about feminism and to become more specific about their focus on women and women's concerns.[31] Eventually, for every institution seriously engaging the principle of equality, that specificity led to a recognition that women's identities are multiple, defined by more than gender alone. Women from marginal societal positions—women of color, lesbians, working-class women, older women, women with disabilities, women from religious minorities, and others—brought particular strengths and needs to the movement and to institutions with which they interacted.

In considering the diversity of students, standpoint theory provides a framework for facing tensions and flaws in the work of St. Catherine's and other women's colleges that were not resolved in the 1970s, and that continue to provide challenges today. The minute standpoint theory enters our thinking, the question of whom the college was *for* becomes complex.

The insight that women's colleges continue to have something important to contribute after coeducation has become widespread is connected to the idea that an institution itself has a prevailing standpoint. In an unequal society, men's colleges that have become coeducational must struggle to expand their perspectives in order to move beyond a narrow approach to curriculum, policies, ways of working with students, and other institutional characteristics. Women's colleges within patriarchal societies also are faced with challenges regarding gender; working at a women's college or being a Sister did not make a person immune to sexist ideas or other influences of a male-dominated society. But the experience of working to educate women, in a context of relative freedom, provided a counterbalance to such ideas and influences. Responding to students' experiences led many women's colleges to be better than the former men's colleges at "taking women seriously."

If we understand this analysis related to gender, we should not be surprised that similar issues related to racial/ethnic exclusion have arisen at St. Catherine's and other women's colleges. The College of St. Catherine was built for, and largely by, Catholic women of European American ancestry. Providing a college education to that group was a profound contribution at the turn of the last century. The College did not set out to exclude other groups; in fact it made some courageous moves over the years, such as Sister Eucharista Galvin's leadership during her presidency in admitting the College's first African American students in the late 1930s and providing scholarships to Japanese American students during World War II.[32]

Japanese American students, invited to attend the College during World War II. Photo courtesy of St. Catherine University.

Indeed, from the beginning St. Catherine's student population included some forms of diversity: students came from different economic backgrounds and ethnic groups. In the early twentieth century, differences among European American ethnic groups often were socially divisive, and economic differences, while rarely effectively discussed, always had been sources of stress within U.S. higher education. Moreover, the College reached out internationally beginning in 1908, its third year of existence. The list of "foreign students" began with two Canadians,[33] but by 1976-1977, the roster of 30 international students included women from the following countries: Austria, Brazil, Chile, Cyprus, Ecuador, France, Germany, Haiti, Hong Kong, India, Iran, Korea, Liberia, Macao, Mexico, Nigeria, Panama, Peru, Rhodesia, Trinidad, Uganda, and Vietnam.[34] The College's identity during its first 70 years, nonetheless, was primarily built around its majority population, and the student population remained predominantly European American.

RECOGNIZING DIVERSE WOMEN'S IDENTITIES

During the 1960s and '70s, justice movements helped College leaders to develop greater awareness of multiple elements of women's identities. New programs and other initiatives focused especially on age and race/ethnicity. The Reentry Adult Program (REAP) was established in 1971 to support women beyond the traditional college age. With respect to women of color at the College, a Coordinator of (American) Indian Activities position was established in 1972, and a Counselor for African American and African students was added in 1973.

While those actions indicate that St. Catherine's leadership was beginning to move forward with direct efforts at welcoming a more diverse student body, the College's accreditors soon provided additional motivation, noting in a 1974 report: "The student body at St. Catherine's is quite a homogeneous group; there is a notable lack of minority group students and older women."[35]

In fall of 1977, Sister Alberta appointed a "Committee on Evaluation of the Institutional Commitment to Minorities." Its report stressed three assumptions:

- St. Catherine's is a college for *all* women who can meet its admissions standards;
- The College's homogeneity does not accurately reflect the diversity of American society;
- The College's social justice mission leads to its responsibility to erase the effects of past discrimination.

The committee report called for a "complete support system" for that effort, including initiatives and infrastructure in recruitment, admissions, financial aid, counseling, placement, support services, curriculum, student affairs, faculty hiring, and administrative policies. The positions focusing on particular groups were replaced in 1978 by the Office of Intercultural Student Affairs, which later became Multicultural and International Programs and Services. The changes were not universally embraced. As Sister Alberta remembers, "We had a hard time convincing some people that getting a diverse student body was a good thing."[36] This is reminiscent of the resistance to women in some men's and coeducational colleges.

The College of St. Catherine's economic limitations, combined with the complexity of standpoint among groups served by the Office of Intercultural Student Affairs, created pressure regarding how much to bring groups together and how much to address the specific needs of different populations of women. A 1979 Intercultural Student Affairs report reflected concern over inadequate staffing to administer "in effect five separate programs: American Indian Program, Black American Program, Hispanic-American Program, Vietnamese and Asian-American Program, and a Foreign Student Program."[37] The next year, Director June Noronha focused on the philosophy of bringing groups together, as she noted that four years earlier the College had two and a half FTE staff "working with 60 students in fragmented programs. At present, we have a unique and good program that does not separate minority populations."[38] The 1978-1979 report notes "unresolved problems/concerns," including the following:

- "No formal institutional policy on financial support for minority students which is basic to their recruitment and retention"; and
- Absence of "a wide range of curricular offerings that promote the awareness and appreciation of the students' (majority and minority) cultures and heritage."[39]

Even as institutional change was slow, the new Intercultural Office efforts played a part in increasing student numbers. From 1978 to 1982, the number of international students and U.S. students of color increased from 88 (3.9 percent of the student body) to 160 (5.2 percent).[40]

Sister Alberta and others also focused during this time on establishing a Weekend College, which began in 1979 and became a major vehicle for the education of working students and re-entry students. While the weekend format itself attracted women with multiple responsibilities, faculty and staff who developed the program responded to students' ideas and lives with an array of innovations over the ensuing years, from "highly personalized recruiting and admissions processes" to courses structured around a range of different learning styles. The learning environment was intended to value women's experiences and "[recognize] that their multiple worlds of family, community and work have and continue to build relevant knowledge."[41]

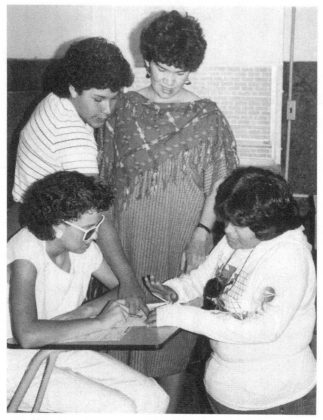

Multicultural and International Programs and Services staff member Dunia Berganza Ruff with students, 1980s. Photo courtesy of St. Catherine University.

Building intellectual work on both experiential and text-based knowledge, the program sought to

> [challenge] women to think more analytically and critically about their experiences, to find their own voice in the midst of multiple demands and responsibilities, to express their opinions and values more clearly and confidently, and to strengthen their ability to apply new learning in their family, social, community and career worlds.[42]

From the beginning, Weekend College courses at St. Catherine's were taught by the College's regular faculty. This fostered a rich pedagogical atmosphere, as faculty members carried teaching strategies back and forth between the weekend and weekday programs, testing their effectiveness with different student populations.

While those major programmatic initiatives focused primarily on age and race/ethnicity, other elements of women's identities also were becoming more clearly recognized during the era, with varying degrees of institutional conflict. Students from other religions, as well as students with no religious tradition, increased in number. (See Connors et al., in this volume.) Students from working-class and low-income families had greater access to the College at this time than in the past because of federal financial aid programs.[43] Lesbian students and alumnae began to come out of the closet. Because of Church doctrine forbidding sex outside of heterosexual marriage and, at the time, a Church position condemning homosexual identity, the College's Catholicism came into direct conflict with the lives of lesbian students.[44] A cutting-edge feminist project in the art department was shut down, in part because of concerns that lesbian themes were being addressed in the art. These and other complexities of women's identities affected their student experiences and the College as a whole.

With respect to age and race/ethnicity in particular, the presence of new student populations challenged long-standing structures and practices at the College. Standpoint theory helps us to understand why women in nondominant groups continued to struggle and to challenge the system after the College took steps to include them. New programs and services for women who were not at the center of attention in the College's early decades were important but incomplete steps toward creating equitable learning environments. Just as feminists knew that coeducational colleges often continued to be male-centered after admitting women and providing a few changes, antiracist activists knew that institutions created with white students in mind would not change immediately or easily as support services were created for students of color. The original steps sometimes made the dominant perspective of the College even clearer to students at the margins.

"BECOMING A WOMEN'S COLLEGE": WIG AND LIBERAL FEMINIST INTERVENTIONS

Even as the College struggled to respond to diverse women, other efforts attempted to strengthen the overall women's college identity. These were not competing initiatives; many of the same people were involved in both. A notable set of tactics emerged when activists took on the idea that St. Catherine's "ought to become a women's college."[45] The challenge inherent in that statement was that the College was not proactive enough in its approach to women's education. Given St. Catherine's 70-year history of educating women leaders, the idea might seem confusing. In the context of the second-wave movement, however, it made sense. The Sisters and others at the College had operated for decades without a powerful women's movement in the wider society. As several essays in this book make clear, they developed ways to encourage women's intellectual growth and career potential in sometimes hostile national contexts, such as at the beginning of the twentieth century and during the 1950s. St. Catherine's faculty members were developing gender-based theories of education before the women's studies movement. (See Fleming in this volume for a discussion of Sister Jeanne Marie Bonnett's contributions in this area.) But when second-wave feminism emerged, engagement in scholarship about women, battling stereotypes, and directly speaking truth to power became hallmarks of the movement. An increasingly feminist consciousness focused people's energy on the need for change.

The intensity surrounding the mission for women's education became clear at a Futures Invention Faculty Workshop in May 1976. Part of a national movement, the workshop brought together faculty from across the College to develop ideas about the future. Participants remember that one group focused on "how we would see CSC's mission for women" by the turn of the century.[46] Workshop participants voted that group's vision as the most persuasive of the day. While the workshop did not result in an overall blueprint for planning, ideas from it inspired actions over the next few years.

Faculty who had focused in the workshop on the mission for women's education joined others on campus the following academic year to form the Women's Interest Group (WIG). In its first newsletter, WIG provided a brief discussion of its origins:

> During the 1976 summer Future's Invention Workshop . . . it became obvious that several people saw St. Kate's as a place to give women the best education possible so they can become political, religious, business and social service leaders. For instance, we envisioned both the first women elected as President of the United States and as Pope as CSC graduates. During the workshop, strategies were planned so that CSC would begin to build that future devoted to women.
>
> Unlike many other good ideas, this one did not evaporate with the new school year. Instead, several members of the workshop issued an invitation for those concerned about women's issues to meet. About thirty people came to the first meeting. Since the fall of 1976, regular meetings of WIG have been held. Membership includes staff, faculty, alumn[ae], and students.[47]

The group, which included mostly women and a few men, at first structured meetings around "problems brought to the group by individuals," but quickly decided to move on to more systematic goal setting. WIG saw itself as "primarily a political action group . . . to assure that CSC fulfills its mission as a women's college."[48] In most of its actions and in statements by its members, WIG reflected liberal feminist commitments.

For example, WIG member Alan Graebner, a faculty member in the history department, presented a position paper at the September 30, 1976, faculty meeting in which he proposed that St. Catherine's "become a women's college."[49] In a passionate discussion of justice and education, Graebner presented seven major assumptions from which he had developed his argument, beginning with the following:

> Women in our society are burdened by serious constraints that are socially rather than biologically induced. This is morally wrong and the results impoverish the growth both of individuals and of the whole society.[50]

Aware of the apparent contradiction between his liberal feminist ideals and the continuing existence of a women's college, Graebner proposed that St. Catherine's build its future around a key aim of liberal feminism: "the sole justification in our times for a college which admits only women is to challenge social stereotypes of women."[51]

To pursue its goals, which "clustered around structural, educational and social issues," WIG developed an array of strategies. The group's regular attendance during the next two years ranged from 10 to 17. An undated list of total members included 36 names. WIG organized three standing committees: College Affairs, Educational Task Force, and Social/Cultural Task Force. In its first policy victory, WIG took on the issue of sexist language. The group introduced at the February 8, 1977, faculty meeting a resolution regarding a policy on nonsexist language and how to implement it. The resolution noted that in its identity as a Catholic liberal arts college for women, St. Catherine's

> demonstrates basic respect for the intellectual, social and creative potential of women (p. 7, CSC Catalogue, 1976–1978). To assure language usage consistent with CSC's commitment to women, the Women's Interest Group requests the adoption of the following recommendations:
>
> 1. The CSC faculty members follow the National Council of Teachers of English (NCTE) "Guidelines for Nonsexist Use of Language" where appropriate for college-related communication.
> 2. The CSC faculty request that administrators and staff members use NCTE guidelines where appropriate for college-related communication.
> 3. The faculty establish an *ad hoc* committee of volunteers to review and revise, if necessary, existing faculty publications according to NCTE guidelines.[52]

The resolution passed, and its implementation ranged from revising the faculty constitution to publishing the policy in the student handbook. WIG's activism contributed to a range of institutional efforts directed toward the mission for women's education, including the establishment of a women's studies minor and consortial major, and the creation in 1985 of the Abigail Quigley McCarthy Center for Women's Research, Resources, and Scholarship.

STANDPOINT AND PURPOSE

While WIG's liberal feminism did not come to define the College, the group's intellectual work and activism reaffirmed an important value: openness to new knowledge and to sometimes controversial views. Like the innovations to include older students and students of color, WIG's initiatives depended on an expansive rather than a defensive engagement with change. That engagement was not perfect or complete, but it was substantive enough to offer the College a future without rejecting its identity.

During the years we have examined in this essay, standpoint feminism was only beginning to emerge nationally as a new theoretical approach; Sister Alberta and others did not explicitly analyze or present their ideas in those terms. But today, analytically, we can consider how St. Catherine's leaders' standpoints shaped their thinking. Those standpoints were grounded in the Sisters' decades of experience as sponsors of a Catholic college for women and centuries of experience as activist and intellectual women religious working within patriarchal European and American societies. With or without an explicitly feminist consciousness, educators who integrated their own experiences with their scholarly knowledge had been fostering women's leadership at the College for years.

Standpoint theory necessarily engages group histories as well as contemporary circumstances. Those histories cannot be dismissed as we think about what St. Catherine's was 35 years ago. Sister Alberta and others knew that the College's history made it possible to continue offering something unique to the world, even as they integrated the insights and goals of '60s-era justice movements. Their gamble to remain a women's college worked, in part because of a willingness to critically examine the institution's limitations and a desire to engage in change. A rich history alone would not have been enough to carry St. Catherine's into a new era.

Looking back on the decision to remain a women's college, three decades later Sister Alberta emphasized her "[interest] in the education of women."[53] Her resolve, influenced by the commitments of many others within the St. Catherine's community, reflects Tidball and her coauthors' argument that purpose is a crucial component of education. Purpose and standpoint are integrally connected. The decision to go forward as a women's college reflected the understanding that a women-focused education was valuable and the confidence that it could be sustainable, even with a small endowment, no financial support from the Archdiocese, and other barriers related to an unequal world. As in past generations and different historical contexts, Sisters and others at the College of St. Catherine considered their options and applied what they knew to their consistent, unwavering purpose of educating women.

NOTES

1. M. Elizabeth Tidball, Daryl Smith, Charles Tidball, Lisa Wolf-Wendel, *Taking Women Seriously* (Phoenix: American Council on Education, 1999), p. 20.
2. Sister Rosalie Ryan and Sr. John Christine Wolkerstorfer, *More Than A Dream* (St. Paul: College of St. Catherine, 1992), p. 103.
3. Sister Karen Kennelly, "Mary Molloy: Women's College Founder," in Barbara Stuhler and Gretchen Kreuter, editors, *Women of Minnesota: Selected Biographical Essays*, Revised Edition (St. Paul: Minnesota Historical Society Press, 1998), p. 116–35, at 116.
4. Thomas M. Landy, "The Colleges in Context," in *Catholic Women's Colleges in America*, ed. Tracy Schier and Cynthia Russett (Baltimore: John Hopkins University Press, 2002), p. 81.
5. Anita Pampusch, e-mail message to Catherine Lupori, August 4, 2004.
6. Aaron D. Anderson and Cherry L. Danielson under the supervision of Prof. Marvin W. Peterson of the University of Michigan's Center for the Study of Higher and Postsecondary Education, *From College to Comprehensive University: The St. Thomas Transformation* (Kellogg Forum for Higher Education Transformation, December 1999).
7. James Cunningham, "Memorandum to Friends and Colleagues on the CSC Faculty and Administration, Re: The Future of CSC," February 28, 1978, Abigail Quigley McCarthy Center for Women files, College of St. Catherine (CSC) Archives, St. Paul, Minnesota.
8. Sister Alberta Huber, interview with Sharon Doherty, August 24, 2006.
9. Ryan and Wolkerstorfer, p. 102.
10. Huber, interview with Doherty.
11. Kathleen Mahoney, "American Catholic Colleges for Women: Historical Origins," in Schier and Russett, *Catholic Women's Colleges in America*, p. 26.
12. Jeanne Knoerle and Tracy Schier, "Conclusion: Into the Future," in Schier and Russett, *Catholic Women's Colleges in America*, p. 333.
13. Tidball et al., p. 14.
14. See Abigail Quigley McCarthy, "Catholic Women's Colleges: Looking at Their Future," *Commonweal*, November 21, 1997 (New York: Commonweal Foundation, 1997), pp. 8–9.
15. *Ibid.*, p. 8.
16. Jane Lamm Carroll, "The College of St. Catherine: Taking Women Seriously for 100 Years," unpublished manuscript, CSC Archives, p. 78.
17. As with other patterns at the College, this involved both money (in the early years, Mother Antonia had raised funds to pay lay faculty) and principle (the Sisters leading the College wanted to offer students an open-minded, expansive education, and they saw lay faculty as contributing to that). Related to a desire for expansive-

ness, the early inclusion of lay faculty also supported the Phi Beta Kappa bid, as the college needed to have ten faculty with the Ph.D. who were PBK members in order to be eligible for a chapter.

18. United States Congress, 1972. *Title IX, Education Amendments of 1972*, Section 1681.

19. Kennelly, "Mary Molloy: Women's College Founder," p. 116.

20. Tidball et al., p. 11.

21. M. Newcomer, *A Century of Higher Education for American Women* (New York: Harper and Brothers, 1959), cited in Tidball et al., p. 11.

22. Tidball et al., p. 54.

23. Sara M. Evans and Harry C. Boyte, *Free Spaces: The Sources of Democratic Change in America* (New York: Harper and Row, 1986).

24. Helen Lefkowitz Horowitz, *Campus Life: Undergraduate Cultures From the End of the Eighteenth Century to the Present* (New York: A. A. Knopf, 1987), p. 86.

25. Patricia Hill Collins, *Black Feminist Thought: Knowledge, Consciousness, and the Politics of Empowerment*, Second Edition (New York: Routledge, 2000), pp. 10–12.

26. Sandra Harding, "Introduction," in *The Feminist Standpoint Theory Reader*, ed. Sandra Harding (New York: Routledge, 2004), p. 8.

27. Sister Mary Thompson, Interview with Sharon Doherty, August 24, 2006.

28. *Ibid.*

29. Greta Bahnemann, "Finding Aid for Faculty Advisory Committee on Women papers, 1972–2001," University of Minnesota Archives, Minneapolis, MN, Collection Number 2002–34.

30. See Audre Lorde, *Sister Outsider: Essays and Speeches* (Trumansburg, NY: Crossing Press, 1984), and Sara M. Evans, *Personal Politics: The Roots of Women's Liberation in the Civil Rights Movement and the New Left* (New York: Vintage Books, 1980).

31. Anita Pampusch, Interview with Catherine Lupori, July 13, 2004.

32. Karen Kennelly, "Faculties and What They Taught," in Schier and Russett, *Catholic Women's Colleges in America*, p. 119.

33. File P 71, Friends International, CSC Foreign Students, 1908–1928, CSC Archives.

34. File P 71, Friends International, CSC Foreign Students, 1970–1978, CSC Archives.

35. File P 71, "North Central Accreditation Team Report to the College of St. Catherine, 1974," CSC Archives.

36. Huber, interview with Doherty.

37. File P 71 A, "Intercultural Affairs Annual Report, 1978–79," CSC Archives.

38. File P 71 A, June Noronha, January 31, 1980, memo to Robbie Hart, Intercultural Affairs, CSC Archives.

39. File P 71 A, "Intercultural Affairs Annual Report, 1978–79," CSC Archives.

40. File P 71, Intercultural Affairs File, notes for accreditation self-study, 1982, CSC Archives.

41. Joan Robertson, "Open Doors, Open Minds, Open Weekends," in *Colleagues Newsletter* (Vol. 13, #1) (St. Paul: The College of St. Catherine, 2003), p. 2.

42. *Ibid.*

43. In this volume, see Balamut and Steinhagen for a discussion of financial aid changes, and see Churchill and Obah for a discussion of economic justice in the development of the CSC Minneapolis campus.

44. Since Church doctrine regarding sexuality also forbade heterosexual sex outside marriage, that conflict did affect heterosexual students. People's prejudices against lesbians, though, combined with Church doctrine to create more intense conflict about their lives than about the activities of heterosexuals.

45. Alan Graebner, "Position Paper," CSC Faculty Meeting, September 30, 1976, Abigail Quigley McCarthy Center for Women files, CSC Archives. Similar language also appeared in Women's Interest Group (WIG) meeting notes.

46. Julie Belle White-Newman, Interview with Catherine Lupori, July 13, 2004.

47. *Womanline*: WIG Newsletter, Vol. 1, April 19, 1978 (St. Paul: College of St. Catherine, 1978), p. 3.

48. *Ibid.*

49. Graebner, Position Paper, CSC Archives.

50. *Ibid.*

51. *Ibid.*

52. "Nonsexist Language Resolution," Faculty Meeting Minutes, College of St. Catherine, February 8, 1977, CSC Archives.

53. Huber, interview with Doherty.

II

INTELLECTUAL LIFE: IN AND
OUT OF THE CLASSROOM

5

What a Woman Should Know, What a Woman Can Be

Curriculum as Prism

Joanne Cavallaro, Jane Lamm Carroll, and Lynne Gildensoph

"The real test [of a curriculum is] the kind of lives students live after they leave college."[1]

Opening a college for women in the early years of the twentieth century posed many challenges, not the least of which was this dilemma: What should be taught? The answer might seem obvious today: teach women whatever they need to know. But in 1905, when the Sisters of St. Joseph founded the College of St. Catherine, the answer was anything but obvious. Of course, this question entailed others: What is woman's proper role in society? What do women need to know? What should they be and what can they become?

These and similar questions preoccupied not only the leaders of women's colleges but society as a whole, and the more so as women began entering realms previously reserved for men, including higher education. During the mid-nineteenth century, a few institutions of higher education began opening their doors to women, especially those of upper- or upper-middle-class backgrounds who demanded access. At the same time, numerous women's colleges were being founded, starting with Mount Holyoke Academy in 1837. Indeed, the number of women's colleges grew so rapidly that, by the end of the nineteenth century, 150 of them had been built in the United States, a figure that includes a slowly rising number of Catholic colleges for women.[2]

Clearly, when it came to joining this national trend toward providing higher education for women, Catholics did so slowly. In 1884, although there were many Catholic colleges for men, none existed for women. Within a little more than 40 years, however, well over 40 Catholic colleges for women had been established.[3] What accounts for this marked change in attitude? At a quickening rate, Catholics began opening colleges for women in reaction to the growing number of Catholic women enrolling in secular or Protestant institutions of higher education. As a consequence, both the benefits and perils of so many Catholic women attending non-Catholic colleges were hotly debated. Conservative Catholics saw the perils: they feared a loss of faith among young Catholic women and tried to protect them—and the Catholic faith—from outside forces. For conservatives, the solution to the problem was to encourage the development of colleges created specifically for Catholic women.

Paradoxically, the same solution was offered by progressive Catholics, who saw the distinct benefits of increasing educational opportunities for Catholic women. In the view of one such progressive—Archbishop John Ireland of St. Paul, Minnesota, a self-described "firm believer in the higher education of women"—Catholic colleges for women would have a liberating potential.[4] In their support of Catholic colleges for women, both conservative and progressive Catholic leaders were able to join together on the question of women's higher education, yet they did so without giving up their divergent views about women's proper place in society.

For conservative Catholics of the time, a woman's natural function was reproduction; thus, her proper role was as wife and mother who passed on the Catholic faith and Catholic traditions. However, progressive Catholics envisioned a more expanded role for women; her proper sphere was "wherever she can live nobly and do useful work," according to Bishop John Spalding, a prominent Catholic bishop.[5] The Catholic women's college adroitly served the purposes of both perspectives: it protected women from secular influences, thus protecting their faith, and it opened women's horizons to new knowledge and skills, thereby offering them opportunities for work or activity outside the domestic realm. These competing views of what women should be were reflected in the colleges that were built for Catholic women, including the College of St. Catherine.

In light of the shifting balance among these competing views of women's roles and the tensions created by them, this essay examines the curriculum and co-curriculum developed at the College of St. Catherine over the last century. The College of St. Catherine created its curriculum based on a conception of women's roles that was both liberatory and conservative, the balance between the two shifting from decade to decade, neither aim ever managing to eradicate the other.

THE EARLY YEARS: SERIOUS WOMEN DOING SERIOUS WORK

In founding the college in 1905, the Sisters of St. Joseph may not have thought of themselves as radicals, but the founding was a radical act in and of itself. In the Catholic Church at that time, women were seen as "pre-ordained to social roles of loving, nurturing, and caring for life, while their capacity for thought and active leadership counted for little worth. This obviously translated into the domestic and private spheres of life as . . . the woman's proper domain."[6] In addition, the Church assumed that women were inherently less capable than men in intellectual matters. Founding a college for women challenged these traditional ideas on women's abilities in that it recognized women's intellectual capacities and aspirations and took them seriously.

Taking women seriously meant recognizing the capacity of women to engage in rigorous and far-ranging intellectual inquiry and to take on roles other than those of wife and mother. The very act of creating a college for women challenged the widespread perception that women could not and should not learn subjects common in higher education for men: philosophy, literature, science, Greek, Latin, and history. As the College noted in its 1935 report to the Phi Beta Kappa Qualifications Committee, "Our College is not a finishing school. It is distinctly for intelligent and cultured women," in other words, for serious women who would play a part in their world.[7]

The Sisters who founded and did most of the work of the College served as immediate role models of serious women, demonstrating in their works and lives that women could be defined by what they did rather than by familial or relational roles only. As Ruether and McLaughlin point out, religious sisters, because they were outside of traditional gender expectations, were in some ways allowed more freedom of action: "Catholic nuns, though they belonged to an extremely patriarchal church whose male hierarchy defined female roles according to medieval notions that women were irresponsible, soft-brained and incapable of logical thought, were in some ways the most liberated women in nineteenth-century America."[8]

Indeed, students at the College of St. Catherine, unlike those at many secular and Protestant women's colleges, would see women performing nearly all the duties and tasks required to manage and run a complex institution; from its beginning, the college has had women presidents, women deans, women administrators; women formed the majority of its faculty, a situation highly unusual in coeducational or men's colleges. As Ker Conway notes, women religious "offered a counter social model" in that they lived the reality of a "vocation outside marriage" where the purpose of an educated woman was not "being a good companion to an educated male."[9] Ker Conway suggests it was the Sisters' experiences that helped Catholic women's colleges avoid much of the "hidden curriculum" designed to teach women that their proper place in life was solely in the domestic sphere. The Sisters put a lie to this claim by their very existence. During the College's first four decades, students would also see Sisters leaving to pursue graduate education. These sisters, interestingly, rarely did so at Catholic institutions; instead, they attended such secular institutions as the University of Chicago, Juilliard School of Music, and Columbia University, and often traveled abroad to such elite universities as Oxford University and Universite de Louvain. (See Carroll, this volume, for further discussion of early faculty development at the College.)

Surely seeing such intellectual pursuits and administrative abilities in women might have helped students at the College begin to view women as capable of doing important things in the world. It may also have accounted for the emphasis placed on encouraging students to pursue graduate studies. According to Kennelly, from 1913 to 1935 at least 21 percent of St. Catherine's graduates went on to postgraduate studies, at a time when the vast majority of Midwest female college graduates went into teaching. In contrast, during the same period, less than 5 percent of the female graduates of nearby coeducational Hamline University pursued graduate studies.[10] Moreover, graduates of Catholic women's colleges, like graduates of non-Catholic women's colleges, pursued professional degrees in law and medicine at proportionately higher rates than alumnae of coeducational institutions.[11] The Sisters, as one early alumna noted, "inspired generations of young women to take an active part in the world."[12]

LIBERAL ARTS CURRICULUM:
WOMEN CAN DO PHILOSOPHY TOO

The education offered at the College was, from the beginning, based firmly in the liberal arts. The course of study was meant to be of the same high standards as that at men's or coeducational colleges. Early leaders rejected the very notion that courses of study at a women's college should be specifically designed for them. (See Carroll, this volume, for further discussion.) Believing that women could rise to "the higher planes of intellectual life" just as men could and that "the career open to ability applies to her not less than to man," they insisted that providing women with a higher education equal to that of men meant offering a curriculum identical to that offered at men's and coeducational institutions.[13] Although they would not have called themselves feminists, the framework within which the early leaders worked predicts that of second-wave liberal feminism: women should have rights and opportunities equal to those offered men. In this case, it was educational opportunity that needed to be equalized. The College's belief in women's ability to learn whatever men learned was the basis for the curriculum it created. Women at St. Catherine's were expected to learn what men learned, though not, as we discuss below, necessarily to become what men could become.

The early curriculum of the College mirrored the standard liberal arts courses found at secular and Protestant liberal arts colleges and universities of the time. Majors listed in the 1906 catalogue were philosophy, Latin, Greek, history, history of art, English, German, French, mathematics, chemistry, physics, and botany. By 1910, the College required a total of 126 credits as well as noncredit courses in elocution and physical culture for the bachelor of arts degree. St. Catherine's students chose one major and four minors, with at least 12 credits in each of the minor departments.[14]

In 1914, Sister Antonia, the College's profoundly influential leader who served as dean and later president in the years spanning 1911 to 1937, altered St. Catherine's curriculum to emulate the rigorous requirements and course offerings of the University of Chicago. Although she retained the major subject areas from the 1906 curriculum, Sister Antonia added new courses, upgraded or augmented the level of work required in existing courses, and expanded prerequisites for some courses. In particular, she oversaw significant revisions in botany, geology, and geography to make those courses comparable to the University of Chicago's curriculum.[15]

Derham Hall classroom, 1912. Photo courtesy of St. Catherine University.

In the 1920s and '30s, as the College's faculty developed under Sister Antonia's leadership, the liberal arts and sciences curriculum evolved and expanded. English, art, and chemistry were especially noteworthy for their growth, advancements in curriculum, and added academic rigor during this period.[16] Sister Antonia established a broad variety of fine arts offerings, which had always been available at the College as extracurricular courses but now became fully integrated into the curriculum. Music and Art became distinct departments. In 1937, the Theater Department became professionally organized when the College hired Mabel Frey, a professional producer and director who would lead the department until her retirement in 1971.[17]

From the mid-1930s to the early 1980s, the liberal arts and sciences curriculum at the College of St. Catherine, with a few notable exceptions, remained largely unchanged. The humanities, which encompassed languages, history, classics, philosophy, the fine arts, and literature, dominated the liberal arts curriculum, constituting its own division among four major divisions in the curriculum and offered as either a major or minor. One three-part interdisciplinary humanities course, especially popular among students and faculty from 1942 to 1962, asked students to not only study music, art, and literature, but to connect all three fields in their exploration of what was called Western civilization.[18] In 1935 Sister Jeanne argued in her report to the Phi Beta Kappa Committee on Qualifications that it was the College's emphasis and strengths in the humanities that recommended it more than anything else for membership in the prestigious liberal arts honors society.[19] (This argument proved successful: in 1937 the College of St. Catherine became the first Catholic college or university in the U.S. to be awarded a Phi Beta Kappa chapter.)

Later additions to the liberal arts and sciences curriculum included American Studies in the late 1950s and several Area Studies programs that focused on Russia, the Far East, and the Middle East, developed in conjunction with other area colleges, in the early 1960s. The College also developed independent departments of Theology, Philosophy, Political Science, Economics, and Classics in the 1960s and 1970s, although all of these subjects had been taught for decades under various disciplinary labels. Communications, Women's Studies, and Critical Studies of Race and Ethnicity have all been introduced to the College curriculum since 1980, as have two bookend liberal arts courses, *The Reflective Woman* and the *Global Search for Justice*.

PROFESSIONAL CURRICULUM:
EDUCATING FOR ECONOMIC INDEPENDENCE

Catholic colleges for women faced challenges in terms of their curricula that elite women's colleges of the East, the so-called Seven Sisters, did not.

For those elite colleges, the aim of higher education was to produce intelligent and cultured women who could be cultured mates for successful men and educated mothers to future male leaders. The future for most of these students did not include having to earn a living or contributing financially to family income; their contributions would be as wives and mothers. Students at Catholic colleges for women had more varied futures ahead of them: career women, wives and mothers, single women responsible for their own financial affairs, continuing contributors to family incomes.

Although the first students to attend St. Catherine's were most likely from middle- or upper-middle-class families, by the 1920s, students were increasingly working class and children of immigrants. The College's response was to begin developing a curriculum and co-curriculum that were not only grounded in the liberal arts and sciences, but also professional.[20] Indeed, as discussed below, the cultural graces and moral virtues taught at the College were meant, perhaps as much as the professional subjects were, to help students from immigrant, rural, and working-class backgrounds learn the skills necessary for employment that would allow them a life free of the physical drudgery so common in rural and working-class jobs at that time. Through much of the College's history, only certain professions were deemed acceptable in American society for women: nursing, home economics, library science, education, secretarial/clerical work, and social work. Like all Catholic women's colleges, in the 1920s St. Catherine's began adding vocational courses and programs in these female-dominated professions to meet the needs of their students. It continues to offer majors in professional fields dominated by women: nursing is the largest undergraduate department; social work, education, and home economics (now expanded and renamed Family, Consumer, and Nutritional Science) continue to attract large numbers of students.

Financial concerns of the institutions also required them to respond to the needs of all Catholic women, not just the affluent. According to Karen Kennelly, "purism in the liberal arts mode was a path Catholic women's colleges could ill afford to follow."[21] As Schier and Russett note, in the early days, Catholic women's colleges had two models to chose from in developing their curriculum: either offering a "rigorous liberal arts education with an admixture of theology and spiritual guidance" such as that offered at elite secular women's colleges; or "providing skills and training to young Catholic women of the working and lower middle classes, often the first in their families to attain a college education."[22] It was those who followed the latter model that served as "engines of social mobility" for Catholic women. The College of St. Catherine decided to follow both models simultaneously: students were expected to follow a rigorous liberal arts education, one modeled not on elite secular women's colleges but on elite secular coeducational institutions such as the University of Chicago; and they were offered training in such fields as nursing, librarianship, teaching.

This decision allowed the College not only to help their students achieve some economic independence but also to introduce them to broad cultural ideas. The St. Catherine's student was to be a lady of culture, broadly educated and able to pursue a professional career.

The College set about preparing students to be the best in what were the relatively few professional occupations considered socially acceptable for women.[23] As early as 1909, the College *Yearbook* informed prospective students concerned about their future employment that "a judicious choice of subjects and earnest, persevering study will enable a young woman to be successful in the work for which she is fitted."[24] The following two decades saw the establishment and growth of eight new fields of professional study at the College, including kindergarten education, home economics, foods and nutrition for dieticians, nursing, social service, physical education, library science, and secretarial studies.[25] In addition, recognizing that more women were interested in journalism as a career, St. Catherine's offered a course in journalism in the early 1930s. In subsequent decades, as women's occupational choices broadened, the College's curriculum expanded to include additional health science, business, and pre-professional programs, as well as graduate professional programs in nursing, occupational therapy, and education.

As early as the 1930s, the development of professional curricula alongside the traditional liberal arts curriculum, one of the hallmarks of St. Catherine's, created tensions among and between administrators and faculty at the College. In a 1939 report, the dean, Sister Ste. Helene Guthrie, expressed her concern about the increasing demands for "vocational fields" and their threat to "the liberal arts character of the College." The response of the faculty and administrators was to require all upper division students "entering upon a vocational field" to "also carry a major field of study in a purely academic subject."[26] Sister Jeanne Marie had been compelled, four years earlier, to defend the College's professional studies curriculum to Phi Beta Kappa, the national liberal arts honors society, by arguing as follows:

> Curriculum studies yield evidence of adaptability without sacrifice of integrity. Only those vocational courses have been admitted which require a maximum of general culture and a minimum of specialization. Emphasis has definitely been maintained on the humanities, with the social studies and biological and physical sciences given about equal secondary importance, and with philosophy and religion kept instructive and inspirational.[27]

In the College administrative reports of the 1940s and 1950s, references are made to internal battles among faculty and administrators regarding the proper balance of professional and liberal arts curricula. According to Sister Rosalie Ryan, during the 1950s, the "College became the scene of a struggle between proponents of the liberal arts and those of the professional fields."[28] To assure a proper balance between the two curricula, the faculty studied the liberal arts curriculum for several years in an effort to reassert its primacy in the face of encroachment of the professional programs. In her 1956–1957 report, the Dean of Professional Studies, Sister Annette Walters, described significant problems in successfully integrating the various professional curricula with not only the liberal arts core, but with the existing administrative and faculty structures of the College.[29] In 1960, however, Sister Mary William Brady, then President of the College, reported that "the central curriculum, liberal and cultural, has persisted and survived all attempts at dilution or elimination."[30]

Through the 1970s, the College's bulletins described St. Catherine's as a liberal arts institution, but in the 1980s it began to represent itself as both a liberal arts college *and* a professional college.[31] This shift in language signified a real and dramatic change in the makeup of the student body at the College; after 75 years, the balance between the number of students in professional programs and the number of liberal arts majors had finally shifted in favor of the former group. Since 1980, concomitant with this shift in the student body, the number and variety of liberal arts courses and programs offered at the College have decreased, while professional curricula and departments have expanded.[32] In response, since 2000, the College has been engaged in a focused effort to reinvigorate the liberal arts, making it central to its mission to teach women to lead and influence.

GOOD POSTURE AND CULTURAL GRACES: EDUCATING FOR CHARACTER

In the early years, St. Catherine's, like other women's colleges that aimed to teach women such subjects as philosophy, science, and literature, had to demonstrate that "women could be both educated and womanly."[33] Indeed, all colleges for women in the late nineteenth and early twentieth centuries had to counter widespread fears that encouraging intellectual pursuits for women would be detrimental not only to their health but to their morals as well. Concerns were especially strong around supposed connections between higher education for women and lesbianism. As Gibson notes, a "taint of lesbianism . . . surrounded the . . . female college student in the late nineteenth and early twentieth century." To many in the medical field and the general public, the "connection between intelligence and degeneracy" in women was well established, "the apparently innocuous goal of higher education" automatically leading to degeneracy in women. As some medical writers at the time put it, education "was a process by which women might become masculine, and therefore lesbian, and ultimately degenerate."[34]

From the beginning, the Sisters' aims for their students included not only intellectual development but character development as well, character development as women. As Sister Marie Phillip Haley, an alumna and faculty member, noted about President Sister Antonia McHugh:

> To Sister Antonia, the mere accumulation of knowledge was not the sole purpose of a college education. Character training or the building of a life was almost the unique subject of her assembly talks. . . . She drove at practice, at homely virtues—honesty, cleanliness, industry, dependableness, a nice consideration for others. Who could ever forget her urging us to chisel our characters, to accomplish hard things, to be women of good sense?[35]

So what did women of good sense look like at the College of St. Catherine? What qualities of character did the Sisters seek to instill in their students? Their aims were threefold: to develop students' physical health, "cultural graces," and moral virtue.[36]

Physical health: Late nineteenth- and early twentieth-century concerns about educating women did not just focus on fears of degenerate sexuality; women were warned that higher education posed great dangers to their female bodies. "The female brain, according to Clark (a professor at Harvard Medical School in 1873), could only be used at the expense of physical feminine qualities, since energy devoted to study would be diverted from the development of the healthy reproductive system that was so essential to society."[37]

Students playing field hockey, 1928. Photo courtesy of St. Catherine University.

Student archers, 1937. Photo courtesy of St. Catherine University.

To counter these perceptions that rigorous intellectual study was detrimental to female health, colleges for women began requiring of their students what would now be called physical education courses. By 1905, when the College of St. Catherine was established, the physical cultivation of students was assumed to be necessary to the female college experience, and throughout its history, the College has maintained a physical education requirement for its students. In addition, there was a variety of outdoor and sports activities of which students could partake: horseback riding, field hockey, basketball, tennis, archery, and after 1931, required swimming classes.[38]

Physical health included more than sports and required classes. Sister Antonia McHugh, then President of the College, in her address to the National Catholic Council of Women in the mid-1930s, elaborated upon the need to attend to students' posture. She noted that "at certain times of the year, students have, what they call, Good Posture Day. Slumping, slovenly attitudes, slouching gaits, bent shoulders and cramped necks are attacked through amusing drawings and through verbal discipline."[39] Indeed, one alumna recalls that Sister Antonia was always telling students to correct their posture; another remembers Sister reprimanding her style of walking, saying, "Stop swinging your arms when you walk. A lady never walks like that!"[40]

Cultural graces: How a lady walked was important; even more important was how a lady behaved. A graduate of the College should exhibit what Kennelly calls "cultural graces."[41] Although the College claimed not to be a finishing school, finishing did indeed take place there, at least up to the late 1960s. Students were taught lessons on proper attire, manners, poise, speech, and ladylike behavior, such lessons taking place both in and out of the classroom. The Sisters admonished students to be proper ladies at required weekly convocations, in casual encounters with students in the College's hallways and dormitories, and as part of the wisdom imparted in the classroom and in private advising meetings. As one alumna from the 1920s puts it, the clear message was "at no time can you refrain from being a lady."[42] Another alumna recalls of Sister Antonia, "Her emphasis on good speech always impressed me, as well as her stress on personal neatness and grooming. She spent several minutes during one talk telling us how to pronounce *first*." Another alumna, in reminiscing about the convocations Sister Antonia gave, said, "She taught us the importance of little things: the importance of a clean uniform; the holding of a door; the friendly smile— all of which are bases for character building."[43] Clearly, being a lady meant staying clean, standing up straight, and having gracious manners.

Being a lady also meant having refined tastes. The development of such taste in music, art, and literature was an important part of the formation of students' character. From its inception, the College has offered an array of courses in music and art both for credit and as extras. In the 1920s and 1930s, the College made tickets to the Minnesota Orchestra available to students, brought noted writers and musicians to campus, prominent among them Edna St. Vincent Millay, Marcel Dupre, Ethel Barrymore, Hugh Walpole, Sheila Kaye Smith, Evelyn Waugh, and May Sarton.[44] (See Farr, this volume, for more about the College's curricular and extracurricular literary life.) A journalist who visited in 1940 remarked on the emphasis the College placed on cultivating the artistic and literary sensibilities of faculty and students:

> One of the expressed purposes of the College is to develop the creative abilities of each student. It is no wonder the girls, even those of no recognized talents, here learn the art of self-expression: for creativeness, in one form or another, is in the air. Many a parlor, office and classroom has beauty that has been created by the quiet, unassuming teachers of art—paintings, heads and figurines of madonnas tiled relief plaques over the fireplaces, yes, and even the Stations of the Cross in the chapel. The publications of the Sisters reveal a sensitiveness to things immediate and things of the past, as in Sister Maris Stella's collection of sonnets.[45]

An early advertisement for the College cites as one of the outcomes desired for its students the ability to count "art an intimate friend." This objective appeared repeatedly in College literature through subsequent decades. The 1938 *College Bulletin* noted, "The curriculum is organized to meet the special demands for the trained mind with its keen perceptions . . . and deeper appreciation of aesthetic pleasure." Similarly, the Home Economics

Art classroom, 1920s. Photo courtesy of St. Catherine University.

Department's stated aim in 1938 was "to ensure scholarly intellectual perceptions, social sympathy, and refined personal tastes" of its students. The 1940 *Bulletin* cited the aim to develop in students "truly liberal tastes," and in 1944 the *Bulletin* emphasized that graduates of the college will live "rich lives, pursuing intellectual and aesthetic interests that are enduring, leisure activities that are satisfying and worthwhile."[46]

When the College taught students "refined personal tastes," manners, and other cultural graces, it was not just an aesthetic enterprise, nor just a gendered one, but one that was closely tied to social class in U.S. society. The College was teaching its students those personal and social skills necessary for them to obtain and retain jobs that would not only allow them to support themselves as single women and contribute to their family income as married women, but also allow them to attain the types of jobs that could move them beyond their class of origin. Indeed, early advocates of higher education for women noted that a college education is necessary for any women "who must provide for themselves and who would rise above the rank of clerks and domestic servants."[47] An emphasis on the proper pronunciation of *first* was not just about talking like a lady; it was about not talking like a lady's maid. Such pronunciation, like manners and graces, signaled membership in a middle-class America that for many students differed from the rural, immigrant America they had been born into.

As such, efforts at teaching cultural graces were assimilationist in purpose, at least in terms of class assimilation. At the same time, however, the College's aim was decidedly antiassimilationist in terms of religion. Like all Catholic colleges for women, St. Catherine's was a space in which women could be protected from the mainstream Protestant culture that threatened to absorb Catholics into its dominant embrace. This threat, though generally perceived to be of import to all Catholics, was seen as more dangerous when it came to Catholic women, even though Catholic men were attending Protestant or secular institutions of higher education at far higher numbers than were Catholic women.[48] Issues of religious assimilation were, then, deeply gendered. It was important to safeguard women's religious identity in a way that it was not so important to safeguard men's: "the case of young men is different" when it comes to the temptations of a Protestant or secular institution.[49]

Women needed the spiritual and moral safeguards of a Catholic institution because they were seen as more susceptible to temptations; the idea of "blurred or permeable boundaries [inherent in] the female personality" meant that they were easily open to persuasion and thus needed special protection.[50] Echoes of this need to protect women from temptation can be seen as late as the 1950s, when the president writes in her annual report that with the four new required courses in philosophy and theology, students seem to "go out now with more mature understanding of their religion and better equipped to meet the inevitable false philosophies of the secular world."[51] Women were also seen as the ones who preserve and pass on religious values to the family. Their assimilation into Protestant culture was, thus, triply dangerous: for them, for their future families, and for the Church.

Moral virtue: These antiassimilationist tendencies were evident in the moral virtues explicitly taught and implicitly promoted. It was not enough to ensure students were physically healthy, refined, and lady-like. The graduate of St. Catherine's should be a woman of "serious dignity" as well as "charming grace," able to exercise "habitual self-control and self-restraint," to "display mutual courtesy and honor," to be "solidly virtuous and religious." She should have "a strong sense of reliability and responsibility" that relies on "Catholic principles and ideals of conduct of life."[52] In other words, she should be a woman of outstanding moral virtue and spiritual depth.

As a Catholic college, it is no surprise that one of the College's stated goals from its beginning was to enhance the spiritual development of its students. Bulletins from the 1920s through the 1960s emphasize its importance, noting the connection between intellectual, social, physical, and spiritual development within a Catholic community. Attention to religious values was an integral part of both the curriculum and what we would now call the co-curriculum. Religion courses, their focus changing over the years, were required of all Catholic students, though not of non-Catholic students until the 1960s. Multiple extracurricular religious activities were also offered for students. (See Connors et al., this volume, for further discussion of religious teaching at the College.)

Interestingly, the stated aims of such courses and activities, as expressed in early College bulletins and catalogues, defined spiritual development as much in terms of action in the world as of contemplative learning, perhaps because of the founding congregation's emphasis on service—to "serve the dear neighbor" is a key value of the Sisters of St. Joseph. The College clearly expected its graduates to be of service outside the home, to have a profession through which they would not only earn a living but also contribute to society. A morally virtuous graduate should have the personal resources and qualities of mind that would, in the words of a catalogue from 1920, enable her "to do her fair share of the world's work in a gracious, generous, beneficent spirit."[53]

In its concept of spiritual and character development for women, the College managed for a while to partially resist the dominant notion of women's roles promulgated by the conservative wing of the church. As Mahoney notes, in the early twentieth century "officially and unofficially, the church promoted a traditional, conservative domestic ideology," one that limited woman's roles to that of wife and mother and sought to inculcate "typical" women's virtues of nurturing, loving, maternal care, all part of what the Church called "women's special nature."[54] Johnson notes that within this special nature, women's "capacity for thought and active leadership are counted of little worth."[55] The College did not so much challenge the idea of women's "special nature" as enlarge it to include women's capacity not only for intellectual "thought and active leadership" but also for meaningful work outside of the home, work that would make the world a better place.

The Sisters led by example in connecting moral/spiritual development and social justice/action in the world. They hosted the first African American art exhibit in Minnesota at the College during the 1930s, and invited Dorothy Day, founder of the Catholic Worker movement, to address the College community about their responsibilities to the homeless and jobless three times between 1937 and 1947. St. Catherine's also admitted its first African American student in 1937 at a time when many other Catholic colleges and universities in the United States still discriminated against Black applicants. During World War II, in response to the social injustice of the forced internment of Japanese Americans in government camps, the Sisters invited eight Japanese American women to attend St. Catherine's on scholarships.[56]

In the 1945 *Bulletin*, students were told that the College "will make [you] the very best possible person of which you are capable and you must make the community in which you live a better place because you have lived there." The College considered this critical for its graduates because "unless the young people of today know the meaning of justice and understand equality they will not insure democracy for tomorrow." History courses in the 1945 *Bulletin* specifically mentioned the analysis of current social problems in their course descriptions. Similarly, political science courses were "designed to prepare the students for public service, for citizenship, and for society." Courses in Catholic Social Thought were offered through the Sociology Department and nursing courses exposed students to factors influencing the health of communities. Education students were encouraged to get out into the community so that they would become aware of various social forces at play in the Twin Cities.[57] New courses addressing the societies and economies of nations in Latin America and the Far East, race relations, labor problems, and social philosophy were introduced during this decade. The College also assessed how well students were prepared to make a contribution to social justice out in the world. In the late 1930s and early 1940s, the College required students to take the "Life Situations Test," which was used to evaluate "students' attitudes toward interracial justice, social responsibility, moral courage, economic fairness."[58]

In the late 1940s and through much of the 1950s, the woman of good sense was redefined according to a conservative Catholic perspective. The emphasis on developing "all aspects of [the students'] personality" and contributing to society remained, but it was muted by the dominant "cult of domesticity" that became ascendant in American society after World War II and by the increasingly conservative bent of the Catholic Church. During the early Cold War years, both American society and the Catholic Church asserted a traditional view of women's proper role in life, one that saw women as destined for the domestic sphere with little or no role in the wider society, except perhaps as an occasional volunteer in charitable causes. Ironically, this definition of women's proper role was one which women's colleges had directly challenged and actively undermined in the first half of the twentieth century.[59]

The Education Plans of those years note that the education a student received would "instill in her a realization of her role in life *as a woman*—her capabilities and her insights, her duties and privileges, her dignity and *her special vocation of motherhood*, natural and spiritual" developed "in realms of nature and of grace"[60] (emphasis added). Indeed, for the first time a course on "Christian marriage and family life" is required; each student is also required to take four years' study of philosophy and theology, both of which are at this time dominated by conservative Catholic doctrine.[61] The 1955–1956 *Bulletin* defines women's roles in clearly traditional ways:

"Women must do their share and contribute their special talents to work which is particularly suited to them as women. Homes, hospitals, libraries, schools, and offices need leaders whose ideal is instructing and serving others with Christ-like understanding and charity."[62]

The upheavals that gripped American society and campuses in the 1960s and 1970s left their mark on the College as well. The civil rights, women's, and anti-Vietnam war movements did not convulse the campus with protests, sit-ins, and strikes, but student life at the College was nevertheless transformed as changes in social mores made their way onto campus. Students chafed at the paternalism of rules meant to isolate them for their "own protection" and demanded the freedom other college students already enjoyed. Codes of conduct were relaxed; strict rules governing when and where students could go—and what they could wear—were abolished. According to one faculty member teaching at the time, "the dress code disappeared overnight." Students who had previously come to class well groomed in skirts and carefully ironed blouses "from one day to the next" appeared in unkempt jeans and scruffy tops.[63]

The goal of teaching students cultural graces, good manners, and refined tastes died away for good by the mid-1970s. The goal of teaching students to be women of good sense did not die, however; it was, instead, transformed. As cultural graces became less of a marker of the St. Catherine education, moral virtue became more paramount. The virtuous woman of good sense was redefined as one who knew something of and was willing to do something about deep social injustices that plague societies, here and abroad.

SOCIAL JUSTICE: EDUCATING TO SERVE

Catholic colleges for women began early in their history to use Catholic social teaching as a "major source of intellectual stimulation" for their curricula. They took seriously Pope Leo XIII's call to "involve themselves in action to alleviate social ills" and saw higher education as an important tool in this effort. St. Catherine's was no exception in this endeavor.[64]

From its first decade, the faculty at the College included discussions of social justice issues in various courses across the College curriculum. Early courses that addressed social justice issues included *Elementary Sewing*, in which "factory conditions and laws governing the production of such garments is discussed," and *Advanced Sewing*, which considered the "economics or conditions governing the production of readymade garments, and the work and wages of women and children."[65] The 1921 catalogue included courses on "Racial Backgrounds" and "Americanization" that were meant to help women learn to solve social problems and promote social justice. According to Kennelly, the curriculum developed at St. Catherine's, and other

Catholic women's colleges, encouraged women to analyze "causes of unjust conditions, [reflect] on remedies, and [act] to effect societal change." In the 1930s, the Spanish department began teaching Latin American authors who focused on social themes, a departure from the standard curriculum. During the 1940s courses from disciplines such as history, economics, political science, and education addressed relevant social issues. At that time, the Sociology Department had a cluster of courses discussing contemporary social problems and solutions. In the 1960s, Area Studies courses (taught in collaboration with four other local colleges) were designed to focus on Africa and Latin America and to "reflect multicultural perspectives."[66]

Faculty, staff, and students also designed and participated in a variety of extracurricular forums and actions addressing social justice issues.[67] Beginning in the early 1960s, speakers such as Dr. Jose Maria Chaves, an educator and diplomat from Colombia, spoke on such topics as "The Church and Social Change in Latin America."[68] A number of students (mostly social work majors) traveled to the southern U.S. or to Bogota, Colombia, to work with community members. President Alberta Huber, CSJ, noted in her 1964–1965 report that many CSC graduates joined the Peace Corps and an organization named Teachers for East Africa after graduation.[69]

During the 1965–1966 academic year, faculty and students held a two-day institute entitled "The College Community and Christian Responsibility," which included a talk by Rev. Daniel Berrigan, and discussions of the books *The Other America* by Michael Harrington and *The Rich Nations and the Poor Nations* by Barbara Ward. According to the student newspaper, *The Catherine Wheel*, the institute was very well received by both students and faculty.[70] Mary Land, a sophomore, said about the institute, "It offered us an opportunity to gain insights into the problems of poverty and discrimination in America. . . . We have a serious obligation to educate ourselves and take our places in the community." Sr. James Agnes, who had just spent several weeks working in poor communities in Philadelphia, stated, "This experience sharpened my sensitivity to the poor and dissolved my stereotypes of them." Another successful student-faculty institute, "The People and the Power," took place during the 1968–1969 academic year.[71] Students themselves established a Social Action Committee during these years. They also participated in lay mission trips to Mississippi, Alabama, Arizona, and Harlem during the summers and worked with the local Urban League, tutoring African American high school students. The Social Action Committee placed student volunteers in the Twin Cities community, including the Shakopee Women's Reformatory.[72]

Student activism and curricular focus on social justice were responses not only to the societal changes of the late 1960s but also to deep changes within the Catholic Church. The Second Vatican Council of the early 1960s opened the Church up to accommodations with modern thought, heightened the power of the laity, and dramatically altered the roles of clergy and women religious. Subsequent Papal encyclicals advocated for human rights, expressed support for movements addressing social and economic injustices,[73] and stressed the need to address the growing gap between rich and poor nations with a "call to action to Christians to participate and contribute to solving the many problems facing individual countries and the world."[74]

The College of St. Catherine made its call to social action explicit in the 1974–1975 *Bulletin,* in which students were encouraged to think critically about how "the educated person of today . . . [can become] not only a judge of the 'instruments of the good life' but also a producer or distributor of those instruments for the benefit of others . . . [to] effect desirable social change."[75] Course offerings addressing diversity and social justice issues included *Black African Literature* (English), *Women in America* (History), and a course called *Women: An Interdisciplinary Perspective,* taught by a collaborative team from history, literature, psychology, sociology, and theology. The MUST program (Metro Urban Studies) recruited students from St. Catherine's for a semester of concentrated coursework and community partnerships during the 1970s. Other courses focusing on alternative social and political theories and systems included *Radicalism in America* (History) and *Social and Political Philosophy* (Philosophy). Meanwhile, the campus community participated in teach-ins and invited speakers to educate themselves about issues such as the Vietnam War, feminism, and civil rights.

After the killing of students by National Guard troops at Kent State in 1970, students went to Washington, D.C., to speak with their government representatives, and other students helped a Vietnamese student and her family move to St. Paul after she had been imprisoned in Vietnam. St. Catherine's students also participated in an exchange program with students at Xavier University (a historically Black university), and heard Eldridge Cleaver, the former Black Panther leader, speak to a packed house on campus.[76]

An emphasis on social justice continues to this day. In 2005, when the College faculty voted to accept a set of liberal arts outcomes that formally included a subset of goals addressing ethics and social justice, it was not a departure from previous practices but rather an attempt to formalize what had been going on informally since the 1910s. The College's current capstone course, *The Global Search for Justice,* exposes each student to social justice issues related to various topics, including immigrants, women's health, women's work, and the environment, among others. Catholic Social Teaching, the role of the Catholic Church, and an array of alternative justice theories are presented and discussed in *The Global Search for Justice* as a means to encourage students to take action to solve what are seemingly intractable global problems.

WOMEN'S MISSION IN A MAN'S CURRICULUM:
A PHILOSOPHY FOR HER TOO?

A student entering the College from its early years until the late 1970s would find a wide array of classes designed to teach her liberal arts skills and content and, in some cases, prepare her for a professional career. She would find courses infused with social justice and an expectation that she herself contribute to making the world a more just place upon graduation. What she would not find was a curriculum that focused on women's concerns, experiences, knowledge. Indeed, in founding the College, the Sisters rejected any notion that courses for women should be so designed. When it was founded, the College set out to demonstrate that women could learn whatever men could; it was a mark of faith in women's abilities to demand of them the same curriculum as that demanded of men.

Having the "same" curriculum for women and men, however, did not mean the curriculum was not gendered. In examining the professional fields offered at CSC, one can see quite clearly their gender specificity: library science, nursing, occupational therapy, education, all fields dominated by women. The liberal arts curriculum, though not so overtly gendered, was still deeply so, for until the mid-1970s, the curriculum at the College of St. Catherine, like that at most colleges, whether they be women's, men's, or coeducational institutions, was basically a men's curriculum. The authors taught in literature courses were almost exclusively male; the artists studied in art classes were equally so; the focus of science and social science was men's roles; economists studied the work of those who were paid for their labor—men. With minor exceptions, this "men's curriculum" continued to be the norm both at St. Catherine's and nationwide until well into the 1980s. One exception to this norm at St. Catherine's was a relatively early focus on Catholic women authors, including Sigrid Undset and Flannery O'Connor, in English courses.[77]

Beginning in the late 1960s, women in institutions of higher education in the U.S. began to create a curriculum that was more inclusive of women's experiences, issues, history, lives, concerns. (The first Women's Studies Program was introduced at San Diego State University in 1970.) The rise of the women's movement nationwide had led to increased scholarship on women and increased demand to include that scholarship in college courses. It also led to a rethinking of how knowledge is made, and by whom, in an effort to correct the male bias that has traditionally valued men's experiences, work, contributions, roles. This rethinking included investigating the ways in which that bias has shaped truths, theories, observations, questions, interpretations in academic fields and beyond, and infusing what came to be known as the new scholarship on women into the curriculum at colleges and universities.

A further impetus impelled the College of St. Catherine toward questioning whether the curriculum offered could be or should be so revised: the decision in the late-'70s to remain a women's college in face of social and financial pressures to change. (See Doherty and Lupori, this volume.) Discussions leading up to and following this decision engendered debates and heated arguments among both faculty and administrators about the purpose and nature of an all-women's college.

St. Catherine's was an early leader in revising its history and literature courses to be more inclusive of women. Courses on the history of women were offered beginning in the mid-1970s, among them *Women in America to 1920* and *American Women since Suffrage*. A course on women's literature soon followed, as did a composition course which focused on women's writing, both fiction and nonfiction. More courses followed: by 1983, there were courses focusing on women in history, English, speech communication, social work, sociology, and one, *Human Sexuality*, listed as interdisciplinary.

In the late 1970s and early 1980s discussions around what it meant to be a woman's college became not only more heated but more widespread as the College sought to clarify what it meant to teach women in a women-centered environment. Several ad hoc committees were formed to explore this issue: Women's Interest Group (WIG), Ad Hoc Committee on Women's Studies, a multi-college consortium committee on Women's Studies and Gender Related Issues.[78] In addition, standing faculty committees such as the Educational Policies Committee and the Curriculum Committee also addressed the question of curricular revision. In 1977, the faculty passed a resolution making nonsexist language official policy at the College in all internal and public documents in order to "assure language usage consistent with CSC's commitment to women."[79] The College encouraged and funded attendance at several national conferences and workshops for faculty to learn more about scholarship, research, and pedagogy by, on, and for women. In November 1982, a faculty, student, and staff workshop, The Institute on Women's Studies: Integrating the New Scholarship on Women, was held to "acquaint the campus community with . . . aspects of the new scholarship on women." Classes were cancelled for this day-long event that was extensively covered in the student newspaper.[80]

The results of these discussions and activities on campus were many. An ad hoc committee on women's studies was formed, charged with carrying forward the work begun at the institute. The report from this committee to the Educational Policies Committee (EPC), the faculty committee overseeing the curriculum, noted that "in recent years, scholars and teachers in nearly every academic discipline have come to realize that the liberal arts, as traditionally defined and taught, have inadequately dealt with the status, roles, concerns, and contributions of women." The committee recommended "a consistent and on-going effort to incorporate the new scholarship into already existing courses" and "an interdisciplinary minor in women's studies" to be "introduced into the curriculum as soon as possible."[81]

The College's Strategic Long Range Plan developed through 1983–1984 contained several goals related to this issue, including that the College work to become "a center for research on women" and to "integrate research on women into the curriculum."[82] Two Educational Policies Committee recommendations were accepted into the Plan in 1984: "To include among criteria for program review the degree to which the scholarship and research on women and social justice have been integrated into [every] department" and to create as a new liberal arts outcome, "an appreciation of how the scholarship on women is related to both the liberal arts core and studies in major fields."[83]

One immediate result of the strategic plan was the establishment of the Abigail Quigley McCarthy Center for Women's Research, Resources, and Scholarship, named after a prominent alumna. In 1983–1984, a women's studies minor was created; deliberately interdisciplinary in nature, it required an introductory course in women's studies and four courses cross-listed in women's studies and another discipline. In its first year, eight courses were offered as cross-listed, coming from history, sociology, communications, and English, including literature and composition. In the 1984–1985 academic year, eleven new cross-listed courses were added, including three in the newly created Weekend College meant to serve non-traditional-aged women. As the committee that proposed the new minor stated, the minor would serve as a means of "organizing and regularizing a group of courses that already exists and providing a focus from which we can begin to address the other imperative—the integration of new scholarship on women into already existing courses."[84]

Reflecting a commitment on the part of the College's administration and president, in 1984 Elizabeth Minnich, a leading feminist philosopher and author of *Transforming Knowledge*, was invited to the College. Her visit was used by many as a way to understand the new scholarship on women and the ways in which that scholarship was transforming knowledge in the academy. She met not only with faculty interested in women's studies, but also with standing faculty-governance committees (Educational Policies Committee and Curriculum Committee), top administrators, student affairs staff, and students. The curricular revisions undertaken at this time included new courses not only in the liberal arts but also in professional disciplines, a fairly unusual circumstance in women's studies departments. Two new courses, *Career Development for Women*, which is still taught today, and a social work course were approved to be cross-listed in women's studies, a fairly unusual action in that few women's studies departments included professional courses.

Interestingly, during this time, the term "feminism" was widely used to describe the efforts being undertaken. The national backlash against the word had not yet occurred; *femi-nazi* was not a common term then. Those seeking to enlarge and deepen the impact of women's studies scholarship on the entire curriculum and learning environment could use the word with ease: The Institute on Women's Studies was unofficially known as Feminist Research Day. Such ease of terminology does not indicate, however, that the meaning of integrating feminist or women's scholarship was clear or agreed upon by all. For some, it simply meant adding women's voices and experiences within existing disciplinary boundaries: adding women artists and writers to art history and English or seeing women's lives, not just the lives of male leaders, as worthy of study in history. To others, it meant challenging what was seen as official knowledge within a discipline: asking whose perspective is dominant in judgments of literary quality, for example; or questioning deeply embedded beliefs about citizenship in political science, beliefs based on Greek ideas stemming from a society that devalued women to such an extent they were not seen as fully human; or demanding that economic theory take into account not just paid work but the unpaid work of many women throughout the world; or offering alternative theories on human development to the dominant male-based ones in psychology. One notable challenge to existing epistemology was the creation of a new course, the *Biology of Women*, that not only revised the content of an introductory biology course to make it more relevant to women, but also transformed the pedagogy to be more feminist, including student-initiated research projects.[85]

The College was more successful in adding women's experiences than in challenging traditional knowledge, perhaps because much of the momentum working to transform the curriculum in the early 1980s came to a halt by the late 1980s. At that time, the College underwent a major financial crisis, one that forced the attention of top administrative officials away from matters of curriculum and onto matters of financial survival. The repercussions for curricular transformation were great. New initiatives were curtailed, as few resources and little attention could be spared. Few new faculty were hired. Although this limitation affected all disciplines to some extent, it affected women's studies more than most. Women's studies was a fairly new field at that time, and faculty with expertise in it tended to be young, adjunct, or new to their profession. Curtailing new hires resulted in fewer faculty interested in expanding women's studies.

By 1990, the College was on more secure financial ground and interest in developing a women's studies major arose. Despite the work of the early 1980s, however, the College did not believe it had enough depth in the field to offer such a major on its own. The same held true for other colleges in the Associated Colleges of the Twin Cities, a consortium of five small, liberal arts colleges in Minneapolis and St. Paul who coordinated calendars, allowed easy cross-registration among students, and offered a few consortial majors (e.g., Russian Studies, East Asian Studies). Representatives of the five colleges came together in the late 1980s and developed an interdisciplinary consortial major in women's studies that was approved in 1990. The major consisted of courses offered at four colleges (one college dropped out of the major after the first year) that students at any college could take. This arrangement ensured that the depth and breadth necessary for a major could be maintained. St. Catherine's first listed the women's studies major as available to students in its 1992 catalogue. At that time, the College offered eleven cross-listed women's studies courses, fewer than in 1986.[86] The number of courses cross-listed in women's studies and other disciplines has steadily increased so that now it stands at 32.

The discussions, debates, and curricular revisions at the College took place within the context of a Catholic hierarchy also struggling with redefining issues of women's "natural" or proper role. Not until 1971 did the Vatican begin to state that women have an equal right to participate in "cultural, economic, social, and political life."[87] Pope John Paul II, in 1981, reaffirmed this right, but he also emphasized the "traditional" role of women to be responsible for the family. In 1986, the U.S. Catholic Bishops addressed the issue of equality for women, and discussed the feminization of poverty in their report *Economic Justice for All*.[88] In the late 1980s, the National Conference of Catholic Bishops constituted an ad hoc committee on the Role of Women in Society and the Church, which, although it involved thousands of women from approximately 100 dioceses, was released in 1992 only as a report, not as a pastoral letter as originally planned, and only after most of the women's voices had been excised.[89]

Regardless of the Catholic Church's *official* teaching about women's proper roles in society, the College of St. Catherine saw women as complete human beings, people who were not necessarily limited by either the Church or the broader society's narrow expectations of what women could and should be. The Sisters of St. Joseph of Carondelet created and maintained a curriculum where women were encouraged to learn and use the tools of critical analysis and judgment. They prepared women, through both the liberal arts and the professional studies curricula, for work outside the home, apart from duties as wife and mother. And they insisted that part of women's work was to contribute to making the world a better place.

CONCLUSION

The tensions arising from the compromise reached between conservatives and progressives when the College was founded continue to be apparent today. Landry's summary of the early Catholic college for women, as "both a liberating and conservative institution," still holds true.[90] Although St. Catherine's has long been thought of as a good school for good girls, the "white glove" image has never fully captured either the intent of its founders or the effects of its education on students. The curriculum created by the Sisters and continuously refined and developed by the faculty taught students to be "Katies"—to believe in themselves as individual women, capable of managing complex institutions and of undertaking intellectual endeavors, able to define for themselves who they are and what they want. It taught them to care for and work toward social justice as they learned the skills necessary for a career. Like liberal arts education at its best, the education they received taught students to challenge authority. It is this call to challenge that forms a key part of the inheritance the University relies on today.

NOTES

1. "President's Report," 1939 College of St. Catherine *Administrative Reports*, CSC Archives.

2. M. Elizabeth Tidball, Daryl G. Smith, Charles S. Tidball, and Lisa E. Wolf-Wendel, eds., *Taking Women Seriously: Lessons and Legacies for Educating the Majority* (Phoenix: American Council on Education and The Oryx Press, 1999).

3. Kathleen Mahoney, "American Catholic Colleges for Women: Historical Origins," in Tracy Schier and Cynthia Russett, editors, *Catholic Women's Colleges in America* (Baltimore: John Hopkins University Press, 2002), pp. 25-54, at 49-51.

4. Reverend John Ireland, *The Church and Modern Society* (St. Paul: Pioneer Press, 1904).

5. Mahoney, p. 46.

6. Elizabeth A. Johnson, "Feminism and Sharing the Faith: A Catholic Dilemma," in Thomas Masserro, SJ and Thomas Shannon, editors, *American Catholic Social Teaching* (Collegeville, MN: The Liturgical Press, 2002), p. 114.

7. Sister Jeanne Bonnett, "General Report of the College of St. Catherine to the Committee on Qualifications of Phi Beta Kappa" (1935), College of St. Catherine Archives, St. Paul, Minnesota, p. 121.

8. Rosemary Ruether and Eleanor McLaughlin, *Women of Spirit: Female Leadership in the Jewish and Christian Traditions* (New York: Simon & Schuster, 1979), p. 256.

9. Jill Ker Conway, "Faith, Knowledge and Gender," in Tracy Schier and Cynthia Russett, editors, *Catholic Women's Colleges in America* (Baltimore: John Hopkins University Press, 2002), pp. 11-16 at 13, 15.

10. Karen Kennelly, "The Dynamic Sister Antonia and the College of St. Catherine," *Ramsey County History* (Fall/Winter 1978): pp. 3-18, at p. 18, footnote #40.

11. Karen Kennelly, "Faculties and What They Taught," in Schier and Russett, editors, *Catholic Women's Colleges in America*, pp. 110-111.

12. Margaret Petrich, Class of 1927, Reminiscence of Mother Antonia McHugh, Alumnae Reminiscences File, Box #8, Mother Antonia McHugh Papers, CSC Archives.

13. Mahoney, pp. 46, 51-52; Karen Kennelly, "The Dynamic Sister Antonia," pp. 12-13.

14. College of St. Catherine *Yearbooks*, 1906, 1909-1910, CSC Archives.

15. Kennelly, "The Dynamic Sister Antonia," p. 12.

16. Sister Rosalie Ryan and Sister John Christine Wolkerstorfer, *More Than a Dream* (St. Paul: College of St. Catherine, 1992), pp. 11-17.

17. Ryan and Wolkerstorfer, pp. 15, 19, 38-39, and 48.

18. Kennelly, "Faculties and What They Taught," p. 116.

19. Bonnett, p. 33.

20. Sister Teresa Toomey, "Material Collected on Mother Antonia McHugh," Box #8, Mother Antonia McHugh Papers, CSC Archives.

21. Kennelly, "Faculties and What They Taught," p. 103.

22. Schier and Russett, "Introduction," *Catholic Women's Colleges in America*, p. 5.

23. Nancy Woloch, *Women and the American Experience*, third edition (Boston: McGraw-Hill, 2000), pp. 225-254; 275-306.

24. 1909-1910 *College of St. Catherine Yearbook*, CSC Archives.

25. Sister Helen Margaret Peck, "The Growth and Expansion of the College of St. Catherine to the End of the Presidency of Mother Antonia McHugh," (unpublished manuscript, 1982), CSC Archives, p. 73.

26. 1939 "Dean's Report to the President," CSC *Administrative Reports*, CSC Archives.

27. Bonnett, p. 2.

28. Ryan and Wolkerstorfer, *More Than a Dream*, p. 54.

29. Sister Annette Walters, "Dean of Studies Report," 1956-57 CSC *Administrative Report*, CSC Archives.

30. Sister Mary William Brady, "President's Report," 1960-61 CSC *Administrative Report*, CSC Archives.

31. See CSC bulletins, circa 1960s-1980s, especially the sections in the beginning describing the nature of the College, CSC Archives.

32. The most significant losses in the liberal arts have been in the number and variety of languages taught at the College, as well as the number and variety of music, history, and classics courses. Also lost have been interdisciplinary humanities courses that were the mainstay of the liberal arts curriculum in the 1940s, '50s, and '60s. Professional programs have expanded mainly in the health fields, including physical therapy, holistic health, health care interpreting, occupational science, and respiratory care.

33. Thomas Landy, "The Colleges in Context," in Schier and Russett, editors, *Catholic Women's Colleges in America*, pp. 55-97, at p. 65.

34. Margaret Gibson, "American Doctors Define the Lesbian and Her Intellect, 1880-1949," in Mary Beth Norton and Ruth Alexander, editors, *Major Problems in American Women's History*, Third Edition (New York: Houghton Mifflin: 2003), p. 313.

35. Sister Marie Philip Haley Oral History Interview, May 6, 1934, Box #8, Sister Antonia McHugh Papers, CSC Archive, p. 61.

36. Bonnett, p. 33.

37. Gibson, p. 313.

38. College of St. Catherine Bulletins and Catalogs, 1904-1980, CSC Archives.

39. File of Mother Antonia McHugh speeches, Box 9, Mother Antonia McHugh Papers, CSC Archives.

40. Helen Stewart Flynn, Class of 1921; Adelaide Darcy Whalen, Class of 1932; Alumnae Reminiscences of Mother Antonia McHugh, Box 8, Mother Antonia McHugh Papers, CSC Archives.

41. Kennelly, "Faculties and What They Taught," p. 108.

42. Phyllis Sweet, Class of 1924, Alumnae Reminiscences of Mother Antonia McHugh, Box #8, Mother Antonia McHugh Papers, CSC Archives.

43. Florence Wolters, Class of 1932; Gertrude Fink McIntosh, Class of 1926; Alumnae Reminiscences File, Mother Antonia McHugh Papers, CSC Archives.

44. Anonymous, "Faith in Good Works: Mother Antonia McHugh's Accomplishments," circa 1930s, undated manuscript, Biography File, Box #9, Mother Antonia McHugh Papers, CSC Archives, p. 2.

45. Sally Michener, "The College of St. Catherine," *Sports Magazine* (Winter 1940), p. 46.

46. Bonnett, quoting an early College advertisement written by Sister Antonia McHugh, p. 33; 1938 CSC *Bulletin*, p. 40; 1940 CSC *Bulletin*, p. 39; 1944 CSC *Bulletin*, p. 7; 1938, p. 40, CSC Archives.

47. Mahoney, "Historical Origins," p. 48.

48. Landy, "The Colleges in Context," p. 61.

49. Mahoney, "Historical Origins,"p. 50.

50. Jill Ker Conway, *A Woman's Education* (New York: Borzoi Books, 2001) p. 133.

51. "President's Report" 1950-51, College of St. Catherine *Administrative Reports*, p. 3.

52. First quote: Mother Antonia McHugh, "Address to National Council of Catholic Women," Speeches File, Mother Antonia McHugh Papers, CSC Archives, p. 9; Other quotes are taken from the Purpose and Ideals Section of College of St. Catherine Bulletins in the years between 1914-1921, CSC Archives.

53. Purpose and Ideals sections of 1920s CSC Catalogues, CSC Archives.

54. Mahoney, "Historical Origins," p. 50; Johnson, "Feminism and Sharing the Faith," in Masserro and Shannon, p. 114.

55. Johnson, "Feminism and Sharing the Faith," p. 114.

56. Kennelly, "Faculties and What They Taught," p. 119.

57. 1945 *Bulletin* of the College, Series XXVI, No. 1, CSC Archives.

58. "President's Report," 1941-42, CSC *Administrative Reports*, CSC Archives.

59. Woloch, pp. 281-288, pp. 507-523.

60. "Educational Plans," CSC *Bulletins*, 1949-1958, CSC Archives; Quote from 1955-56 *Bulletin*, p. 5.

61. 1955-56 *Bulletin*, CSC Archives.

62. 1955-1956 *Bulletin*, CSC Archives.

63. Personal Interview with Catherine Lupori, April 8, 2005.

64. Kennelly, "Faculties and What They Taught," p. 117.

65. College of St. Catherine Catalogue, 1921-22, CSC Archives.

66. Kennelly, "Faculties and What They Taught," p. 118-119.

67. "Dean's Report," 1967-68 CSC *Administrative Reports*, CSC Archives.

68. "President's Report," 1967-68, CSC *Administrative Reports*, CSC Archives.

69. "President's Report," 1964-65, CSC *Administrative Reports*, CSC Archives.

70. *The Catherine Wheel*, October 1, 1965, p. 3, CSC Archives.

71. "Dean's Report," 1968-69, CSC *Administrative Reports*, CSC Archives.

72. *The Catherine Wheel*, October 22, 1965, p. 3.

73. Charles E. Curran, *Catholic Social Teaching: A Historical, Theological, and Ethical Analysis* (Washington, D.C.: Georgetown University Press, 2002), p. 2.

74. Edward P. DeBerri and James E. Hug, *Catholic Social Teaching: Our Best Kept Secret*, fourth edition (Washington, D.C.: Center of Concern, 2003), p. 9.

75. 1974-75 *Bulletin*, p. 10, CSC Archives.

76. Ryan and Wolkerstorfer, *More Than a Dream*, pp. 98, 105, 108.

77. Kennelly, "Faculties and What They Taught," p. 116.

78. Abigail Quigley McCarthy Center for Women files, CSC Archives.

79. CSC Faculty Minutes, Nonsexist Language Resolution, February 8, 1977, CSC Archives.

80. *The Catherine Wheel*, October 1, 1965, p. 3, CSC Archives.

81. Memo to Educational Policies Committee from AdHoc Committee on Women's Studies, Chair Gretchen Kreuter, February 18, 1983, CSC Archives.

82. The College of St. Catherine Strategic Plan, 1985, CSC Archives.

83. Educational Policies Committee Meeting Minutes, Note 4, September 1984; October 1984, File 7, Box 645, CSC Archives.

84. Report to the President from the Task Force on the College's Commitment to Women, May 15, 1980, CSC Archives.

85. Personal Interview, Deborah Wygal, Professor of Biology, September 25, 2007.

86. College of St. Catherine Catalogue, 1992-1994.

87. Marvin L. Krier Mich, *Catholic Social Teaching and Movements* (Mystic, CT: Twenty-third Publications, 1998), p. 353.

88. National Conference of Catholic Bishops, *Economic Justice For All: Pastoral Letter on Catholic Social Teaching* (Washington, DC: United States Catholic Conference, 1986), pp. 358; 359-363.

89. Mich, pp. 357-363.

90. Landy, "The Colleges in Context," p. 63.

6

Theology Fit for Women

Religious Wisdom, St. Catherine's Style

Russell Connors, Joyce K. Dahlberg, Catherine Litecky, CSJ, Mary Lou Logsdon, and Thomas West

When the Sisters of St. Joseph of Carondelet established the College of St. Catherine, they did so to ensure that Catholic women had an opportunity to attend an institution of higher education especially suited to them as women and as Catholics. Although the college that they created was, as several essays in the present volume note, what we might now call *implicitly* feminist, it was *explicitly* Catholic. The College Plan of 1925 makes this clear: "As The College of St. Catherine is distinctly a religious college, its aim is to have the college life, studies, and activities permeated by Catholic ideals."[1]

How that aim was translated into practice has varied over the century-long history of the College, but throughout that time, one key aspect was the insistence that religious studies (later known as theology) be part of students' experiences and learning. This essay explores how the teaching of religion and theology at the College has served the ideals of the Sisters as it responded creatively to the mission of guiding women spiritually and educationally. Indeed, to chart the changes in the teaching of religion/theology during the past century is, in some measure, to chart the ways in which both the mission and identity of the College have remained the same, even as they have evolved.

THE COLLEGE'S EARLY YEARS: 1905–1947

From the founding of the College in 1905, the religious studies requirement for Catholic students was a cornerstone of the College.[2] The Sisters of St. Joseph stressed a dual approach: both learning about the Catholic faith and experiencing it. These two intellectual threads would later find expression in courses of study in theology and spirituality.

123

Convocation in Our Lady of Victory Chapel, 1930s. Photo courtesy of St. Catherine University.

As an indicator of their importance to the College, courses in religion and philosophy were required of all Catholic students from the beginning. These courses were open to non-Catholic students, of which there were increasing numbers throughout the past century, but were not required for them until 1949. All students, however, were required to attend chapel and convocations, underlining the Sisters' conviction that "classroom religious instruction was only one side of a humanistic approach that placed equal stress on character formation, or the application of philosophical and religious truths to the daily circumstances of life."[3] The College sought to make the practice of religion an integral part of every student's daily experience. What was taught in religion and philosophy courses constituted only one part of a broader focus. The Catholic religion served as the core of the educational and community experience of the students, and religious instruction was included in such fields of study as literature, art, music, and history, as discussed below.

From the early years through the early 1920s, required courses included *Old Testament* and *New Testament, Sacraments, Christian Life, Logic, Ethics,* and the *History of Philosophy.* In 1914–1915, the four courses included in the College *Bulletin* were *Old Testament, New Testament, Revelations,* and *The Church and the Divinity of Christ.* These courses met two or three hours a week, but students received no academic credit for them.[4] As can be seen from this list, courses that might now be taught in the philosophy department were then part of a religion department that included both religious studies and Catholic philosophy. No separate department of philosophy existed at St. Catherine's, as at many Catholic colleges, until the 1960s.

Students on the lawn in front of Chapel during festive event, circa 1925. Photo courtesy of St. Catherine University.

Old and New Testament studies continued to be foundational courses required of first- and second-year students throughout the 1920s and 1930s.[5] First-year students studied *Old Testament*, with the specific aim of building character by studying the patriarchs and prophets. Sophomores studied the *New Testament* to build religious ideals. Beginning in 1925, students in their junior year undertook *Logic, Social Ethics,* and *Church History* to learn the principles of religious thought and action. Finally, seniors completed their religious education with courses on the *Mass, Christ's Earthly Life,* and the *Human Soul.* The goal of this course program, which was reviewed every year, was to develop "The Religious Attitude" in students, summed up as "God is the scope of one's life—not just 'God exists,' but 'God exists for me and I exist for God.'"[6]

The intentional infusion of Catholic religious values into student life was meant to connect students to the founding mission and purpose of the College. Religious values were expressed not only in the classroom but in morning and evening prayers, daily celebration of the Eucharist, and an all-campus retreat during Lent, usually ending on the Feast of St. Joseph. The Sodality of the Blessed Virgin Mary, a Catholic action and spiritual life group, became the largest extracurricular activity on campus. Even non-Catholics participated in campus prayers, some religious services, and retreats.[7]

Initially, priests from the St. Paul Seminary of the nearby St. Thomas College, not Sister faculty, directed and taught the religious studies courses. Women, including Sisters, were not allowed to teach religion. As Kennelly notes, "a common exception to sister-faculty teaching all required courses was that of religion and philosophy, the teaching of which had to be confined to priests, since advanced degrees in those areas were available only in seminaries which excluded women."[8] The Sisters did manage to find a way to teach religion at the College, however. As at many Catholic women's colleges, the teaching of religion was not confined to religion courses per se. Courses in literature, art, music, and history were used by the Sisters to teach religion. The English department, for example, offered courses such as *The Bible as Literature* and later *Catholic Literary Revival,* and Church history was taught in the history department.

Eventually, Sister faculty from various fields began to teach religious studies, despite the fact that they were forbidden to do so. An academic history of the College written in 1980 refers to religion courses taught not by visiting priests, but by Sister faculty: "From 1914–1915 on, *Bible I* or *Old Testament* was consistently taught, but *not* by the visiting lecturers"[9] (authors' italics). Between 1914 and 1920, the instructors included Sister Clara Glenn, Sister Antonia McHugh, and Sister Ste. Helene Guthrie. Sister Clara also taught the *Gospels* and *Acts.* Sister Jeanne Marie Bonnett taught *New Testament.* For these and later Sisters, teaching these courses was not just teaching about the Bible, but like all of their work at the College, part of furthering "the work of God through Catholic education."[10]

A 1925 thesis by Sister Jeanne Marie, "The Teaching of Religion," begins with an introduction entitled, "The History of the Teaching of Religion by the Sisters of St. Joseph." Her thesis clearly indicates that the Sisters not only served as religious instructors but were known for their pedagogy in doing so. The teacher of the first-year course, for example, chose *Old Testament* "as her special field of inquiry," concentrating on the great ideas and great "personages" of the Old Testament, using maps, charts, diagrams, and projection slides.[11] Some of these audio-visual aids may have been obtained from Sister Julienne Foley, whose accurate and well-researched biblical maps and charts received wide acclaim during the 1930s, as few audio-visual materials were then available for classroom use.[12]

The sophomore course, *New Testament*, was similarly taught by a Sister-Instructor, ensuring students became familiar with the Gospels and learned how to use inductive reasoning. In their junior year, religion students studied *Logic, Thought, Ethics*, the *Religion of Acts*, and a *Survey of Church History*. The instructional method included individual work and small discussion groups.[13] Instructors worked to unite practice with theory.[14] Students studied the Mass, memorizing all its major prayers and reviewing its history, and they learned to prepare the altar and vestments. Seniors studied courses such as *The Human Soul* and *The Life of Christ*.

By the early 1940s, things had changed. Priests most likely again taught the lecture part of required religion courses.[15] Sister faculty were still part of the courses, however. Lecture classes often included a "Quiz Class with Sisters" in which the lecture was reviewed through discussion and quizzes. At this time, first-year students took a Religious Placement Test to identify their preparation and place them correctly in classes. Among the subjects that students were asked to identify were prayers and creeds, sacraments, commandments, beatitudes, precepts of the Church, the meaning of sanctification, the Rosary, and Old and New Testament figures.[16] Other assessments were created to discover students' attitudes toward justice, social responsibility, and the Church. Sister Marie Philip Haley created a "Religious Attitudes Questionnaire," and Sister Annette Walters developed a "Life-Situations Questionnaire." In June 1941, Sister Marie Philip and others wrote "An Attitude Scale in Religion for Catholic Colleges," which was published in the *Journal of Religious Instruction*.[17]

In the 1940s first-year students studied *Worship of the Christian Religion*, which included liturgical elements of the Church and the Mass.[18] Sophomores studied the *Truth of the Christian Religion*, which examined "The Catholic Church, Dispenser of the Christian Heritage." Catholic students were taught how to talk with non-Catholics in the outside world. A note at the bottom of this course description refers to Catholic truths and the non-Catholic learner:

> The general theme of the apologetics course will be rather the manner in which Catholic truths may be presented to non-Catholics; thus, throughout the year, a great deal of Catholic dogma can be reviewed by way of examples or object of defence [sic]; ample opportunity should be afforded especially in this second year for the presentation of objections and questions.[19]

No coursework is listed for the junior year. The senior course, *Teachings and Practice of the Christian Religion,* included a review of dogma, sacraments, and "our membership in the Church as the Way; the Last Things as the End."[20]

THOMISTIC THEOLOGY AND STUDENT REVOLT: 1947–1966

After World War II, the teaching of religion changed dramatically at the College. Students entering the College in 1947 were required to study a four-year theology curriculum devoted to the *Summa Theologica* of St. Thomas Aquinas. This program, taught exclusively by Dominican priests, replaced the courses on Scripture, Church and sacraments, and Christian life taught primarily by priests from the St. Paul Seminary and a few Sisters. Faculty members who argued for the curriculum change "pointed out the superior organization of the proposed program, its intellectual discipline, and solid foundation of thought."[21] They insisted that "the religion course must actually have primacy among the studies constituting a Catholic college education" and "must be on the same educational level as the other college courses and must be capable of being a principle of unification for the other studies in view of the purposes of a Catholic education."[22]

The decision to rely on Thomistic theology reflected Catholic academia at the time. Pope Leo XIII's 1893 encyclical, *Aeterni Patris,* "exalted St. Thomas and proposed his teachings as the very touchstone of Catholic orthodoxy. Thomism interpreted in the narrowest and unhistorical way took possession of all the chairs and schools of Rome and from there conquered the rest of Catholic academia."[23] Thomistic theology would dominate the theology curriculum at St. Catherine's as well.

At the same time, the philosophy curriculum underwent changes that would support those being made in theology. Thus, the philosophy curriculum began to focus on scholastic philosophy, that is, Thomistic philosophy. A document that reviewed the first four years of this curriculum stated:

> It is an innovation to give a full course of scholastic philosophy in a women's college. The prejudices of the past would deny woman an intellect capable of

speculative truth. This fallacy shaped the curriculum of girls' colleges when they were to be finished not educated.[24]

Similarly, while Thomistic theology would not be regarded as feminist today, the fact that St. Catherine's students had now begun learning the same theology being taught at virtually all Catholic seminaries reflected the founding attitude of the College: women were capable of doing rigorous and demanding scholarly work, including theological scholarship. Seminaries still excluded women during this time, and Catholic institutions did not admit women to graduate programs in theology. However, with the 1941 opening of the Graduate School of Sacred Theology at St. Mary's College, Notre Dame, Indiana, women finally had the opportunity to do graduate studies in theology. Within the next two decades, a number of Catholic universities would also begin admitting women.

Thomistic philosophy and theology were not new to the curriculum in 1947. The 1943 catalogue identified a philosophy class entitled *Introduction to the Philosophy of St. Thomas Aquinas*, wherein questions raised by students were answered by passages from the *Summa Theologica*. In 1944, when the departments of philosophy, psychology, and religion all resided within the same division, the Thomistic philosophy, class was eliminated, and a psychology class, *Aristotelian-Thomistic Psychology*, was added. This class, however, was dropped a year after the Thomistic theology series was initiated.

The reading list for the class *Introduction to Psychology* included texts on Thomistic psychology, Aristotle, and St. Thomas—but no theory by or about Freud, Jung, Skinner, or Adler. The philosophy, psychology, and theology curricula all emphasized St. Thomas Aquinas, as did the Catholic teaching of the time.

The decision to use St. Thomas's teachings exclusively was met with dissent by some faculty members. Though some faculty argued that Scripture and Church life should be part of the curriculum, the dissenters persisted in their protest, and the theology department's *Report of 1959–1960* notes some variation from the strictly Thomistic course offering:

> A course change, on a trial basis, was set in motion, to be completed for the school year 1961–1962. The change invloves [sic] the introduction of Sacred Scripture into the program as a required course; and the introduction of Apologetics as an elective. Scholastic Theology will be given to Sophomores, Juniors and Seniors.

The department tried to keep the number of course offerings to a minimum so as to not tax the priest faculty, the only ones teaching these courses. The Sister faculty, who had earlier found a way to teach religion despite prohibitions on their doing so, were effectively sidelined by the reorganization of the curriculum and could no longer offer their expertise.

In studying the *Summa Theologica*, students were led through a series of theological questions set forth by St. Thomas, which were followed in the text by reflections from other contemporary thinkers. St. Thomas then responded to their answers, typically drawing upon St. Augustine and Aristotle. Though many have argued that the *Summa* is the most brilliant summary of Catholic theology ever compiled, it is also single-voiced and based on a 700-year-old worldview that was far removed from the daily lives of St. Catherine's students. For all its spiritual and intellectual worth, the focus on St. Thomas excluded female voices, Protestant theologians, Jewish wisdom, contemporary authors, and non-Western cultural and spiritual experiences.

Responses to this single-focused approach to teaching theology were mixed. Some faculty members warned that the new program would mean the loss of attention to Scriptures or the sacraments; some students objected to a rational, patriarchal, authoritarian theology taught by clerical men to classrooms filled exclusively with women. Other students responded positively to the academic rigor, at least initially, before the winds of change that blew across Catholicism in the 1960s. *More Than a Dream*, the history of the first 85 years of the College, quotes students from the late 1940s:

> One said, "Theology is the substance of our religion; once we have some understanding of it the liturgy becomes much more meaningful and beautiful." Another was sure that "If I had learned nothing else, the program would have made the four years [at the college] worthwhile."[25]

Sister Vera Chester, not a Catholic when she arrived at the College in 1948, described her experience of the Dominican priests this way: "The Thomism taught by the Dominicans convinced me that the choice for faith was reasonable. Reason worked with faith, not against it. Learning this was what first drew me to Catholicism."[26]

Thomistic theology, which was never meant to be practical, was viewed by many as separate and distinct from the religious activities of students. According to Father E. M. Burke, CSP, "Theology is an intellectual science whose purpose is to order and relate all knowledge to God." Therefore, to judge its effectiveness by "the increase or decrease of the religious activities of the students" would be dangerous, for "to formulate a religion course in terms of moral activity is to run a real danger of forming a Protestant cast of mind whereby you have intense moral activity without a corresponding intellectual level."[27]

Societal norms for women changed in the post–World War II years. Women were encouraged to marry and return home rather than work. Theology coursework also reflected this movement. *Christian Marriage* became a required course for all seniors from 1947 through 1953. A new class, *Christian States of Life*, replaced *Christian Marriage* at the end of 1953 and was offered through 1956. The course carried this description: "The role and status of the Christian Woman in modern society. The states of life suited to her nature and destiny." In 1957, *Christian Marriage* returned as an elective.[28]

During the 1940s and 1950s, the College's focus on Catholic identity was not limited to the religion department. For instance, a popular upper-division English class, *The Catholic Literary Revival*, traced the development of a Catholic point of view in fiction, poetry, essays, biography, and drama. A seminar on *World Literature* included such Catholic wisdom figures as St. Augustine, Dante, St. Teresa of Avila, and Jacques Maritain among its authors. Among Latin courses was one on *Christian Hymnology* that examined the great Latin hymns, including their Scriptural basis, linguistic qualities, and authorship, as well as their place in literature and in liturgy. The music department offered a class in *Liturgical Choir* and six four-credit classes in Gregorian chant. The Social Science Survey classes included an analysis of the Catholic social encyclicals, while Social Philosophy compared Catholic social theory, individualism, socialism, and totalitarianism. But while the Catholic theology curriculum was squarely aimed at the education of Catholics, in 1952 a course was again added for non-Catholic students on readings from Scripture and the Fathers of the Church.[29]

In 1958, the department name was changed from religion to theology, a direct reflection of the decision to hire Dominican priests to teach the *Summa Theologia*. The Thomistic series remained part of the religion curriculum until the mid-1960s. In 1962, theology department classes were also renamed; *Theology I*, for instance, became *God and His Creation*, but the course description still began with these words: "The first part of the *Summa Theologia* . . ."[30]

By the 1960s, criticism of the teaching of Thomistic theology had grown into a groundswell. In addition to the objections raised earlier, students criticized what they considered to be irrelevant subject matter. However, something more than impatience with Dominican Thomism was affecting the attitude toward theology at the College of St. Catherine. Certainly, the Catholic Church was feeling the winds of change. Sister Vera Chester remarked on the liturgical reforms that had their beginnings years earlier: "One of the centers of this reform was St. John's University up in Collegeville [Minnesota] and we Sisters were often exposed to what the Benedictines were doing up there."[31]

Throughout the 1940s and 1950s, a significant minority of very creative theologians, whose ideas for renovating theology had been poorly received in Rome (in some cases, these theologians were silenced and prohibited by the Pope from writing about current theological questions), turned away from contemporary theology to the study of Scripture and early Church theology. This turn became widely known under the French term *rassourcement*, "back to the sources."

This *rassourcement*, which engaged these theologians with a kind of thinking quite different from that of Thomas Aquinas, stimulated them to frame questions such as, "Why does Thomism have to be the only way of doing theology? They did it much differently in the fifth century. And Thomas himself did it his way in the 13th. Why can't we do it our way in the 20th century?" In their own way, St. Catherine's students had started to raise the same thoughtful questions.

Even at the level of institutional structure and policy, one could feel the stirrings of renewal in the Catholic Church. Sister Catherine Litecky remembers that in the mid-1950s Pope Pius XII, often considered a religious conservative today, urged religious sisters to "return to the original charism of their order"[32]; for an "apostolic order" (as contrasted with a "monastic order"), this meant turning outward to the world, thereby engaging the needs of all people in all classes and circumstances. Here the Pope foreshadowed the turn toward the world that characterized the Second Vatican Council of Pope John XXIII.

The Pope's initial call for a council aroused little excitement. But while the bishops were gathered in Rome from 1962 to 1965, they composed and issued an extraordinary set of decrees, all of which affirmed the trend toward a deep renewal of the Church. The effect among Catholics was electrifying, and it charged the atmosphere at the College of St. Catherine.[33] Leading spirits among the Sisters took immediately to Vatican II. Catholic laypeople at the College, both faculty and students, now felt empowered, for Vatican II not only opened the Church to the modern world, but also to lay Catholics who worked in that world. It was no accident that the most talked about decree, "The Church in the Modern World," asserted the importance of laypersons.

On campus, student complaints about the theology department increased in volume and intensity. Sister Rosalie Ryan, academic dean at the College from 1958 to 1963, told the Dominican in charge of sending priests to teach at St. Catherine's that future replacements would be handled through the College's regular hiring process. The Dominicans refused to submit their candidates to this process, so they withdrew from teaching in the theology department.

In the autumn of 1965, Sister Rosalie—a scholar who had turned from English to theology as her chief academic interest—became acting chair of the department to deal with the situation. Later she would write: "Before classes had really begun there was a rebellion among the seniors over the choice of theology texts by the two full-time Dominicans."[34] With determination and tact, she set out to restructure the department. She also hired a layman, Donald E. Byrne.

Sister Rosalie then recommended that the contract of only one of the Dominicans be renewed. A year later, in a memo to the then-president of the College, Sister Alberta Huber, Sister Rosalie left no doubt that she would be eager to replace the remaining Dominican: "His range is limited and his thinking from my observation is not profound."[35] By 1964, all references to the *Summa* were removed from the class descriptions. However, it was not until the Dominicans left their teaching positions in 1966 that the department eliminated from the curriculum what students considered to be the "rigid Thomistic viewpoint and a lack of relevance to contemporary thought."[36]

THE POST–VATICAN II ERA: 1967–1989

The theology requirement was now completely revamped, and a major in theology was introduced in 1968. Within the theology department, a doctorate became the minimum degree required for achieving academic promotion and tenure. Several instructors in the department quickly achieved that degree: Sister Vera received a doctorate in theology, the first Sister from the St. Paul Province to do so, and Joan Timmerman, who was hired as the department's first laywoman in 1968, returned to Marquette University for her doctorate. Meanwhile, course offerings changed to reflect the spirit of Vatican II, and Thomism faded from the department with astonishing rapidity.

When one talks to friends and colleagues of Sister Rosalie, the woman who led the change away from Thomism, they do not speak of her as a feminist. Sister Catherine Litecky explains this seeming paradox: "We were always committed to women reaching their full potential. Our feminism was implicit, as it had been since we Sisters founded the College. Rosalie was not driven by feminism as an explicit ideology when she set about transforming the department."[37] Yet looking back at what Sister Rosalie and her Sister colleagues accomplished in the department, it is evident that they were serving the second-wave feminist cause of women's liberation by emancipating the theology department from male clerical domination. By the 1960s, women, both religious and lay, could finally earn degrees in, and teach, theology—and not only at St. Catherine's but at other Catholic colleges as well.

New political forces and social movements swirled around the campus in the 1960s. The student movement, the antiwar protests, the struggle to free individuals from the oppressions of color and class—all had their effects on campus, which became a vibrant place politically. In the early 1970s, feminism on campus became more explicit.[38] Joan Timmerman credits Alan Graebner, in the history department, and Catherine Lupori, in the English department, for making feminism an ongoing subject of campus discussion. Theologians, "who began to look at theology from an explicitly feminist perspective,"[39] were also affected by these discussions, though the department did not adopt a pervasively feminist ideology. In the words of Dr. Joan Timmerman:

> We decided not to see ourselves as teaching feminist theology. Indeed, we never offered a course in feminist theology per se. We wanted above all to be professionals in our discipline. We wanted to be regarded first as biblical scholars, historians of theology, systematic theologians, and so on, and not first as spokespersons for feminism. We wanted to *do* theology and hire the very best people—men and women, religious and lay, married and single—to do it with us. And yet in all our classes we incorporated, more or less, a feminist critique of the prevailing approach to the subject matter. When I taught a course in Sexuality and Spirituality, for example, I did not teach a feminist sexuality or a feminist spirituality, but introduced to students a feminist critique of both. Even later, when we, with the help of women both inside and outside CSC, reached out to women in the wider community with our ongoing series entitled "Theological Insights," we were not driven by a feminist agenda. What drove us was the desire to show women the dignity that comes from the disciplined search for theological truth.[40]

Evident in these remarks is a conscious effort to place feminism *in* theology rather than to make feminism the prime shaper of theology. Perhaps this reflects a sensibility that is more reformist than radical, a sensibility that predisposes one to viewing the Catholic tradition as not so pervasively patriarchal that a person must break with it. This sensibility also leads to an inclusivist approach to men and to a "mediational" interpretation of history, where suspicion of the past is complemented by an appreciation of it.

This inclusivist and mediational approach was clearly revealed in the department's proposal for a graduate program, a Master of Arts in Theology (MAT), in the early 1980s. In addition to offering three courses in Scripture, three in Historical Theology, and three in Systematic Theology, the program would be open to both women and men. However, at that time, the College did not offer graduate degrees, and faculty opposition to the proposal was vigorous. Opponents feared losing the undergraduate character of the College and a dilution of the liberal arts if additional professional MA programs were to follow. And some did not want the College to grant degrees to men. Thomas West, a layman hired by the theology department in 1979, recalls the debate at a faculty meeting:

> We were surprised at the contentiousness evoked by the question of admitting men. When we in the department first put the proposal together, that question was decided in five minutes: of course we would admit men. We did not believe for a second that all men were irredeemable patriarchs. We assumed that self-selection would draw men who were committed to women's flourishing and unafraid of an academic environment where the fundamental equal-

ity of men and women was unquestioned. And if occasionally a man came in infected with patriarchal attitudes, well, we would de-patriarchalize him![41]

After heated debate, the MAT program was approved by a vote of 53–39 in May 1982.[42] Present at that meeting, and casting a vote in favor of the program, was Sister Rosalie, still teaching though nearing retirement. From the beginning of departmental planning for the new program, she had been its most passionate supporter.

The first classes in the MAT program were offered in the autumn of 1983. Enrollment was good, but not spectacular. By its second year, the program began to sputter and was losing money. Spurred by its chair, Joan Timmerman, the program was expanded to include a Concentration in Spirituality. The result was an immediate upsurge of enrollment, which saved the program.

Some faculty, though, were concerned that the study of spirituality would tarnish the reputation of the MAT program as academically rigorous. Others in the theology department were more optimistic. A few made the feminist epistemological point that the study of spirituality forces one to attend to the full complexity of the human person; that is, not only to human reason, but also to human feeling and will. This argument won out. Not only was the Concentration in Spirituality embraced by the department, but a graduate certificate program in Spiritual Direction was also added several years later.

Meanwhile, in the undergraduate theology courses, the faculty were increasingly attentive to feminism, both in method and content. A key addition to the curriculum was *Women and American Christianity*, constructed by Sister Catherine Litecky and first taught by her in 1978–1979. Later, Chris Franke added *Women and the Bible*, and Sister Shawn Madigan added *Christian Women Mystics*. Today, five theology courses are cross-listed with the women's studies program. Edward Sellner, in his *History of Spirituality* course, emphasizes the role of women leaders and writers in shaping that history. In *Issues in Pastoral Theology*, he also includes the topic of "Women's Leadership." In 2004, St. Catherine's Master's of Art in Organizational Leadership offered women and men in the business world a Spirituality Concentration through the theology department. Indeed, the theology department aims to inspire in its women students the belief that their full advancement and unfolding is fully consonant with deep and disciplined theological study.

A Pastoral Ministry Certificate, first envisioned in 1925, became a reality in 1978. This ecumenical program was created to prepare individuals, especially laywomen, for modern ministry. Over the years, this program has produced hundreds of qualified pastoral ministers, many of whom hold key positions in the St. Paul-Minneapolis Archdiocese, as well as leadership roles in retreat centers, hospitals and hospices, and congregations. Through required theology courses and internships, the program encourages women to become change agents.

To meet the growing interest in spirituality among the laity, the department established the Spiritual Direction Certificate program in 1996–1997. Through theology courses—especially in spirituality, Jungian psychology, and spiritual direction—many women have developed skills in guidance and spirituality. According to Professor Sellner, "These programs provide women the theological depth, as well as the professional skills, to function competently in corporate and church settings."[43]

Two outreach programs, the Theological Insights Program and the Wisdom Ways Resource Center for Spirituality, involved the leadership of Professors Joan Timmerman and Edward Sellner. From its beginning in the autumn of 1987, Professor Timmerman initiated and guided the Theological Insights program, which was based on a program created by Elizabeth Dodson Gray at Harvard. At each of four sessions in the autumn and spring, two speakers tackled the same subject, one from the perspective of personal experience, the other from an academic or professional viewpoint. According to Kay VanderVort, a graduate of the MAT program who later became the director of the Theological Insights program, its mission was to provide a public forum for women to reflect on the meaning of their lives, to engage in a collaborative process that values all persons equally, and to influence traditions and cultures toward acceptance of a diversity of views within a unity of spirit.

Wisdom Ways Resource Center for Spirituality began in 1994 as a cooperative ministry of the College and of the Sisters of St. Joseph. The ministry responds to the spiritual needs of our times. Wisdom Ways programs integrate spiritual growth with intellectual depth and a passion for justice. Thousands of participants have attended its summer institutes, short courses, workshops, spiritual offerings, retreats, works of justice, and special events. Eventually, Wisdom Ways became solely a ministry of the Sisters of St. Joseph at the Carondelet Center.

THE CONTEMPORARY MOMENT: 1990–PRESENT

The earlier sections of this chapter trace how religion and theology have been taught at the College of St. Catherine during its first one hundred years. In this final section, we identify the most important questions facing the theology department as the University moves into its second century. We reflect on "the contemporary moment" and ask: *What is theology? Whom do we serve? Who are our students? Who shall teach? What does it mean to be Catholic?* We seek to address these questions in ways that are both *faithful* to the College's past and *creatively responsive* to its mission of guiding women "to lead and influence."

What Is Theology?

For some, teaching theology or teaching catechetics (the method used in the early years of the College) means providing *religious instruction* for the spiritual and moral edification of those under instruction and for the well-being of the community itself. For others, theology refers to a revered body of wisdom and truths that experts attempt to pass on to their students. Theology was understood in this way in the period of Thomistic teaching, which emphasized academic rigor. Teaching this vision of theology assumed that young women were well capable of such academic rigor. But with the changes to the world and the Church in our modern era, students at the College became dissatisfied with this approach to theology.

The third period of our history recounts a sea change in the teaching of theology, involving nothing less than a radical rethinking of the very meaning of theology. For many students, the Thomistic teaching by the Dominicans lacked relevance. As students described it, this approach to theology disconnected them from the real world in which they were living and from their deepest questions and concerns. These students gave voice to one of the central convictions of Catholic theologians today: theology means reflecting on our experiences in the light of faith.

The theology engaged in by white, male clerics of the thirteenth century is undoubtedly different, in important ways, from the theology engaged in today by the poor and oppressed peoples of Latin America; or from the theology engaged in by women, including women of color, seeking liberation today from the unjust and oppressive network of social structures in society and in the churches. After the Second Vatican Council, these new kinds of theology emerged at St. Catherine's.

Our theology attempts to build bridges between contemporary experience and Catholic Christian theological insights and traditions. Indeed, the theology department today embraces wholeheartedly the mission of this University, a mission aimed at promoting the ability of women to lead and to influence in our contemporary society and, as they wish to do so, to lead and to serve in the churches.

Whom Do We Serve?

During St. Catherine's past one hundred years, much has changed regarding the kind of theology that has been taught. But what has persisted is the conviction that religious or theological education can contribute to the flourishing of women. Both the women being educated and the theologians educating them are part of several larger contexts that significantly shape how theology is taught and how it is engaged in by students. As contemporary Catholic theologian David Tracy has suggested, the work of theology is always related to "three distinct and related social realities—the wider society, the academy, and the church."[44] These three contexts (or "publics," as Tracy calls them[45]) shed important light on the contemporary moment in which the theology department today finds itself.

Students and teachers of theology everywhere are obviously part of the wider society. To "do theology," as the late Bernard Lonergan argued, is to dialogue with one's culture, to do so with both an open and a critical eye, including an open and critical eye of faith.[46] The liberal arts foundation of the Unviersity has always presumed this, as does the University's vision statement to educate women to lead and to influence. Theological education at the University must teach a theology that is attentive to the intellectual and social movements of the day. Students need to understand themselves and their world better, to know how to take their place in that world and to serve as leaders.

Theologians are also part of "the academy." Their teaching, scholarly research, and publications are responsible to, and contribute to, the community of scholars. Mother Antonia understood the importance of this community when she sent future faculty members to some of the most important educational institutions in the world to study for graduate degrees. She could not, of course, send Sisters, or any women for that matter, to do graduate study in theology during her time. She did encourage Sister Jeanne Marie Bonnett's graduate work in religious pedagogy, however. And Sister Jeanne Marie insisted that the teaching of religion or theology be *academically credible* and based on excellent teaching, a challenge that has been embraced by the theology department's men and women today.

In a way that is analogous to its relation to the academy, Catholic theology "happens" in responsible relation to the Church. Sometimes in clear and explicit ways, theology is at the service of the Church, even though a fear remains that ecclesiastical authorities will intrude inappropriately into the work of theological inquiry or into the lives of students.

For contemporary evidence of theology's relation to the Church, one need only look at the theology departments of colleges and universities, including St. Catherine's, which now train educational and pastoral ministers for leadership in the Church. Taking up the charge of Vatican II, St. Catherine's theology department has embraced this service to the Church in a host of ways, particularly through the graduate and undergraduate certificate programs in Pastoral Ministry, as well as through the graduate certificate program in Spiritual Direction. Presently, the theology department is about to launch a new certificate program in Catechetical Ministry. Thus, our relationship to ·
the Church remains important, a fact that is unlikely to change.

Who Are Our Students?

In the earliest years of the College, the vast majority of the students—though not all—were Roman Catholic. However, as evidence clearly shows, the Sisters were respectful of religious differences and tried to make appropriate religious instruction available to non-Catholics. Nevertheless, early religious education at the College was directed at a largely Catholic student body.

As enrollment at the College grew, so too did the religious diversity of the student body. Today, the majority of students do not claim Catholicism as their religion. As St. Catherine's gained an increasingly fine reputation for excellence in several professional fields, notably health care and education, it started to attract students who were seeking an education that was unrelated to the College's Catholic identity. In the 1960s, enrollment also increased among students who perhaps had been baptized Catholic, but who now increasingly voiced their discontent with, and their alienation from, the Church and traditional religious faith and practice. Their criticisms were often feminist in nature, and a growing number of students—as well as faculty and staff at the College—started to speak out about the sexism they saw in the Catholic tradition. These criticisms, which remain today, are beneficial to the University and the theology department as they directly challenge both professors and students to engage in theology honestly and critically.

St. Catherine's has also promoted religious diversity by actively recruiting students from countries in Asia, Southeast Asia, and Africa. Though a comparatively small group of students, they are still a highly visible and highly respected group on campus who represent religious traditions from Buddhism and Hinduism to Islam and Shamanism. Also among our students are those who identify themselves as being agnostic, atheist, or humanist.

The challenges and the opportunities that come with a religiously diverse student population are enormous. All students are required to take one course that offers "an intellectual account of some of the key elements of Christian theological tradition."[47] This means that, among a class of 25 students enrolled in an introductory religion or theology course, eight or nine students may identify themselves as Catholic, four or five as "former" or estranged Catholics, six or seven as members of another Christian denomination, two or three as worshippers of a non-Christian religion, and another two or three students who acknowledge no religious affiliation and who might be atheist. Thus, in a course such as *New Testament Studies*, which explores the ministry and teachings of Jesus, diversity in the classroom, if acknowledged and honored by a skilled teacher, can turn out to be a gift and a resource that brings fresh eyes and insights to bear on Biblical texts. However, the result could also verge on the chaotic at times, so responding creatively to the diverse backgrounds of our students remains one of the greatest challenges and opportunities facing the theology department.

Who Shall Teach?

In the earliest years of the College, even though priests from the St. Paul Seminary provided the "formal" religious instruction on campus, the Sisters found ways to participate in this work. No doubt the Sisters were convinced that they could—and should—make their mark on the religious formation of their students. By the middle of the twentieth century, St. Catherine's leaders sought to bolster the respectability and academic rigor of religious instruction at the College. They did so by inviting Dominican priest-theologians to teach Thomistic theology in the theology department from 1947 to 1966. Eventually, though, it became evident that the "academy" of the Dominicans was far too small. In the language of the Second Vatican Council, Thomistic theology was not always in dialogue with "the joy and hope, the grief and anguish of the people of our time, especially the poor and afflicted."[48] As a result of student protests and through the leadership of Sister Rosalie, Thomistic theology gave way to new theological approaches, which are being taught in the theology department today.

As the department grows, and in light of its history and the broad diversity of the student population, what qualities are needed by future members of the theology faculty? We will need faculty who engage in a theology that stands in active dialogue with the issues and concerns of the world at large, a theology that stays open to the insights and wisdom of all the human sciences, and a theology that remains attentive to both the New Testament and everyday life. We will search out faculty who are comfortable with religious diversity and who welcome it as an opportunity for honest exchange and growth. And we will recruit faculty who embrace the feminist ethos of the College, theologians who teach and engage in scholarly work that contributes to the flourishing of women and their ability to lead and influence.

What Does It Mean to Be Catholic?

In another one hundred years, our future colleagues may be sorting through the University's archives as they prepare a volume entitled *Two Hundred Years of St. Catherine University*. They will find that, from the 1990s to well past the year 2000, issues revolving around the Catholic identity of the College preoccupied the administration and faculty. These are some of the questions being tackled today:

- What is academic freedom and what does it mean in a Catholic university?
- Who can and cannot speak on campus? If there are limits, what are they and why?

- Who can be hired as a faculty member, and what weight should be given to religious affiliation in making these hiring decisions?
- What does critical inquiry in the classroom mean in a Catholic context?
- Can there be legitimate dissent from Catholic teachings, especially about moral matters? If so, how does one "negotiate" this dissent?
- What kind of religious pluralism or diversity should exist on campus? In campus ministry? Among administrators, faculty, and staff?
- Is Catholicism hostile to the flourishing of women, or might the traditions and resources of the Catholic Church be used to promote women's abilities to lead and influence?

The theology department embraces its important role in addressing these issues. That role, however, is not to provide easy answers to these critical and complex questions, but rather to serve as a resource for all our colleagues as we investigate together how the Catholic identity of St. Catherine's might best evolve in the years ahead.

NOTES

1. College of St. Catherine Bulletins and Catalogues, 1904–1980, College of St. Catherine (CSC) Archives.

2. Sister Helen Margaret Peck, CSJ, "An Academic History of the College of St. Catherine, 1905–1920," (unpublished manuscript), June 1982, p. 7, CSC Archives.

3. Sister Karen Kennelly, CSJ, "Faculties and What They Taught," in Tracy Schier and Cynthia Russett, eds., *Catholic Women's Colleges in America* (Baltimore: The Johns Hopkins University Press, 2002) p. 111.

4. Sister Helen Margaret Peck, CSJ, CSC Archives, pp. 257–259.

5. *Ibid.*, p. 8.

6. *Ibid.*, p. 25.

7. Sister Rosalie Ryan and Sr. John Christine Wolkerstorfer, *More Than A Dream* (St. Paul: College of St. Catherine, 1992), p. 44.

8. Sister Karen Kennelly, CSJ, "Faculties and What They Taught," p. 105.

9. *Ibid.*, p. 260.

10. Sister Antonia McHugh, CSJ, panel, *The Dream: A Centennial Photographic Exhibit*, Carondelet Center, September 2004–June 2005.

11. *Ibid.*, p. 15.

12. Sister Ann Thomasine Sampson, CSJ, *Seeds on Good Ground* (St. Paul, MN: Self-published, 2000), pp. 318–320.

13. *Ibid.*, p. 17.

14. *Ibid.*, pp. 17–18.

15. "Suggested Class Methods," Re: College Education for Women, Sisters of St. Joseph of Carondelet, St. Paul Province (CSJ) Archives, Sister Jeanne Marie's box.

16. "The College of St. Catherine Religious Placement Test," CSC Archives, "Teaching of Religion" box.

17. Ryan and Wolkerstorfer, p. 34.

18. *Ibid.*

19. *Ibid.*

20. *Ibid.*

21. Ryan and Wolkerstorfer, p. 49.

22. "Comments on the Tentative Outline of Courses in Theology and Philosophy adopted in September of the Year 1947 At the College of St. Catherine," CSC Archives.

23. Thomas Bokenkotter, *A Concise History of the Catholic Church* (Garden City, NY: Double Day and Company, 1977), p. 326.

24. "Comments on the Tentative Outline of Courses in Theology . . . ," CSC Archives.

25. Ryan and Wolkerstorfer, p. 49.

26. Sister Vera Chester, CSJ, Interview, January 18, 2005.

27. Fr. E. M.Burke, CSP Catholic University, in *The Philosophy of Catholic Higher Education* by Roy Deferrari, Dean, Catholic University from a document, "Comments on the Tentative Outline of Courses in Theology and Philosophy adopted in September of the Year 1947 At The College of St. Catherine," CSC Archives.

28. College Catalogues, 1947–1956, CSC Archives.

29. *Ibid.*

30. College *Catalogue*, 1962, CSC Archives.

31. Sister Vera Chester, CSJ, Interview.

32. Sister Catherine Litecky, CSJ, Interview, January 19, 2005. See also Sisters of St. Joseph of Carondolet, St. Paul Province, *Eyes Open on a World: The Challenges of Change* (St. Cloud, MN: North Star Press, 2001), pp. 16–26.

33. Ryan and Wolkerstorfer, pp. 86–87, 91–92.

34. Sister Rosalie Ryan, CSJ, "Annual Report of the Department of Theology for 1965–66," CSC Archives, p. 6.

35. Letter to Sister Fides Huber, CSJ, President, February 22, 1967, CSC Archives.

36. Ryan and Wolkerstorfer, p. 89.

37. Sister Catherine Litecky, CSJ, Interview.

38. Ryan and Wolkerstorfer, pp. 86–87.

39. Former Professor Joan Timmerman, Interview, September 5, 2004.

40. *Ibid.*

41. Professor Tom West, Interview, January 25, 2005.

42. On the evening of the day of the vote, Sister Rosalie recorded a vote count of 53–39 in her private journal. Her count, however, differs from the count given in *More than a Dream*, p. 121, which records it as 57–37.

43. Interview with Professor Edward Sellner, Spring 2005.

44. David Tracy, *The Analogical Imagination: Christian Theology and the Culture of Pluralism* (New York: Crossroad, 1981), p. 5.

45. *Ibid.*, pp. 3–31.

46. Bernard Lonergan, SJ, *Method In Theology* (New York: Seabury, 1972), p. xi.

47. College Catalogue, 2003–2005, CSC Archives, p. 190.

48. "Pastoral Constitution on the Church in the Modern World," *Gaudium et Spes*, 1965, par.

7

Communion with Books

The Double Life of Literature

Cecilia Konchar Farr

In 1958 the writer May Sarton, like many authors before and after her, visited the College of St. Catherine as a Phi Beta Kappa lecturer. She delivered her lecture, but she also had tea with a group of English majors, taught a literature class, and spent some time with the faculty before returning to New England. May Sarton found something extraordinary at the College during that visit, something that drew her back again and again over the next 20 years. As she wrote to her dear friend and fellow poet Sister Maris Stella (later, Sister Alice Gustava Smith), a Sister of St. Joseph and English professor at St. Catherine's, "Sometimes I long to hop a plane and come and see you all, taste your silences and rest my heart near your altar. 'Behold I make all things new again.'"[1]

May Sarton's words echo those of Mary Ellen Chase, another non-Catholic writer, who, in her 1940 memoir, described what drew her to St. Catherine's:

> I liked the peace of its chapel, the quiet of its garden, the friendliness and fun of its nuns, the good manners of its students. I like the shuffling off of a hundred trivialities, the release of which seemed not only possible but inevitable within its gates. . . . I like the long talks with Sister Lioba about all manner of books, of which she knew more than I. I like our occasional mad games of tennis in which nuns in heavy habits could beat me in a cotton dress to nothing. I like the single-mindedness at St. Catherine's, the sense that religion was not something to be seized upon in uneasy moments, but natural, like one's hands and feet, and waiting only to be discovered.[2]

These passages and others like them in letters, reports, lecture notes, and memoirs depict an atmosphere of "goodly fellowship," as Chase wrote, an atmosphere both lively and contemplative where women writers felt nurtured and where book talk flourished in and out of the classroom. What Sarton and Chase found at the College in the 1920s and 40 years later was the unique result of a confluence of forces that made St. Catherine's an exceptional environment for the education of women and, as a result, for the nurturing of a distinctive and significant sort of literary work.

EDUCATING WOMEN

In their introduction to *Catholic Women's Colleges in America*, Tracy Schier and Cynthia Russett note that religious sisters started more than half of women's colleges in the United States. In the last half of the nineteenth century, when women's education was still a controversial concept, Catholic religious were uniquely positioned to sanction women's education. To begin with, the authors point out, "their religious vocation allowed them to transcend gender roles considered normative."[3] No one expected them to marry or have children, a remarkable freedom given the cultural strictures of the time. And their call to religious service became their chosen profession, freeing them from having to rely on family for support and opening opportunities for single-minded dedication to their work, an especially precious prospect for scholars.

Their vocation also gave them access to a history of learned women stretching back beyond the Middle Ages—"the Hildas, the Liobas, the Marcellas, the Paulas, the Eustochiums, the Catherines, and hosts of others"—who could serve as both inspiration and justification for their work.[4] This history of sisters doing intellectual work in community became foundational for single-sex education. Monika Hellwig points out that in Catholic tradition, "Habits of concentration and reflection were cultivated, and in the medieval monasteries of women as well as men, scholarship was highly prized."[5] She explains that these traditions were passed from generation to generation among the religious, but that they were also shared with children of various faiths who came to the monasteries for schooling. "Then, as now," she concluded, "communities of vowed religious were obvious groups to undertake education because their community life offered a stable base for collaborative work."[6] Even in a predominantly Protestant U.S., the fact that nuns were leading the effort helped to weaken conservative objections to women's education.

Calling on this tradition of scholarly life in community, many Catholic women's colleges in their early days aspired to the intellectual rigor of the finest liberal education in the U.S. and modeled themselves on elite women's colleges like Smith, Vassar, and Wellesley, with, as Schier and Russett point out, "an admixture of theology and spiritual guidance."[7] Other colleges responded to conservative pressure to remember that women's "destiny was home and family, for which a more modest level of education sufficed," and offered the equivalent of a finishing school education. Still other institutions, called to serve the poor, as many religious orders were, set out to educate the daughters of immigrants and the working classes into professions and offered coursework mainly in nursing and teaching.[8]

Thus, by 1905, when the founders of the College of St. Catherine looked around for models of women's education, they already had options. The early St. Catherine's, in what we now recognize as its signature style, set out boldly for the middle; sidestepping the either/or quandary, the Sisters decided to offer, in essence, every option: a rigorous liberal arts curriculum, social education or polish, *and* training for a profession. The College's mostly Irish nuns took a democratic view, saying that the daughters of immigrants deserved the same education as that generally reserved for the privileged—and they aimed to educate both. Their intention was to establish a place where women students were taken seriously, where scholarship was nurtured and ideas were sacred. (See Cavallaro et al., in this volume.) As the Sisters of St. Joseph write in their 2001 history, *Eyes Open on a World*, "The college administration and faculty have always put the students first, thereby aiming to be true to its roots by helping women 'be all of which woman is capable'—strong, independent, competent, and caring."[9] This mix of clear-sighted practicality and intellectual audacity has always defined the College, and, I will argue, ideally situated it to embrace a distinctly democratic approach to books and reading even when such an approach was being shunted aside by conservative forces wedded to more traditional models.

TEACHING ANTONIA

If there was profound disagreement over the social and moral ramifications of women's education in the late nineteenth century, there was an equally intense conversation occurring about the political and cultural importance of an American literature. Drawn to European standards based on classical scholarship, nineteenth-century critics in the newly established republic attempted to situate a national literature both within and beyond that context. They longed for a literature having the seriousness of Milton or Wordsworth, yet demanded texts responsive to the idea of "America," of vast lands sparsely peopled with free, independent souls. James Fenimore Cooper seemed a hopeful candidate for canonization early on, but even those who admired his iconic Americans were put off by his appalling prose. For many years, Henry Wadsworth Longfellow was our country's poet-in-chief, but he fell out of fashion when American style demanded less overt romanticism and moralizing. By mid-century, our current tradition tells us, Ralph Waldo Emerson and Henry David Thoreau, Herman Melville and Nathaniel Hawthorne had established themselves as the forerunners of a truly serious American literary tradition.

Yet recent work on American literary history reveals the extent to which this story is a twentieth-century invention. Feminist literary historians have demonstrated that the books Americans read, valued, and took seriously in the nineteenth century tended to be those we now dismiss as sentimental and unimpressive, as not serious. Studies by Nina Baym, Jane Tompkins, Sandra Gilbert and Susan Gubar, Judith Fetterly, Cathy Davidson, and Janice Radway have presented convincing evidence that this division between what the literary and educational establishment called excellent and what most people read and appreciated was, among other factors, gender-based. In some cases, the judgment was as simple as this dictum: if women write it or read it, it probably isn't good.

There were reasons, of course, for this gendered division. Classical education, the basis of most of our aesthetic theory and practice, was available only to men through the nineteenth century. Rare was the white woman who could read Latin and Greek, even among the privileged, where educated women were not scarce. And Black women were forbidden to be literate by law in most of the U.S. before the Civil War, and many forbidden in practice long afterward. Other women of color, poor, rural, working-class, and immigrant women and men had little access to education beyond the basic literacy skills, even well into the twentieth century. I think of the immigrant Bohemian father in Willa Cather's *My Antonia*, a starving Nebraska farmer, beseeching the well-fed white neighbor boy Jim Burden to "teach, teach my Antonia," as he thrust a book into Jim's hands.

While farm girls like Antonia learned to read, they rarely achieved a level of education that would allow them to read, for example, Henry James or James Joyce. The works of such authors contain allusions and metaphors, plots, characters, and concerns that assume a level of education achieved by few Americans and a knowledge of classical texts not generally part of the curriculum for most students. Instead, American women read popular novels.

The rise of the popular novel paralleled historically the rise of democracy and universal literacy and benefited from the mass production of the industrial revolution. As Nina Baym writes in her study of reviews of nineteenth-century novels, the novel was always considered the province of women and "the newly literate masses," and "its dominant position represented less a change of taste in an existing audience than *a change in the makeup of the audience for the written word*."[10] From the beginning the novel attracted the audience that ensured its survival. Even today scholars estimate that women buy 90 percent of the novels sold.[11]

Even as the late nineteenth century saw the expansion of women's colleges and opportunities for higher education increasing nationwide, it also saw a growing recognition of the novel as central to the study of American literature. As young colleges and universities established their curricula, many began including not just classical literature, but also novels, essays, and poetry from the evolving American tradition, texts that would appeal to "the newly literate masses" they aimed to educate. But while the texts in the new courses shifted and their national and cultural contexts changed, the modes of teaching and judging them did little to adjust to the shift. Instead of asking what the novel did differently (and did very well), critics tended to classify and evaluate novels by the standards they knew from classical and European texts. Thus, novels like Melville's and Hawthorne's, which never sold well in the nineteenth century (and, one could argue, were unsuccessful as novels), became the cornerstones of twentieth-century courses on the American novel because of their complex language, careful literary allusions, and serious philosophical and theological explorations. The values of the writers and readers who made the novel the dominant genre were sidelined.[12]

It has been the focus of my scholarly work for several years to examine what makes novels work for those who read them—my students, book group members, what critics call "general readers," even the many women who read along with Oprah Winfrey—and to integrate their values with my training in a more traditional aesthetic assessment of novels. What I have found we left behind in legitimating the novel for scholarly study were, not surprisingly, given our literary history, the novel's feminine qualities: its aim for connection and compassion ("sentimentalism"); its intimacy or frequent location in domestic situations (such as Jane Austen's "tiny canvasses"); its sociability and the way it inspires readers to talk to each other and to pass books along to encourage new conversations (think *The DaVinci Code* or *Harry Potter*), and its demand for engagement in repeated calls to action or social justice (as in *Uncle Tom's Cabin*, *The Good Earth*, or any Alice Walker novel).

I maintain that there is something insistent about a good novel, something that pushes beyond the boundaries of the classifications and evaluations of our scholarly methods. The novel's predominance in more democratic forums—women's improvement societies, the Book-of-the-Month Club, and today's ubiquitous book groups—is unquestionable. A successful novel has ever been a cultural phenomenon, with its realistic characters and compelling stories inspiring readers to belief, action, literacy, and conversation. Nina Baym quotes a reviewer in *Harper's* in 1853, who noted that novels work because "hundreds of readers who would sleep over a sermon, or drone over an essay, or yield a cold and barren assent to the deductions of an ethical treatise, will be startled into reflection, or won to emulation, or roused into effort, by the delineations they meet with in a tale which they opened only for the amusement of an hour."[13]

CROSSING BOUNDARIES

At first blush, the history of literary instruction at the College of St. Catherine suggests that the Sisters followed the established twentieth-century
path of serious study; that is, to teach classical and European literature
(with a preference for Catholic authors) via traditional aesthetic standards,
paying some attention to American literature and mostly ignoring popular novels and women writers. The coursework, as Cavallaro et al. point
out, was masculine; "the authors taught in literature courses were almost
exclusively male," and Greek and Latin were among the early majors. The
authors note, however, that "one exception to this norm was a relatively
early focus on Catholic women authors, including Sigrid Undset and Flannery O'Connor, in English courses."[14]

This exception is crucial, because it hints that events outside the classroom, in that lively and contemplative environment of goodly fellowship,
where visiting women writers thrived and book talk flourished, sometimes
affected life inside the classroom. It confirms that being a women's college
within the Catholic tradition allowed St. Catherine's to cross boundaries
that other institutions vigilantly policed.

Anne Ruggles Gere describes these boundaries in *Intimate Practices: Literacy and Cultural Work in U.S. Women's Clubs, 1880-1920*. She notes that
women's book groups, although serious in their intellectual pursuits, carefully distinguished themselves from more masculine academic models:

> Gathering in one another's homes, libraries, or club rooms that carried a do-
> mestic imprint, clubwomen assumed a less formal posture than that enacted
> in the classroom. Academic discipline of the body was supplanted by com-
> fortable chairs, handwork such as sewing or knitting, and the consumption
> of food and drink. These accommodations to the body never appeared in the
> classroom, where students occupied hard seats in lined rows, with the figure
> of the instructor often towering over them on a dais, and where handwork and
> refreshments of all sorts were explicitly forbidden.[15]

Academic institutions were careful to draw the same lines between their
work and the more feminine world of club women, which explains why nee-
dlepoint, stuffed armchairs, or tea and cakes were not just frowned upon but
"explicitly forbidden" in classroom space, as was the study of popular women
novelists. Larger academic culture, like its literary subculture, was hard at
work at the beginning of the last century building distinctively American
institutions based on masculine values—and purposefully separating itself
from anything that smacked of femininity. The values the academy left out
when judging novels—connection, intimacy, sociability, and engagement—
were also what it left out in constructing its educational spaces.

But if your goal as an academic institution is both strict academic discipline and the warmer "finishing" work of the women's improvement societies of the time, if you have tea and cakes with living writers then invite them to join in your (strictly disciplined) classroom discussion of Dante, lines will get crossed; distinctions will be blurred. The result for the College of St. Catherine was a unique environment for reading and valuing literature that, throughout its first hundred years, moved quietly against the grain of the mainstream of American academic culture.

Because the founding Sisters were women in community whose charism centrally included hospitality, whose values embraced both the practical and the traditional, and whose pursuits ranged from scholarship to social justice to contemplation to lively bouts of tennis, St. Catherine's was bound to become a college unlike most others. It could be attentive both to what women read and to what educated people of any gender should read. Its spaces could be both masculine (the classrooms) and feminine (lounges, clubs, libraries). And its literary experiences could embrace both the American aesthetic of the new college curricula and the feminine values that this aesthetic was intended to counter.

Students in College Hall (Whitby Hall) dormitory, late 1920s. Photo courtesy of St. Catherine University.

Perhaps the most distinctive of these feminine characteristics was the College's often sisterly connection with popular novelists such as May Sarton and Mary Ellen Chase. Other writers—Edna St. Vincent Millay, Hugh Walpole, Evelyn Waugh, Willa Cather, and later Flannery O'Connor, Meridel LeSueur, Judith Guest, Maya Angelou, Toni Morrison, Amy Tan, Rosa Guy, Patricia Hampl, Sue Monk Kidd, and Lois Lowry—spent time at the College. While some delivered a lecture and left, as they were expected to do, others stayed on—then visited again, corresponded with the Sisters, connected with students, and continued their relationship with the College for years. Alumna Regina Nolan Connors, Class of 1930, remembers Mother Antonia McHugh having "a down to earth quality, very like that of her long-time friend Willa Cather." The popular poet Edna St. Vincent Millay was also a frequent visitor in the 1920s. She, too, was remembered as "a personal friend" of Mother Antonia, though her most significant connection to the College was by way of Sister Ste. Helene Guthrie, an English professor and later dean.[16]

Mary Ellen Chase stands out among these writers with connections to St. Catherine's for several reasons. First, although she was a New England Protestant, she found community among the Sisters. She met Sister Lioba, who taught English at St. Catherine's, in a graduate class at the University of Minnesota, and the two quickly became friends. "Her vow of poverty did not deny her the wealth of Henry Fielding," Chase remembered years later, "or her vow of chastity shut her from his distinctly unchaste situations. In fact, the best paper written in our seminar that year was written by Sister Lioba on the humor in *Tom Jones*." Chase wrote vividly about her frequent stays at the College in her 1940 memoir *A Goodly Fellowship*. Her memories of Mother Antonia ("a perfectionist in every sense of the word") are still quoted at convocations at the College, and her depiction of the nuns as full of humor and playfulness as well as devotion and faith is delightful. "I have never seen happier people, or funnier for that matter, than the nuns at St. Catherine's," she wrote. "I have never known so much laughter elsewhere or such good, rich cause for it."[17]

Chase also stands out as one of many successful mid-century American woman novelists that literary tradition and history quickly sidelined. Though she taught at Smith College for many years, went on national lecture tours, earned numerous literary awards and honorary degrees, and was considered among the best writers of her day, Chase is all but lost to today's students. And, though she taught courses at St. Catherine's (she was one of the poet Sister Maris Stella's early mentors) and lived among the Sisters for several summers, I can find no evidence that her novels were taught in English classes. However, throughout the 1920s and 1930s in issue after issue of the students' literary publication, *Ariston*, there are repeated mentions of Chase and her influence on students. The February 1929 issue, for example, includes her advice to young writers that "the true value of learning how to write is learning how to read." In April 1929 the *Ariston* reports that she stayed at the College for two weeks while lecturing in the Twin Cities, and she "talked about Woolf's *Orlando* and . . . also talked about [popular poet and essayist] Louise Imogen Guiney with great respect."[18]

Chase's relationship with the College demonstrates how a feminine literary culture could flourish happily on the borders of serious academic life and how it could, in its more hospitable situations, ignore the rigid categorizations of American aesthetic practice—the practice that has written the much-admired Guiney (and Chase herself) out of literary history. By developing an intimate setting for writers and writing, the College allowed its women students to, as advertisements for the College claimed for years, "count art an intimate friend."[19]

Sister Margery Smith, who was first a student, then a Sister and English professor, now the Archivist at St. Catherine University, affirms that this atmosphere of intimacy was nurtured at the College at all levels. In her student years, 1945-1949, "we felt like guests," secure and comfortable, and the College operated "as a home into which we were invited," she says. For both boarders and commuters, "it never felt like a commercial arrangement." Most distinctive in her memory, however, is how the College "rang with music." In the familial atmosphere, "literature and music were culti-vated—if you didn't have it in your life before, you got it here."[20]

One of Sister Margery's most vivid memories is of the British writer Ev-elyn Waugh on his visit to the College in 1947. In the lovely, upholstered, homey space that is still the Derham Hall Parlor, he joined students "while we were trudging through Milton," she recalls. "The nuns were in the chairs and the students on the floor. I was on the floor at his knee." What ensued was compelling conversation (though, confesses Sister Margery, the stu-dents mostly listened while the Sisters talked with Waugh). Again, this easy blending of academic and domestic space, this combining of the popular (Waugh) and the canonical (Milton), this engagement of both students and Sisters as novices sitting at the feet of the master and apprentices shar-ing in the conversation transgressed the boundaries of masculine academic culture. And while other institutions also had visiting writers and interac-tions like this one, such scenes seem typical of the atmosphere which St. Catherine's, as a women's college run by women, purposefully cultivated.

Such exchanges, Sister Margery says, were among the best moments of her College years. As Mary Ellen Chase writes of St. Catherine's:

> I have never known better conversation than went on within its walls in the hours given to conversation. Sister Antonia had high ambition for her nuns, and several of the best teachers among them had studied in Europe, the teacher of psychology at Louvain, the teacher of music in France and Germany.[21]

These Sisters, in their unique roles and with their particular training, seemed well prepared to stand toe-to-toe with contemporary writers and intellectuals. As teachers, they also invited their students in. When Edna St. Vincent Millay came to the College in 1927, for example, senior students got to pick her up and escort her back to campus. She had dinner with them, and, at 10:30 a.m. on a Friday morning, she led a discussion "for the American Literature class and others interested," as reported in the *Ariston*.[22]

Like Mary Ellen Chase and May Sarton, Edna St. Vincent Millay formed a particular bond with one of the Sisters, Sister Ste. Helene. In a letter soon after Millay's 1927 visit, the poet addresses the Sister as "Darling, darling Sister Saint Helene." In the years of correspondence that followed, Millay often consulted Sister Ste. Helene on Catholic characters and situations in her poems and plays and had her read early drafts of her writing. In a letter dated December 3, 1940, she writes, "The lovely nun in the little play *The Crooked Cross* is of course named for you."[23]

Poet Edna St. Vincent Millay at the College, 1927.
Photo courtesy of St. Catherine University.

How Edna St. Vincent Millay came to visit the College in the first place is a testament to its unique position among educational institutions of the time. The *New York Times* reported in 1924 that Millay, whose popularity was on the rise, was reading before an appreciative audience in Minneapolis when the Mother Superior of the Sisters of St. Joseph contacted her to say that the Sisters weren't allowed to go out at night, but that they dearly wanted to hear Millay read her poetry. Millay then "went to St. Paul and gave a special reading within the walls of the convent." Later, she left a signed portrait, still in the College archives, which reads: "To my dear friends at the College of Saint Catherine, with my love." It is striking, first, that the Sisters were engaged enough in contemporary literary culture to seek out Millay, and, second, that Millay would respond so quickly and warmly to their request.[24]

It is also striking that this incident marked only the beginning of a long relationship with the College. Like Chase, Millay visited again and again. In February 1928, the *Ariston* reported that, during her November visit, "she read poems favored by the girls and requested by them. Her delightful informality linked her immediately and warmly to her audience, and created a most individual love for her in their hearts." While the language is mildly overblown (indeed, sentimental), the sentiment is significant in that it places Millay not in the role of visiting dignitary or Literary Authority, but as a participant in the familial arrangements of the College. Writing for the *Ariston*, Alumna Sister Helen Angela Hurley echoes the style of women's fiction popular at the time throughout her report on the visit. She muses, "Dusk closed us in quickly and there was a delicious coziness about the way we drew up our chairs for a chat. There is that about Miss Millay which makes you love her. . . . She makes you feel that she likes you and that she is interested in what you have to say."[25]

While Millay commented on literature—"poems, plays, novels . . . she reads everything, apparently, with amazing intellectual acumen"—again, I find no evidence that her poetry was taught in the College's classes. She was a friend of the College; students and Sisters read her poems as part of their literary life, but it was a life outside the curriculum. In the curriculum, as Sister Margery recalls from the 1940s, "We studied World Literature—*The Divine Comedy*, the Greeks, and Cardinal Newman."[26]

Given this leaning, it is not surprising that later, when the curriculum opened up to more contemporary writers, the first women writers to enter were not Chase and Millay, but Sigrid Undset and Flannery O'Connor, whose themes and concerns were Catholic. O'Connor, who first visited St. Catherine's in the late 1950s, also returned several times. The *St. Catherine Wheel* reports on October 20, 1960, that O'Connor stayed from Wednesday evening until Friday at noon, during which time she delivered two convocations, visited literature and creative writing classes, and led several informal discussions with students. She even read student writing, and, the *Wheel* reports, "her criticism was direct and to the point."[27]

This engagement with student writing also attests to an unusual atmosphere for a Midwestern women's college. Here, student writers took their work seriously, and they saw themselves as the potential professional writers many of them would become. Sister Margery recalls that several of the women in her undergraduate English classes became published writers, including a longtime columnist for *Commonweal* and a popular mid-century poet. The College's Women's Center is named for Abigail Quigley McCarthy, a promising undergraduate writer who became a best-selling memoirist and novelist. Others student writers took the Sisters as their models and themselves became Sisters and scholars, doing graduate work in literature. Sister Margery, after taking her vows as a Sister of St. Joseph, went on to the University of Chicago for her Ph.D. in literature.[28]

Clearly, these young women who studied Milton and Dante in the classroom could still envision literary production and scholarship as women's work. The goodly fellowship with visiting writers, the role models such as Sisters Lioba, Saint Helene, and Maris Stella among the Sisters of the College's English Department, and their own work on the campus literary magazine, *Ariston*, brought students together as writers in serious engagement around literature. Students freely encouraged and published one another in this venue. And they were not just playing at writing. As Sister Margery recalls, "Anyone in any major felt free to participate. Teachers would say of a good paper, 'Why don't you turn this into the *Ariston*?'" And, she adds, "It was a big deal to get into the *Ariston*."[29]

Thus, while students of St. Catherine's attended learned lectures and knew their literary icons as well as any students from the first half of the twentieth century, they also had unique access to the writers who weren't taught, the writers their mothers (and teachers) were reading, the writers beloved of American book club women—the writers they aspired to become. While students writing for the *Ariston* were engaging in impressive literary criticism and sophisticated analysis of texts, they were also reading contemporary literature, writing poetry, and holding after-hours teas in "comfortable chairs," with the likes of Mary Ellen Chase, Edna St. Vincent Millay, and May Sarton. Some early St. Catherine's students even brought Dante out of the classroom and into this feminine space. Most likely inspired by women's clubs of the time, they organized a Dante Reading Circle that lasted for years.

The ability of this women's college to claim both the disciplined space of the classroom and the domestic space of the women's club was amplified by the Sisters' commitment to community and hospitality, peace and spirituality, and by their connections to the successful writers of their day. In effect, boundary crossing in literature was as acceptable as it was in women's education generally—when nuns were doing it.

English Majors Club, 1959. Photo courtesy of St. Catherine University.

Thus, literature moved more freely between categories at St. Catherine's and was not so easily contained by the educational and aesthetic practices that preoccupied academic institutions throughout the twentieth century. The both/and approach that continues to serve the College well created an environment that visiting women writers recognized as unique—it honored them and embraced their work in the context of a rigorous academic environment. In this atmosphere of intimacy, connection, sociability, and engagement, literature was allowed to be more than aesthetic artifact. It lived and breathed with its authors in communion with students and Sisters of St. Joseph at the College of St. Catherine.

NOTES

1. May Sarton to Sister Maris Stella, March 21, 1960, College of St. Catherine (CSC) Archives. This is one letter in a decades-long correspondence between the two writers, distinguished by both its expressions of deep affection and its serious exchanges between the two—both working poets and thoughtful intellectuals. For example, a letter from March 1959, addressed to "Darling One," contains a poem called "The Waves" and the following: "I feel that the last two lines . . . are too charming—it is the rhyme and the feminine ending that makes it charming rather than the piercing I feel it should be. . . . Please make suggestions. It is so rare to get any criticism from someone inside one's work." A few months later, in a letter dated

September 28, Sarton apparently responds to Maris Stella's suggestions: "I am sure you are right about the final line in "The Waves"—I wonder if the thing may be to cut the last stanza altogether?" Another letter, from 1974, wanders from poetry to Leonard Wolfe to My Lai to Richard Nixon. The quote "Behold I make all things new again" comes from the inscription on the altar in the College chapel.

2. Mary Ellen Chase, *A Goodly Fellowship* (New York: MacMillan, 1940), pp. 240–241.

3. Tracy Schier and Cynthia Russett, eds., *Catholic Women's Colleges in America* (Baltimore: Johns Hopkins University Press, 2002), p. 4.

4. Kathleen A. Mahoney, "American Catholic Colleges for Women: Historical Origins" in Schier and Russett, pp. 25–54, at p. 28.

5. Monica K. Hellwig, "Colleges of Religious Women's Congregations: The Spiritual Heritage" in Schier and Russett, pp. 17–24, at p. 18.

6. *Ibid.*

7. Schier and Russett, p. 4.

8. *Ibid.*, p. 8.

9. Sister of St. Joseph of Carondelet, *Eyes Open on a World* (St. Cloud, Minnesota: North Star Press, 2001), p. 131.

10. Nina Baym, *Novels, Readers and Reviewers: Responses to Fiction in Antebellum America* (Ithaca, New York: Cornell University Press, 1984), p. 29.

11. The estimation of 90 percent of novels bought by women comes from a statement by Elaine Showalter in a *New York Times* article by Bruce Weber entitled "When the I's of a novel cross over" (February 6, 1999, B7), though the percentage is cited more generally among students, publishers, and scholars of the novel as common knowledge.

12. Baym, throughout.

13. Baym, p. 28.

14. Cavallaro, Carroll, and Gildensoph in this volume.

15. Anne Ruggles Gere, *Intimate Practices: Literacy and Cultural Work in U.S. Women's Clubs, 1880–1920* (Urbana: University of Illinois Press, 1997), p. 35.

16. Alumnae Reminiscences file, Sister Antonia McHugh collection, CSC Archives (Box #8).

17. Chase, pp. 229–30, 240.

18. *Ariston*, February 1929, pp. 35–37, p. 55; *Ariston*, April 1929, p. 28, CSC Archives.

19. Sister Jean Bonnett, "Report to the Phi Beta Kappa Qualifications Committee," (1935), CSC Archives.

20. Interview by the author with Sister Margery Smith, CSJ, March, 14, 2007.

21. Chase, p. 235.

22. *Ariston*, 1927, CSC Archives.

23. Edna St. Vincent Millay to Sister Ste. Helene Guthrie, December 3, 1940, Letter #227, CSC Archives.

24. *New York Times*, March 9, 1924.

25. *Ariston*, February 1928, pp. 38–39, CSC Archives.

26. Interview with Sister Margery Smith.

27. *St. Catherine Wheel*, Volume XXVII, No. 2, October 20, 1960.

28. Interview with Sister Margery Smith, CSJ. Sister Margery added in a follow-up e-mail (February 2008) that she found in the "Student Aid/Financial Aid" file from 1930 "a contract for Susan Vander Koor. Clipped to it are the yellow (undated) newspaper clippings about *The Atlantic Monthly* awarding her the Atlantic Poetry Prize." She also got a $150 award from CSC for "her excellence in verse." Later, Vander Koor's prize poem "beat out the prize short story and prize essay for the scholarship to the Breadloaf School in Vermont," Sister Margery wrote. Other St. Catherine's students were also cited in the article as placing in *The Atlantic Monthly* contest—Maridee LaPointe in 1937, Catherine Fitzgerald in 1938, Elizabeth Hodges and Abigail Quigley in 1936.

29. *Ibid.*

III

UNIQUE LEGACY: FACULTY AND STUDENT EXPERIENCES

8

Learning and Earning

The Work-Study Experience

Julie Balamut and Virginia Steinhagen

"Come to the College of St. Catherine. Don't put it off. Decide now. If you need financial help, write to us. We will do all we can. Many students earn their way through college. A college education is worth a big sacrifice. Come."[1]

As this 1914 advertisement for the College of St. Catherine indicates, from its earliest years the Sisters of St. Joseph of Carondelet (CSJ) sought to make their new college for women financially accessible for all qualified students. In addition to placing ads in local newspapers and actively recruiting girls in Minneapolis and St. Paul, the Sisters toured Minnesota and neighboring states to find highly talented students. And in cases where these students' families could not afford the cost of a college education, the Sisters offered them the opportunity to work on campus in exchange for part or all of their tuition.

What began as informal agreements made with individual students on an ad hoc basis in the early decades of the College eventually evolved into a broader, more formal work-study program by the 1940s. This program, in turn, constantly evolved in ensuing decades in response to the College's increasingly diverse student body, new state and federal programs, and changes in student attitudes about work. From the 1920s to the present day, the broad availability of work-study as a means of making a St. Catherine's degree affordable has reflected the commitment of the Sisters of St. Joseph to the education of women.

The academic experience of the women who attended women's colleges, such as the Seven Sisters on the East Coast, has been the subject of both scholarly research and personal memoirs. However, the academic and social experiences of women who attended Catholic women's colleges are just emerging as a subject for serious study. Within this subfield, very little research has been done on work-study programs that made it financially possible for women to attend college. What was college life like for students at Catholic women's colleges who worked to pay their tuition? What changes took place when the early informal work-study agreements became more formalized under federal regulation? How did expanding opportunities for women in the workforce and in society affect the way students perceived work-study?

This essay examines the history of work-study financial aid programs at the College of St. Catherine from the early years through the 1970s. While these programs had positive benefits for many students, the nature of work-study, which had some students cleaning classrooms, typing reports, or serving their classmates in the dining room, at times heightened the class disparity among students. Moreover, not all students had positive experiences with work-study, whether due to the undesirable nature of the work or conflicts with faculty and staff supervisors. Many students, however, recount positive and influential experiences related to their work-study at the College. Regardless of the individual experience, work-study at the College of St. Catherine in the decades between 1920 and 1980 made a college education possible for hundreds of women who otherwise would not have been able to afford one.

Student workers preparing 50-pound cake in College kitchen, 1969. Photo courtesy of St. Catherine University.

THE EARLY DECADES

Sister Antonia McHugh helped the College grow with her insistence on having excellent faculty and students. She managed the financial challenges with the help of her close friend, Sister Ste. Helene Guthrie, the College financial officer, who matched students in need with on-campus jobs. If Sister Antonia was the heart and soul of the campus, Sister Ste. Helene was her right arm. Sister Ste. Helene, who taught English and Old Testament and also served as registrar, worked closely with the families of students to make sure they could remain at St. Catherine's during difficult financial times.

The earliest St. Catherine catalogues list the costs of tuition and room and board, but do not mention work-study opportunities. In 1906, for example, tuition cost $40.00 for the scholastic year, and board and washing cost $160.00. A private room started at $50.00 for the year.[2] These expenses remained at this level until 1914, when prices were raised to $80.00 for tuition and $200.00 for board.[3] Costs per quarter for 1920 were $35.00 for tuition, $25.00 for room rent, and $85.00 for board and laundry.[4]

The 1920 St. Catherine *Catalogue* was the first to mention work-study opportunities. Under the heading "Facilities for Self-Support" it noted these possibilities while emphasizing the good value the College offered:

> The College desires in every way to encourage self-supporting students. It furnishes a few student-service scholarships. Energetic and faithful women can usually find for themselves opportunity. Some earn enough from term to term to meet a large part of their expenses. A few, by rigid economy and hard work, earn all their expenses, while studying, but in such cases health or scholarship is likely to suffer. No one should come, even for a quarter, expecting to support herself, without at least one hundred dollars at her command for use if needed. The College has funds for aiding needy students to some extent; but the great advantage it offers is the low rate at which all its facilities are afforded. The traditions of the College and the public sentiment of the students favor economy in all expenses.[5]

Students applied directly to the College for aid, and there were no set forms to fill out. Students who could not pay the full amount or whose scholarships did not cover all the costs could supplement their funds by working on campus. This work-study opportunity was beneficial to less well-off students in that it allowed them to attend college, but students did not have the option of refusing work-study and finding a job off campus. As stated in the 1920–1921 *Year Book*, "Freshmen, Sophomores, and Juniors may not leave the campus without permission from a prefect or from the Dean."[6] Students' daily schedules were also regulated; in addition to classes, they had daily mandatory chapel visits, supervised study time, and weekly convocations. The 1920–1921 *Year Book* notes, "Freshmen students spend the five o'clock hour in supervised study in the Library. Students spend the evening study hour in quiet individual study in their own rooms."[7]

In the 1930s, with the United States in the midst of the Great Depression, the Sisters needed to work closely with families to provide financial aid to students.[8] Despite the economic crisis, there was no retrenchment in recruiting or enrollment at St. Catherine's during the decade. Having invested two decades in building St. Catherine's, the Sisters of St. Joseph and Sister Antonia McHugh, President of the College, were determined to increase student enrollment during the Great Depression. In her annual report of the academic year 1931–1932, Sister Ste. Helene, the dean, notes the financial difficulties of the times: "The number of Student Service Contracts, which is necessarily limited by the amount of student help which the College can use, has been strained to the utmost this last year. . . . The total number of students employed this year was 102; the number employed in 1930 was 78."[9] In her report of the 1932–1933 academic year, she notes that 114 of 448 students registered during the regular session held Student Service Contracts. The large number of students working allowed the College "to facilitate the work in several departments, especially by providing stenographic help to faculty members who have large classes and who have been badly in need of such help. In this way, the increase, while it has its disadvantages, has acted to the two-fold advantage of faculty and student."[10]

Sister Ste. Helene's correspondence with students and their families reveals how important work-study opportunities were in making a college education possible. In 1930 she began corresponding with Elinor O'Connor, who was an orphan, and with her uncle Joseph B. O'Connor. Elinor accepted a work-study position, but then tried to change her job. She wrote to Sister Ste. Helene, "I have considered the work you offered me and have decided I would rather wash dishes than wait on table (in the freshman dining hall if possible)." Sister Ste. Helene replied:

My dear Elinor,

I cannot tell you definitely whether your work will be washing and wiping dishes or waiting on table this year as we have to arrange that work after the girls have arrived and we see for which part of the house work they are better fitted. I feel certain that you will be delighted with St. Catherine's and the many opportunities which it affords our Catholic students to receive an excellent education under ideal surroundings.[11]

Elinor did not seem to want the work-study option; her uncle sent a letter to Sister Ste. Helene:

I had a letter from Elinor today. She seems to think we cant affor [sic] to send her to school this year. Says she can't stand to wash dishes and keep up her studies and she thinks she should stay this year with her aunt who is not well.[12]

There is no record of whether Elinor ended up washing dishes or working in the dining room, but she did graduate from St. Catherine's in 1935.[13]

The Sisters' efforts to help deserving students extended beyond offering the opportunity to work. One student's contract contained a hand-written note "To take noon day meal with Freshman Boarders."[14] A letter from this student's mother to Sister Ste. Helene noted, "Today we received from you the second gift of food . . . we are very grateful to you, and don't feel we deserve any more gifts from you than we've had the past three or rather two & half years already, namely Elizabeth's wonderful opportunity there. She is like a different girl entirely, she never was so happy anywhere as she has been at St. Catherine's."[15]

During the 1930s, Sister Ste. Helene wrote most of the student service contracts herself, noting how much she would deduct if the student would successfully complete the tasks assigned. She kept students in school by having them work in the dining room, library, residence halls, laboratories, and in the Sisters of St. Joseph convent. Students typically worked between one and three hours per day, and some students worked during the Christmas, Easter, and summer vacations. On Helen Wenzel's 1931 contract, Sister Ste. Helene crossed out "waiting on table" and "sweeping and dusting stairways and halls" and amended the assigned tasks to "sweep and dust Sister Lioba's classroom, 2nd floor Whitby and German II classrooms." Wenzel's contract for 1935 notes that she will give "3 hours of service a day, in 2nd floor corridor Whitby Hall, rooms 204, 200, and 205." Sister Ste. Helene changed Dorothy Elm's service contract in 1933 from three to four hours a day and wrote, "If four hours a day is too strenuous she may make up hours in summer."[16] In 1935, Emma Suomi spent three hours each day washing and drying dishes in the kitchen. Theresa Giulani's contract for the 1932–1933 academic year was typical of those for commuter students. In exchange for working every day in Caecilian Hall (then the Music Building), cleaning the practice rooms and classrooms and serving as a receptionist, Giulani received a $15.00 per quarter tuition rebate.[17] This system of work-study contracts worked well throughout these years. Given the tight economic times, students must have realized that they needed to do their part in order to help defray the costs of a college education.

Each work-study student received a copy of the service contract with the expectations clearly spelled out:

> The College has devised a system of student service open to bright students who can not attend college without this aid.

We think you are scholastically worthy of this consideration and that you would be deprived of educational opportunities without it. We want you to consider this as your first remunerative position. When you finish college we shall be glad to write the very best recommendation which your service will warrant.

1. Students who sign library and laboratory contracts will be called upon to do whatever routine cleaning is necessary in the library or laboratories as well as the more technical work connected with such contract.
2. One hour a day of service for a week, means 6-60 minute periods or 7-50 minute periods a week. You arrange for these periods with the person in charge of your work.
3. All work missed because of absences must be made up. The one in charge of the student service contracts should be notified of the absences as soon as possible in order that she may arrange for a substitute. Failure to notify the person in charge of the work or failure to make up hours missed will be considered sufficient reason for not renewing contract.
4. Students are expected to give prompt, cheerful, full-time, and efficient service.
5. If the contract states that a student work for some days during vacation, this work is on the basis of an eight-hour-day.[18]

The administration at St. Catherine's retained this ad hoc work-study practice throughout the 1930s even though they also participated in the national programs that were developed at this time. In 1934, Sister Ste. Helene reported that 28 students were able to stay at the College with assistance from the Federal Emergency Relief Administration (FERA) and the State Emergency Relief Administration (SERA).[19] In her report for the academic year 1937–1938, Sister Antonine noted that 79 students received funds totaling $7550.70 from the National Youth Administration program. She characterized this funding as "a very significant factor both in providing college opportunities to students otherwise denied them and in enabling the College to expand its program of helping worthy students."[20] St. Catherine's did not establish any new office to administer the National Youth Administration program. Rather, the College's system of informal work-study agreements continued.

Correspondence between students and the Sisters in the 1930s reveals both the extent of students' financial difficulties and the strength of their attachment to the Sisters and the College. In September 1937, a former St. Catherine's student who had transferred to the University of Minnesota wrote to Sister Eucharista, then dean:

Dear Sister Eucharista:

Sister, three years ago you were very kind to me. Although I had not paid my last quarter's tuition and fees to your college, you forwarded my credits to the

University of Minnesota. Since then, I have always intended to pay that sixty-five dollar debt as soon as I graduated from college.

Now I have graduated and I am still unable to pay. . . . As I do not have a teaching position, I am afraid to ask you to wait any longer for your money. Therefore, I should be very glad to do sixty-five dollars of work at the College of St. Catherine. . . .[21]

In 1939 Sister Eucharista wrote to a student who had graduated in 1933, and offered her a teaching position as a way of paying off her debt:

I am wondering if you would consider coming here next year and by teaching on our faculty with–let us say–a cash allowance of $35.00 to $50.00 a month, maintain yourself, and apply the remainder of your salary on your account. . . . No doubt the time is not far off when you will wish to take on new responsibilities; and if we can help you in any way to clear your account with us, we shall be glad to add you to our faculty for the year 1939-1940.[22]

There were distinctions between students who came from more privileged backgrounds and those who did not, despite the College's efforts to provide equal opportunities. In terms of financial aid, for example, the College of St. Catherine had a few endowed scholarships, which were only available to relatives of the donor. Additionally, beginning in 1938 and continuing through the 1950s, the College offered a tuition reduction for students who were graduates of high schools sponsored by the Sisters of St. Joseph of Carondelet. In the early years this reduction covered 50 percent of the cost of tuition; by 1953 the rebate was only 10 percent of the cost of the tuition.[23] This policy helped the College attract qualified, well-prepared students, but it also may have added to the division between those students who attended private high schools and those who attended public ones.

WORLD WAR II AND AFTER

During the Second World War, the Sisters of St. Joseph continued supporting academically worthy students by offering work-study opportunities at the College of St. Catherine through the same individualized contracts as earlier. The war had a direct impact on enrollment and on students' needs. As Sister Antonine noted in her annual report for the 1941–1942 academic year, there was a slight decrease in enrollment (about 6 percent). She noted the difficulty of keeping students "from succumbing to the temptations of high-paying positions left open by the draft. . . . Where financial need was in question, we made every possible adjustment to enable students to continue their college work."[24] Enrollment decreased again the following year, from 626 students to 556.[25] In her report for that year, College President

Sister Eucharista noted, "The war has accentuated sharply the problem of adequate help in all departments of the College; and drastic changes will probably have to be made in order to meet the shortage of help. A committee has to be appointed to study the possibility of the students being assigned small tasks in order to do the work formerly done by paid help."[26] Sister Antonine's comments in her 1943–1944 report indicate that the shortage of help was an ongoing problem: "There was a marked decrease in the number of students requiring financial help or desiring to do part time work, and this in turn made the shortage of both office and domestic help really acute. A total of 140 students holding part time positions as contrasted with 240 in the year of our heaviest pre-war enrollment will suggest some of the adjustments that were necessary."[27]

During the war, enrollment at St. Mary's School of Nursing in Minneapolis, also sponsored by the Sisters of St. Joseph of Carondelet, boomed because of the national need for trained nurses. St. Mary's adopted an intensive program which offered students financial help from the federal government in order to complete courses and clinical work for a nursing degree, in exchange for serving the war effort after graduation. The Sisters of St. Joseph at the College of St. Catherine seized the opportunity created by the soaring demand for nurses by incorporating St. Mary's School of Nursing and establishing both three- and five-year nursing programs on the St. Paul campus.[28] Although the nursing students remained separate from the other students in many ways, the influx of these students greatly increased the student population on the St. Paul campus.[29] College President Sister Antonius characterized the situation, "A report on the academic year 1944-45, embracing as it did the final year of World War II, can be little more than a chronicle of the valiant struggles of the Faculty and domestic staff to maintain a status quo despite shortage of everything but students."[30]

The stories of the women who were employed in the student work program during this time are as varied and intriguing as the women themselves. Many of the women who worked on campus commented on how the jobs they performed helped them with their major or career, even if the skills weren't immediately transferable. They also talked about the strong influence of their supervisors and how this influence sometimes had a lifelong effect.

Sister Catherine Litecky was a commuter student who began her study at St. Catherine's in 1941. Her work-study job involved helping out in the sacristy, doing ironing and other such tasks, but she also did research at the Minnesota Historical Society for Sister Mary Edward Healy. Sister Catherine described the atmosphere on campus where work was a shared responsibility. She noted, for example, that all the Sisters shared laundry duties; even Sister Eucharista, who was president at that time, put in her hour in the laundry. Similarly, clubs and classes were responsible for cleaning common areas, so if the common area in Mendel Hall was used for a social event, the club or class that was hosting the event helped clean it. At a time when everyone was sacrificing for the war effort, working together was part of the spirit of the times.[31]

Rosemary Balk Lovett was a student from the small town of Waucoma, Iowa, who attended St. Catherine's from 1941 to 1945. Her work-study job was in the library. She remembers dusting shelves and straightening books and, after her excellent typing skills were discovered, typing letters for Sister Maria Cecilia, the director of the library school. She does not remember any divisions between those students who had work-study and those who did not, noting that she had one roommate with work-study and another who did not work, and that some students worked more hours than others. When asked whether she felt at a disadvantage because she had to work, she noted, "I don't think I could have gone to St. Catherine's without work-study. It was just assumed that you would work."[32]

In 1944, the federal government passed the Servicemen's Readjustment Act, better known as the GI Bill, which offered free college and trade school education to all veterans returning from World War II. The GI Bill had relatively little effect on women's colleges immediately after the war. However, because it made a college education possible for an unprecedented number of Americans, a college education now became the norm for a much broader segment of the American society generally, including women. In addition, the need for nurses, teachers, scientists, physicians, occupational therapists, librarians, writers, and other professions continued to grow in the post–World War II economy. St. Catherine's provided a rigorous course of study for those wanting to enter postwar careers.

During the 1950s, work-study remained an important means of financing college. In 1954–1955, 166 students had work-study jobs and earned remuneration ranging from $105.00 to $450.00 for the year.[33] In her report of the year 1955–1956, Sister Mary Edward, the newly appointed Dean of Women, mentioned the financial aid programs: "The scholarship and student service program should be more carefully publicized. Since the funds available for both programs are limited, they should be made available to the most needy and most worthy. . . . Some measures need to be taken in regard to those who cancel contracts at the last minute."[34] In 1956–1957, student service contracts were awarded to 200 students at an estimated cost of $39,528.00.[35] In 1957–1958, 197 contracts were awarded at a cost of $37,523.00.[36] In 1958–1959, the costs rose significantly:

> Student service contracts were given to 231 students at an estimated cost of $54,424.70 per year. This increase was due to a change in the salary scale due to the raise in tuition. According to the present scale the salary is as follows: freshmen–85¢ an hour; sophomores–90¢; juniors–95¢; seniors–$1.00

providing they stay at the same job in consecutive years. Because of the skilled service and excellent supervision in the typing service the students may, after one or more years of experience and on the recommendation of the supervisor, receive half tuition for six hours a week and full tuition for twelve hours. Half tuition was given this year to three students and full tuition to one student. These contracts include service in the dining room, typing, dusting, clerical work, home economics department, nursery school, switchboard, science laboratories, language laboratory, art department, library, post office, reception desk, doctor's office, and speech department.

In 1959, College President Sister Mary William Brady noted that the National Defense Student Loan Program was a mixed blessing, as "more and more underclassmen are asking for larger and larger loans and tending to ignore more and more any suggestion of student service as a means of helping their parents to finance their college education. This should be studied and discussed before any further action is taken on our participation in this loan program."[37] Despite her misgivings, however, the number of students interested in work-study remained strong, with an average of 250 students per year participating in the work-study program in the early 1960s.[38]

THE 1960S AND BEYOND

During the 1960s regulations requiring resident students to get permission to leave campus were relaxed. In 1960 first-year students still needed a permit, signed by a prefect, anytime they left campus, but sophomores, juniors, and seniors only needed signed permits after 7:30 in the evening.[39] By 1970, students were required merely to "leave word where they are when they are not on the residence hall floor. . . . During the day a note posted on your door is sufficient."[40] These relaxed rules gave students the option of seeking work off-campus if they did not like the work-study job to which they were assigned. If students found the off-campus work more enjoyable and could earn more money (and actually receive a check rather than a tuition credit), they left campus to work.

But while students were enjoying less oversight of their activities, work-study and other financial assistance were becoming more regulated. In her annual report for 1961–1962, College President Sister Mary Edward Healy described the growing requests for financial aid and the need for resources beyond the College's:

Each year there is a greater demand for financial help. An increasing number of students are taking out National Defense Loans. More are asking for scholarships and student service contracts. Since these last are taken out of current operating expenses, there is a limit to the amount that can be given. Ninety-four and seven tenths percent of the students who received aid, received some of it from college sources.[41]

In her annual report for 1963–1964, Lorraine Jensen, director of admissions, pointed out the problem with the ad hoc system of awarding the work-study contracts that the College had been using. Jensen noted:

> Our present method of awarding assistance leaves me with a feeling of futility and frustration. It is unreasonable to expect a student or her parents to plan the financing of her education when she is notified concerning a scholarship in March, a student service contract in June, and a loan in August. At least some good students, I am sure, have been lost to us because other colleges informed them early of the total amount of aid which they might expect to receive. I know of no other college which does not use a package plan of assistance and I am most eager to adopt this method.[42]

The College began issuing financial aid packages in 1964–1965.[43] The continuing demand for financial assistance plus the need to coordinate the various components of financial aid packages led to a more formalized system.

During the 1960s, the federal government became more closely involved with educational access and student employment programs, including those on college campuses. The passage of the Civil Rights Act of 1964 opened the door for financial aid and college work-study across the nation. Specifically, the Economic Opportunity Act of 1964 funded and defined college work-study programs.

Students relaxing on the lawn, 1970. Photo courtesy of St. Catherine University.

The Economic Opportunity Act granted work-study to qualifying students, but it also meant that St. Catherine's had to comply with new federal regulations. The federal work-study program added to the overall financial aid budget. In 1969–1970, for example, St. Catherine's provided student service employment worth $76,780.00 and the federal work-study program added another $10,288.00.[44] The work-study program provided funding for about 20 students on campus during summer and for four students to work with the Urban Corps in Minneapolis.[45]

The government regulation changed the way the Sisters of St. Joseph could manage financial aid. In 1971, Sister Alberta Huber, the College President, asked Sister Anne Elise Tschida to organize a financial aid office and formalize the student work program at the college. During her years at the helm of the financial aid office, Sister Anne Elise kept track of the new regulations and the increasingly complicated rules governing who could and could not participate in the work-study program.[46]

The new federal and state programs should have made more funding available for qualified students in the late 1960s and beyond, but this wasn't always the case. There were not large increases of public funding to help private colleges such as St. Catherine's. Sister Anne Elise's biggest challenge was finding enough funds for all the students who needed support. She recalls that "there was never enough money" in the years from 1971 to 1989 that she ran the office. In accordance with its mission, the College reached out to populations of potential students who may never have considered a Catholic women's college, including women of color and older nontraditional students. The message at St. Catherine's to all accepted students was loud and clear: "If you want to come here, we will find a way for you to come here." Sister Anne Elise said that the challenges of trying to find enough money for qualified students didn't detract from her satisfaction helping fund a student through all four years. During Sister Anne Elise's years, federal and state grants plus the student's willingness to do campus work-study and even find jobs off-campus made it rare that a determined student had to leave St. Catherine's because she could no longer afford the tuition.[47]

As head of the financial aid office, Sister Anne Elise assigned jobs to incoming students and tried to match campus needs to the interests of the students. Usually, first-year students were assigned to jobs that required many workers, such as food service, the library, and receptionist work; after the student declared a major, she could try to get work in a department that better fit her interests or her talents. The student employee never saw a paycheck during this time. A supervisor approved a student worker's timecard, and the wage was deducted from the student's balance.[48]

One of Sister Anne Elise's other challenges was finding enough meaningful work for the work-study students as she knew that some of the jobs, although important to the functioning of the College, were hard work and not exciting. During the 1970s and 1980s, in fact, students didn't readily accept some of the jobs in food service, special events, and grounds crews.

Interviews of student workers from the 1970s revealed some tensions as students wanted jobs that matched their talents, and they didn't want to be labeled as financially needy by the College in front of their classmates. Although student workers were grateful for their education, they sometimes felt demeaned by being assigned work instead of choosing it themselves, especially when an administrator assigned a job arbitrarily without regard to the student's interests or talents. Some student workers felt that they were the "have-nots" because they had to work one or more jobs that cut into their study time.

Trudy Schoolmeesters Landgren, Class of 1972, grew up on a farm in Litchfield, Minnesota, and decided to study home economics at St. Catherine's even though her aunt warned her that the College was only for girls from wealthy families and she would feel out of place. Because she was interested in chemistry, she hoped to work in a lab in the chemistry department. She was assigned to the dining room, where meals were still served family-style under the direction of Sister Adriana. Landgren remembers being somewhat disappointed, because it appeared she was given this job because of the stereotype associating home economics with the kitchen and serving; her hunch was confirmed when she discovered that many of her coworkers in the kitchen, the dish room, and dining room were also home economics majors.[49]

Landgren respected Sister Adriana and thought she was a good manager. However, because Landgren was such a hard worker, she not only served her peers, she usually had to work late into the evening to clean the tables and the kitchen. Like some others also doing kitchen work, she said that at times she couldn't help but feel inferior to those she served. But because she was reliable, she was assigned more dining room work. And when Landgren came back for her junior and senior years, Sister Adriana depended on her and wouldn't let her work in a different department. Ironically, Landgren wasn't even a food science major; her specialty was textiles, clothing construction, and home economics education.

As a senior, Landgren worked on a catering team for presidential dinners and special events. One difficult incident occurred when Landgren won the annual "Make It with Wool" contest for a garment that she tailored. She wanted to attend the award ceremony, but Sister Adriana would not excuse her from work because she needed her for an important catered event. Today, Professor Landgren is a faculty member in the Family, Consumer, and Nutrition Science department at St. Catherine's; she values the education she received, but she doesn't think her student job contributed to her career skills and she regrets missing opportunities because of her student employment.[50]

THE LEGACY

As the "living endowment" (see Carroll, this volume) of the women religious orders dramatically decreased in the wake of Vatican II and a strong fiscal endowment became more important, many Catholic women's colleges faced financial difficulties and closed during the 1970s and 1980s.[51] At the same time, more students needed financial aid. Compounding this problem, federal funds for needy students were being cut. In addition, many all-male colleges started to admit women, including the neighboring St. Thomas College in 1977, so the pool of prospective students dwindled. As more women were admitted to previously male-only colleges, the pressure became especially acute at Catholic women's colleges to maintain their enrollments in order to stay viable. Ironically, the strides women made as a result of the women's movement in the 1960s and 1970s led many women to chose secular or co-educational Catholic colleges instead of Catholic women's colleges, which had long nurtured women's leadership and achievement.

Those women's colleges that were able to increase their endowments and to attract a more diverse group of students survived. St. Catherine's remained strong by opening its doors to older, nontraditional women students through its Weekend College in 1980 and by offering graduate programs shortly thereafter. The College also merged with St. Mary's Junior College, another school sponsored by the Sisters of St. Joseph, in 1988. The College's work-study program evolved in the 1980s and 1990s in response to the increasing diversity of its students. By the early 1990s, the student work-study program was transferred to the human resources department, jobs were posted, and students were paid directly rather than receiving a tuition rebate.

As the stories of alumnae who participated in the work-study program show, student work on the St. Catherine's campus has evolved from the informal agreements that the Sisters made with "deserving" students to a more formal program to meet the needs of ever more diverse groups of women. Unwavering for over 100 years has been the collective determination, first established by the Sisters of St. Joseph and continuing at the University today, to remain true to the mission of making a college education available to all promising young women regardless of their finances. As a result of this commitment, thousands of women leaders have worked in a variety of jobs in order to obtain an education at the College of St. Catherine.

NOTES

1. Advertisement in the *Catholic Bulletin* (Minneapolis, MN: 1914), as quoted in Rosalie Ryan, CSJ and John Christine Wolkerstorfer, CSJ, *More Than a Dream* (St. Paul: The College of St. Catherine, 1992), p. 6.

2. College of St. Catherine *Year Book,* 1906, p. 13, College of St. Catherine (CSC) Archives, St. Paul, Minnesota.

3. College of St. Catherine *Bulletin,* 1914, p. 77, CSC Archives, St. Paul, Minnesota.

4. *Ibid.,* p. 102-03.

5. College of St. Catherine *Bulletin,* 1920, p. 22, CSC Archives, St. Paul, Minnesota.

6. The College Association of the College of St. Catherine *Year Book,* 1920-21, p. 23, Box 363, File 6, CSC Archives.

7. *Ibid.,* p. 17.

8. College of St. Catherine enrollment figures rose steadily between 1928 and 1932, from 363 to 669, then decreased to 527 by 1933-34, after which it began to increase again. *Administrative Reports,* College of St. Catherine, 1928-1940, CSC Archives.

9. Report of the Dean, *Administrative Reports,* College of St. Catherine, 1932, pp. 19-20, CSC Archives.

10. Report of the Dean, *Administrative Reports,* College of St. Catherine, 1935, p. 15, CSC Archives.

11. Letter from Elinor O'Connor to Sister Ste. Helene Guthrie, September 1, 1931; Letter from Sister Ste. Helene Guthrie to Elinor O'Connor, September 4, 1931, Box 827, File 32, CSC Archives.

12. Letter from Joseph O'Connor to Sister Ste. Helene Guthrie, September 27, 1931, File 32, Box 827, CSC Archives.

13. College of St. Catherine *Catalogue* 1935, Student Roll, Seniors, p. 131. CSC Archives.

14. Elizabeth Gallagher, Student Work Contract, File 32, Box 827, CSC Archives.

15. Letter from Mr. And Mrs. E. J. Gallagher to Sister Ste. Helene Guthrie, December 22, 1933, File 32, Box 827, CSC Archives.

16. Student Work Contracts, File 32, Box 827, CSC Archives.

17. Helen Wenzel, Dorothy Elm, Theresa Giulani, and Emma Suomi, Student Work Contracts, File 32, Box 827, CSC Archives.

18. Helen McMonnon Student Service Contract, May 1936, File 32, Box 827, CSC Archives.

19. Report of the Dean, *Administrative Reports,* College of St. Catherine, 1935, p. 27, CSC Archives.

20. Report of the Dean, *Administrative Reports,* College of St. Catherine, 1939, p. 101, CSC Archives. For more information on the National Youth Administration program to fund student employment for needy young people, see FDR, *The Public Papers and Addresses of Franklin D. Roosevelt* (New York: Random House, 1938), p. 285-286.

21. Letter of Lorna Teas to Sister Eucharista Galvin, File 32, Box 827, CSC Archives. This particular story did not have a happy ending. The student did some work on campus, but Sister Eucharista wrote a letter in May asking for $25.00 in cash to pay the balance in full, and sent a follow-up letter in July. The student's mother wrote a reply in August 1938, noting that her daughter ". . . died May 27 . . . she had not received your last letter. . . . We feel that our girl certainly would have settled this debt had she lived. She proved that she was the type of girl not to

forget her debts, when she worked her way through St. Catherine's for her room and board during her freshman year.

Then last September she returned to your institution and attempted to balance the tuition debt by working almost day and night for several weeks only to have her health fail her in doing so."

22. Letter from Sister Eucharista to Mary Schiltz Gleason, in Sister Ste. Helene Guthrie file, Box 2000.141 E2 Correspondence with Students, Sisters of St. Joseph of Carondelet (CSJ) Archives, College of St. Catherine.

23. Mention of this rebate is first found in the 1938 College of St. Catherine Catalogue (p. 90); the 1942 Catalogue lists a 30 percent rebate (p. 79); the 1948 Catalogue lists 20 percent (p. 10), and 1949 lists 10 percent (p.11); this is also listed in the 1953 catalogue (p.8). In the President's report for the year 1954-55, Sister Antonine stated: "We have also cancelled the automatic discount which for more than thirty years has been enjoyed by graduates of our own high schools whether they needed such assistance or not." Report of the President, *Administrative Reports*, College of St. Catherine, 1954-55, p. 225, CSC Archives.

24. Report of the Dean, *Administrative Reports*, College of St. Catherine, 1942, p. 153, CSC Archives.

25. According to figures in the College Catalogues, enrollment for 1940-41 was 642; for 1941-42 it was 626; for 1942-43 it was 556; for 1943-44 it was 579, plus 196 nursing students; for 1944-45 it was 654 plus 302 nursing students.

26. Report of the President, *Administrative Reports*, College of St. Catherine, 1942-43, pp. 239-240, CSC Archives.

27. Report of the Dean, *Administrative Reports*, College of St. Catherine, 1943, p. 258, CSC Archives.

28. Sister Ann Thomasine Sampson, CSJ, *Care With Prayer: A History of St. Mary's Hospital* (Minneapolis: St. Mary's Hospital, 1987), pp. 48-50.

29. The separation between the nursing students and the others can be seen by the fact that the nursing students were listed separately from the others in the catalogues. CSC *Catalogue*, 1943-44, p. 106; CSC *Catalogue*, 1944-45, p. 108, CSC Archives.

30. Report of the President [Sister Antonius], *Administrative Reports*, College of St. Catherine, 1944-45, p. 107, CSC Archives.

31. Interview with Sr. Catherine Litecky, March 9, 2008.

32. Interview with Rosemary Balk Lovett, March 12, 2008.

33. Report of the Dean [Sister Cecilia], *Administrative Reports*, College of St. Catherine, 1954-55, p. 258, CSC Archives.

34. Report of the Dean of Women [Sister Mary Edward], *Administrative Reports*, College of St. Catherine, 1955-56, p. 161, CSC Archives.

35. Report of the Dean of Students [Sister Mary Edward], *Administrative Reports*, College of St. Catherine, 1956-57, p. 220, CSC Archives.

36. Report of the Dean of Students [Sister Mary Edward], *Administrative Reports*, College of St. Catherine, 1957-58, p. 351, CSC Archives.

37. Report of the President [Sister Mary William], *Administrative Reports*, College of St. Catherine, 1959-60, p. 201, CSC Archives.

38. Report of the Dean of Students, for 1960-61, 235 students; for 1961-62, 247 students; for 1962-63, 255 students; for 1963-64, 266 students; *Administrative Reports*, CSC Archives.

39. College of St. Catherine *Handbook*, 1960. Box 363, file 6, CSC Archives.

40. College of St. Catherine *Handbook*, 1970. Box 363, file 6, CSC Archives.

41. Report of the President [Sister Mary Edward], *Administrative Reports*, College of St. Catherine, 1961-62, p. 14, CSC Archives.

42. Report of the Director of Admissions, *Administrative Reports*, College of St. Catherine, 1963-64, pp. 216-17, CSC Archives.

43. Report of the Director of Admissions, *Administrative Reports*, College of St. Catherine, 1964-65, p. 466, CSC Archives.

44. Report of the President [Sister Alberta Huber], *Administrative Reports*, College of St. Catherine, 1969-70, p. 8, CSC Archives.

45. Report of the Dean, *Administrative Reports*, College of St. Catherine, 1969-70, p. 115, CSC Archives.

46. Interview with Sister Anne Elise Tschida, CSJ, December 15, 2004.

47. *Ibid.*

48. *Ibid.*

49. Interview with Trudy Schoolmeesters Landgren, 2005. A list of work study recipients for the first semester 1970-71, lists 50 students and jobs ranging from kitchen to Spanish department, to Multilith to receptionist—salaries ranged from $90.00 to $255. Trudy Schoolmeesters earned $130.00.

50. *Ibid.*

51. Rosalie Ryan, CSJ and John Christine Wolkerstorfer, CSJ, p.118.

9

Possumus:[1] Sisters' Education in Feminism

Mary Alice Muellerleile and Joan Mitchell, CSJ

The Sisters of St. Joseph who taught at the College during the second-wave feminist movement were a pivotal generation. While impressive academic achievements characterized St. Catherine's Sister faculty long before the second wave, the movement created a new ethos by focusing on justice for all people and on newly emerging opportunities for women. Both context and consciousness changed.

The story of the education of St. Catherine's Sister faculty during the 1920s is well-known at the University today, in the context of Sister Antonia McHugh's foresighted and ambitious plan: "[to] offer Sisters the opportunity for a wide cultural background and professional education at outstanding American and European centers of learning." (See Carroll in this volume.) That commitment continued to direct the education of the Sister faculty well into the 1970s, the peak of the second-wave feminist movement. While in many ways the educational mission and lives of the Sisters of St. Joseph had always been implicitly feminist, the social ferment of the 1960s and 1970s required the Sisters and their College to be more explicit in defining themselves as women in American society.

To explore the educational experiences of that later generation of Sister faculty, we conducted retrospective interviews with those we could locate 30 years later. In reviewing St. Catherine catalogues from the era, we found that the 1974–1976 catalogue had the most extensive list of Sister faculty, with 54. Based on data provided by the University archivist, Sister Margery Smith, and interviews with Sister faculty listed in that catalogue, this essay tells the story not only of the education Sister faculty received in their graduate school disciplines, but also their education in feminism.

The advanced education of Sisters on the faculty in 1974–1976 was remarkable in comparison to national statistics for both women and men on the faculties of colleges and universities at that time. The percentage of Sister faculty with Ph.D.s far surpassed national percentages of faculty with Ph.D.s. In 1974–1976, 32 of the 54 Sister faculty, 59.3 percent, had Ph.D.s. At that time, only one third of all higher education faculty members nationally had earned a Ph.D. and women were "half as likely as men to hold a doctorate."[2] Even at research universities, less than half of the faculty had Ph.D.s.[3] Four-year colleges had even lower percentages of Ph.D.s. A 1972–1973 report indicated that 31.4 percent of all faculty at four year colleges in the United States had Ph.D.s, including 34.2 percent of men and 21.5 percent of women faculty.[4] Yet at St. Catherine's, a small, Catholic college for women, well over half the Sister faculty had Ph.D.s.

Of the Sister faculty with Ph.D.s, 25 of the 32 were educated at non-Catholic universities (University of California, University of Chicago, Columbia, Laval, MIT, Munich, Oxford, University of Cincinnati, University of Minnesota, and University of Nebraska); seven earned their Ph.D.s at Catholic universities (Catholic University, Loyola, Marquette, and University of Notre Dame). The disciplines studied by the doctoral Sister students included biology, chemistry, education, English, French, German, history, math, music, philosophy, and theology.

The majority of the Sisters who did not pursue doctoral work earned terminal degrees, the highest degree available, in professional studies or fine arts disciplines (art, business, home economics, library science, music, and occupational therapy). Seventeen of these students earned their degrees at non-Catholic institutions (California College of Arts and Crafts, Columbia University, University of Chicago, Cincinnati Conservatory, Ohio State University, Rochester Institute of Technology, University of Hawaii, and University of Minnesota).

Of the 54 Sister faculty named in the 1974–1976 catalogue, 28 were alive in 2004, and we were able to arrange interviews with 20. Between September 2004 and February 2005, we conducted semi-structured retrospective interviews, focusing on both formal graduate education and informal education in feminism. Our agreement with those we interviewed was that we would identify them as participants[5] but keep their individual stories anonymous. Our emphasis is on themes we could identify across the 20 interviews.

The majority of the women interviewed for this essay were the first generation in their families to attend college. Most were from the middle or upper class, and all but two had attended high schools sponsored by the Sisters of St. Joseph and/or the College of St. Catherine. All 20 seemed to be of European American heritage.[6] Their families on the whole expected that they would go to college, but the majority stated that their fathers, rather than their mothers, exerted the most influence on their intellectual aspirations.

The mothers acknowledged to be most influential were women who had degrees, wanted a degree, and/or were interested in knowing what their daughters were learning.

Surprisingly for women religious in that era, the majority of those interviewed stated that they had had a choice of the graduate institution to attend. The reasons they gave for their choices varied. Some were chosen because of the graduate faculty's and/or the graduate institution's reputation. As one interviewee said, "It was, according to national rankings, the best school in my field." Other motivations were less academic and more personal: "I wanted to be close to my family." "It was the institution in which I could get my degree the fastest." "My father spoke of the institution all the time even though he had no college degree."

The reasons why some of the Sister faculty were given no choice or had their choice influenced by the Sisters' leadership also varied. Some were sent to Notre Dame because of a request for Sister students from the University; one went to Catholic University because the congregation had a house of studies for Sisters of St. Joseph students in Washington, D.C. Some were asked to enroll in an institution that offered a major for which the College needed faculty. One was sent to an institution where an alumna chaired the department in which the Sister enrolled. Another was sent to an institution where a Nobel Prize winner taught. The choice for two of the Sisters was influenced by the fact that one of them was under final vows, so both had to be at a university in a city that had a Sisters of St. Joseph convent.

Up until the establishment of the juniorate,[7] the Sisters missioned to teach at the College were generally those women who had attended or graduated from there. Those women, for the most part, did their graduate work in their baccalaureate major. Among our interviewees, there was one exception to this trend. One of the College's departments had lost Sister faculty because of health problems. Our interviewee was chosen to teach in that field because the Sisters discovered her artistic talent when they saw her carving soap instead of darning socks during prayer.

The juniorate gave young women who entered the congregation directly from high school the opportunity to earn a baccalaureate degree while in Sister formation, giving the College a new pool for selecting Sister faculty. In several cases, the juniorate candidate selected for graduate education had not earned her baccalaureate degree in one of the needed fields. To remedy this situation, these candidates were tutored in the summers by College faculty or Sisters who taught in the congregation's high schools. Much of this tutoring prepared the juniorate candidates for their language exams, but in two cases it actually changed the Sister's field of study. One was sent initially to a Catholic university to prepare her for doctoral work; the other went immediately, after one summer of tutoring in her newly assigned field, to one of the most rigorous institutions in the country.

Most of the Sisters interviewed had been taught by earlier generations of the College's Sister faculty during their own college years. When asked which teachers or classes at St. Catherine's opened the intellectual life to them, they named 23 Sister faculty. Some of these faculty were named because of their scholarship and teaching as well as their ability to broaden their subject matter by introducing other disciplines. Music and art, for example, were taught in English courses, and science was introduced to explain scriptural miracles. Besides stating their appreciation for being educated by liberally educated women, our interviewees noted other admirable traits. One Sister was mentioned for her pursuit of truth: "she was the first to teach me that I could use my mind to understand my faith." Another was praised because "she had her two feet solidly on ground." And several were named because they were "so much fun."

To a woman, those interviewed for this article acknowledged that the graduate experience, as one Sister put it, "made all the difference in our personal and professional lives." The effect that graduate education had on their professional lives was described consistently: "it trained me to do high level academic work"; it prepared me to do a better job of teaching"; "it broadened my knowledge and understanding of my field"; "it gave me

Women presidents: Gathering of presidents who served the College between 1937 and 1979, all Sisters of St. Joseph of Carondelet. Seated: Sisters Eucharista Galvin, Catherine McNamee, and Antonine O'Brien. Standing: Sisters Antonius Kennelly, Mary William Brady, Mary Edward Healy, and Alberta Huber. Photo courtesy of St. Catherine University.

the depth I needed for teaching"; "it got me terribly interested in my field." Almost every interviewee acknowledged that the graduate experience also gave her confidence in her abilities.

Many of the interviewees described their graduate experience as exhilarating. It opened the doors of the cloister for them to people (scholars, friends, professional colleagues), resources (the riches of European libraries, travel), and ideas. As one interviewee described the experience, "It was pure bright air, intoxicating, like a trip to Switzerland, a glass of champagne. I was eaten up by it. I could not get enough of it." A peak experience for several of our interviewees was the opportunity to do their dissertation research abroad. Federal and foundation grants (Fulbrights, National Science Foundation, Danforth Foundation) funded such travels.

While the graduate school experience brought depth to the Sister students' academic preparations, it also broadened them by challenging their views of the world. As one interviewee put it, "My graduate school experience changed my ghetto thinking about the world." Exposure to non-U.S. views of the Vietnam War, the story of women's struggles to become educated, Vatican II's questioning about the Church's structure and practices, the civil rights movement, to name but a few issues, forced many of these women to use the intellectual skills they were learning in class to interpret the world outside of those classes. As one interviewee put it, "I began to see that there are often different, legitimate interpretations of ethical issues." Another of the interviewees' intellectual convictions went further, leading to her being jailed for personal involvement in a civil rights protest.

The graduate experience was not all positive. It could be extremely stressful because of the academic rigor demanded. Even for those who lived in convents, it could also be very lonesome. At times the Sisters who offered hospitality were more pious and less open than the home congregation. Others of the Sister students, especially those in residences for graduate student Sisters, found a wonderful and supportive community. This was fortunate for one Sister because most of her classmates were seminarians and she was not permitted to speak to them.

Most of the institutions where the Sisters studied did not discriminate against women religious, but there were exceptions. Some instructors despised Catholics; some openly questioned whether a nun would know anything about a topic such as rape; and one faculty member advised a Sister to leave the convent if she wanted to be successful in her field. On the whole, however, most instructors and classmates displayed little or no prejudice against women religious. In fact, many instructors and classmates were sincerely interested in them and their lives. Such interest on occasion sparked profound discussions about Christianity and Catholicism. One interviewee said perfect strangers approached her on campus to offer condolences at the deaths of Pope John XXIII and President John F. Kennedy. The chair of one department joked that his public institution should become a seminary because the Sisters studying in his department were his best students. A professor at another public institution often prefaced his questions with the statement, "Sister will know."

Although demonstrated religious prejudice was almost nonexistent, the Sisters did not escape gender prejudice. Advisors rejected dissertation topics focusing on women with statements such as, "there is nothing to study there." In a course where one interviewee was the only woman, the professor constantly addressed the class as "Men." One interviewee was one of three women in a program of 250. Although she knew she was a feminist, she did not let her instructors or classmates know.

Most of the Sister faculty teaching at the College in the mid-1970s had completed their coursework prior to the second-wave women's movement. Their feminist commitment started at St. Catherine's during their education there and continued through their teaching of other women when they returned from graduate school. Long before the women's movement, many Sister faculty were teaching women that they could do anything. They were encouraging women studying such fields as education and science not to settle for the traditional roles women usually assumed in those fields. They were mentoring women to stand up for their rights. They were attempting to raise their students' aspirations and help them gain a truer sense of themselves.

One interviewee stated that teaching women at St. Catherine's made her aware that she was a feminist and made her determined to remove the obstacles women faced. For others, it was the women's movement that brought their feminist commitment to consciousness. As one interviewee stated, "I came to realize I was no longer teaching girls, but was teaching women." Another traced her feminist commitment to seeing the salary differential between men and women.

The Sister faculty, for the most part, were primed for the women's movement. Many of its goals were already embraced by the St. Catherine's faculty, so many of the changes the movement recommended were adopted. As the second-wave movement emerged, topics for papers focused increasingly on women and their issues; courses studying women's experience were created; the canons of disciplines were changed to be more inclusive and were read from different perspectives.

For some of the Sister faculty, a commitment to feminism was dictated by their overall commitment to justice. As one interviewee stated, "I learned to treat each student as an individual, no matter what their gender. I came to think that such treatment did not come from a feminist perspective as much as coming from a commitment to justice and fairness." Another stated that she became a feminist from being a reader and from being touched by women who got things done.

Whatever the source of their feminist commitment, the Sister faculty felt strongly that they had to help students to achieve their very best. As one interviewee put it, "We were standing on the shoulders of giants. Others had opened doors for us, so we had to open doors for [our students]." When asked to name former students whom they had influenced, the interviewees mentioned doctors, lawyers, judges, women with doctorates, teachers, emergency workers, peace corps workers, even men whom they made "fit for marriage."[8] One of the interviewees was recognized by her field's professional organization for encouraging women in her field; approximately 20 of her former students have doctorates.

From the College's beginning, Sister faculty dedicated themselves to opening doors for their women students. College leaders also expected Sisters to become highly educated. Indeed, the high percentage of Sister faculty with a Ph.D. in the 1970s was a result of continuity with earlier eras, of commitments made before the second-wave women's movement. But as these Sister faculty members from the 1970s looked back on their experiences, many pointed out that something different was happening during the second-wave women's movement. Influenced by Vatican II and by civil rights, feminist, and other social justice movements, Sisters at the College changed their work and in the process changed themselves. They recognized stereotypes, challenged gendered economic inequality, and came to view their own challenges in solidarity with those of other women. Sister faculty members' consciousness changed as they taught women students and as they applied the knowledge they gained in their Ph.D. programs. But the Sisters' education in feminism did not become institutional data. As is often the case with movement history, the story could have slipped out of sight. These interviews help later generations to recognize both feminism and formal education in the lives of Sister faculty. While a changed consciousness could not be precisely measured in the same way as an earned doctorate, its influence was nonetheless profound.

NOTES

1. The Sisters of St. Joseph of Carondelet, St. Paul Province, took this Latin term from St. Paul's letters, using the plural form to mean "We can do all things in [God] who strengthens us."

2. Lilli S. Hornig, "Untenured and Tenuous: The Status of Women Faculty," *Annals of the American Academy of Political and Social Science* 448, p. 119.

3. *Ibid.*

4. W. Vance Grant and C. George Lind, *Digest of Education Statistics* (DHEW) (Washington, D.C., 1978), p. 96.

5. Names and positions of College of St. Catherine Sister faculty, as listed in the 1974–76 catalogue, who participated in the interviews:

Sister Mary William Brady, Professor of English. B.A., College of St Catherine; M.A., University of Minnesota; Ph.D., University of Chicago.

Sister Vera Chester, Associate Professor of Theology. B.A., College of St. Catherine; M.A., Ph.D., Marquette University.

Sister Helen Coughlan, Associate Professor of English. B.A., College of St. Catherine; M.A., University of Notre Dame; Ph.D., University of Minnesota..

Sister Jean Dummer, Assistant Professor of Education. B.A., College of St. Catherine; M.A., Catholic University of America; Ph.D., University of Nebraska.

Sister Mary Ann Hanley, Associate Professor of Music. B.A., College of St. Catherine; M.Mus., D.M.A., University of Cincinnati.

Sister Alberta Huber, President. B.A., College of St. Catherine; M.A., University of Minnesota; Ph.D., University of Notre Dame.

Sister Karen Kennelly, Academic Dean. B.A., College of St. Catherine; M.A., Catholic University of America; Ph.D., University of California, Berkeley.

Sister Eleanor Lincoln, Professor of English. B.A., College of St. Catherine; M.A., Ph.D., University of Minnesota.

Sister Catherine Litecky, Associate Professor of Theology. B.A., College of St. Catherine; M.S., University of Minnesota; M.A., St. John's University.

Sister Mary O'Hara, Professor of Philosophy. B.A., College of St. Catherine; M.A., Ph.D., Catholic University of America.

Sister Anita Pampusch, Assistant Professor of Philosophy. B.A., College of St. Catherine; M.A., Ph.D., University of Notre Dame.

Sister Annabelle Raiche, Associate Professor of English. B.A., College of St. Catherine; M.Ed., Boston College; Ph.D., University of Minnesota.

Sister Magdalen Schimanski, Professor of Art. B.A., College of St. Catherine; M.F.A., Catholic University of America.

Sister Angela Schreiber, Assistant Professor of Education. B.A., College of St. Catherine; M.A., Ohio State University.

Sister Margery Smith, Assistant Professor of English. B.A., College of St. Catherine; M.A., Marquette University; M.A., Ph.D., University of Chicago.

Sister Carol Ann Tauer, Associate Professor of Mathematics. B.A., College of St. Catherine; M.A., University of Minnesota; Ph.D., Massachusetts Institute of Technology.

Sister Mary Thompson, Associate Professor of Chemistry. B.A., College of St. Catherine; M.S., University of Minnesota; Ph.D., University of California, Berkeley.

Sister Maria Wilson, Assistant Professor of Art. B.A., College of St. Catherine; B.F.A., Art Institute of Chicago; M.S.T., Rochester Institute of Technology.

Sister Esperance Wittry, Professor of Biology. B.A., College of St. Catherine; M.A., Ph.D., University of Notre Dame.

Sister John Christine Wolkerstorfer, Assistant Professor of History. B.A., College of St. Catherine; M.A., Ph.D., University of Minnesota.

6. In Minnesota as in other U.S. states, people's heritages sometimes are more multicultural than they know.

7. The juniorate was "a period of several years for young sisters who have made first, temporary profession of vows. While continuing their spiritual formation be-

gun in the novitiate, they attend[ed] college or other training institutions to prepare for professional certification in the fields in which they [would] be serving." Margery H. Smith, CSJ, College of St. Catherine Archivist and Professor Emerita, e-mail message, June 23, 2008. The Sisters of St. Joseph juniorate existed for thirteen years, between 1955 and 1968.

8. Because of cooperative arrangements with the College of St. Thomas and other private colleges in the Twin Cities, men occasionally attended classes at the College of St. Catherine.

Postscript: Questions for the Twenty-First Century

Sharon Doherty, Joanne Cavallaro, and Jane Lamm Carroll

St. Catherine University Gate, 2010. Photo courtesy of St. Catherine University.

As we were completing this book, one of the editors had a conversation with an undergraduate student leader at the University. A progressive activist, the student was upset about a recent conflict with the administration. They want us to lead and influence, she said, but when it comes to the University itself, they resist it. Why don't they take a stand, she asked, on such issues as reproductive and GLBTQ rights? If St. Catherine's shows reluctance to confront the Catholic hierarchy on these matters, according to this student, then that reluctance represents a contradiction in its stated goal of promoting women's leadership. The University shouldn't recruit students with vastly different ideologies and expectations into such an ambiguous environment, she said; everybody ends up disappointed, because they are not fully supported by the institution. A conversation ensued about the founding of Catholic colleges for women in the United States: how over a century ago the institutions emerged from an uneasy alliance within the Catholic hierarchy, an alliance of conservatives who wanted to guard their women from the forces of secular society and progressives who wanted to open new opportunities to Catholic women. The tension is not new.

People who care about the University—from students and their families to donors, alumnae, staff, faculty, and community members—continue to disagree about its purposes and about what should be going on here. The tensions and their lack of resolution can be viewed as both positive and negative for the University's educational mission. While polarizing conflicts over the years have sometimes seemed like emergencies, the University has managed to thrive in the midst of ambiguities and to live with a coherent identity in the midst of paradoxes. On the one hand, this approach can be interpreted as playing it safe, as lacking the courage to challenge power structures that should be challenged. On the other hand, ambiguity has been vital to sustaining St. Catherine's.

While our book focuses on the College's history and not on recent decades, we find ourselves thinking about the Sisters' cultural heritage in the context of St. Catherine's today. Since the liberatory movements of the late twentieth century, dramatic changes in U.S. society are still being negotiated at St. Catherine's and in the wider society. Have those movements—particularly Vatican II, the civil rights movement, and the second- and third-wave women's movements—created such vast change that the strategies of the past are no longer workable? Or are current tensions best understood as the newest stage of a seamless history?

The tensions inherent in both challenging and compromising with traditional views of women's proper role have changed in the century since the College was founded—as has the traditional definition of what women's proper role should be. Today, of course, many women have more opportunities than did their foremothers. In campus discussions of whether to remain a women's college during the 1970s, one faculty member argued that, given the new opportunities available to women, the only justification for remaining a single-sex institution was to "challenge social stereotypes of women."[1] St. Catherine's challenged the current social stereotypes of women at its founding; it did so in demanding a curriculum equal to that given to men; it did so in teaching women skills for professional careers even as it taught them to be "ladies"; it did so in infusing scholarship around women's issues into its curriculum; it did so in expecting that students use their learning to make the world a more just place. St. Catherine's continues to do so today, even as it also continues to seek compromise with those stereotypes. But as stereotypes have changed, so has the nature of the compromises inherent in the University's mission.

Questions and tensions that arose at the College in the 1970s have yet to be resolved, specifically those around diverse elements of women's identities: Who is the dear neighbor, and who is a St. Catherine student? While St. Catherine's has educated women from oppressed groups since its founding, movements in the 1960s changed expectations, knowledge, and strategies. Liberation became an explicit goal in education. National movements engaged in antiracism and the opening of colleges to working-class students revealed and challenged the traditional power dynamics involved in teaching and learning. Assimilationist strategies were no longer accepted by many members of oppressed groups. Students from marginalized communities wanted voice and power, not just to be helped. The distinction between charity and justice became an issue within the College, as well as in community work beyond its gates.

Another contentious element of women's identity at St. Catherine's is sexuality; it is women's sexual freedom that lies at the heart of much of the tension within the University today. The University still exists as part of a Church that seeks to define "proper" sexuality for students, who increasingly define it differently. More and more, tensions over the proper role for women students center around women's sexuality. Issues of homosexuality, abortion, birth control, and premarital sex are sources of conflict both within the University and between individuals and the Church. Challenges to traditional Church teaching around women's sexuality continue to erupt and to be analyzed within liberal arts courses that form the heart of the University's curriculum.

Are current tensions about sexuality and reproduction comparable to the disagreements 100 years ago about women's intellectual capacity and their proper roles in public and private life? We are not certain. Regardless of the answer to that question, feminist analysis helps us to understand that issues inciting controversy do not define the institution. In a democratic society, the mission of a Catholic institution dedicated to women's education requires engagement with *all* ideas, controversial or not. In fact, the Catholic intellectual tradition demands scrutiny of a broad range of concepts and arguments.

These essays about the College's history have convinced us that the cultural heritage of its sponsors has been a powerful, sustaining force.[2] Since their origins in France more than 350 years ago, the Sisters of St. Joseph of Carondelet, St. Paul Province, have developed intellectual, practical, and relational traditions that continue to shape St. Catherine's, even though few Sisters of St. Joseph remain on the faculty and staff today. As Knoerle and Schier argue, "the legacy of the nuns has within it both staying power and catalysis that can build . . . a vibrant culture" in new contexts.[3]

Central to the Sisters of St. Joseph's legacy is a communitarian ethos. The Sisters' actions over the centuries have involved relationships with, and active concern for, others. Living in community with the purpose of helping the wider society set the tone and context for the Sisters' approach to higher education. St. Catherine University remains a liberating sanctuary, a cultural location that fosters leadership and autonomy within community. *Liberating sanctuary* is both an idea that holds a contradiction within itself and a context in which people are able to live with multiple paradoxes and tensions.

Because of the Sisters' approach to community life, their dedication to women's education, and their spiritual commitment to the dear neighbor, the University has been able to embrace contradictory points and yet remain whole. Today St. Catherine's community can be nurturing as well as infuriatingly restrictive. Students, faculty, and staff find themselves delighted with the community's support and confused or angered by its constraints. In an engaged community, people expect to love and care for each other, even in the face of conflicting doctrines.

The commitment to women's education is as long-standing as the Sisters themselves. As we note in the introduction to this volume, when the Sisters of St. Joseph established their congregation in 1650, one pledge in their constitution was to educate girls wherever they were not being educated. Making and keeping that pledge revealed the congregation's willingness to challenge prevailing ideas from the beginning.

Including but not limited to the realm of education, the Sisters of St. Joseph have made particular efforts to ease the suffering of oppressed populations of women and men. To do their work with the dear neighbor, the seventeenth-century Sisters of St. Joseph needed to be with the people, beyond the cloister; this placed them in conflict with expectations—and rules—for women religious of their era. The Sisters of St. Joseph originally were a secret association, because "at that time the church gave approval only to cloistered communities of women religious."[4] Since conflict over women's role in society was central to the congregation's origins, the Sisters gained some hard-won experience that would be directly applicable to conflicts arising in later eras, including the twenty-first century.

In this twenty-first century, the stakes for women's education continue to be high. Consider a few statistics: In the world today, almost 510 million women do not know how to read or write.[5] More than 1.4 billion people live on less than $1.25 a day.[6] On the other end of the power structure, only 3 percent of Fortune 500 chief executive officers are women.[7] In the United States Congress, 17 percent of senators and 16.6 percent of representatives are women; no senator is a woman of color.[8] In this context, we continue to see the promise of education in a community shaped by the Sisters of St. Joseph, with a commitment to women, a focus on justice for the dear neighbor, and a relentless desire to embrace and learn from contradictions.

Graduate at commencement with her child, circa 1990. Photo courtesy of St. Catherine University.

NOTES

1. Alan Graebner, "Position Paper," CSC Faculty Meeting, September 30, 1976, CSC Archives.

2. For an insightful discussion of heritage among Catholic women's colleges as a group, see Monika K. Hellwig, "Colleges of Religious Women's Congregations: The Spiritual Heritage," in Tracy Schier and Cynthia Russett, eds., *Catholic Women's Colleges in America* (Baltimore: Johns Hopkins University Press, 2002), pp. 17-24.

3. Jeanne Knoerle and Tracy Schier, "Conclusion: Into the Future," in Schier and Russett, *Catholic Women's Colleges in America*, p. 340.

4. Sisters of St. Joseph of Carondelet, St. Paul Province, *Eyes Open on a World: The Challenges of Change* (St. Cloud, Minnesota: North Star Press, 2001), p. 6.

5. United Nations Educational, Scientific, and Cultural Organization, "Literacy." *http://www.unesco.org/en/literacy*. June 19, 2010.

6. United Nations, "The Millennium Development Goals Report, 2009," p. 4. *http://www.mdgs.un.org/unsd/mdg/Resources*. June 19, 2010.

7. Cable News Network, "2010 Fortune 500: Women CEOs." *http://money.cnn.com/magazines/fortune/fortune500/2010/womenceos*. June 19, 2010.

8. Center for American Women and Politics, Rutgers University. *www.cawp.rutgers.edu/fast_facts/levels_of_office/Congress-Current.php*. March 3, 2011.

Selected Bibliography

Baym, Nina. *Novels, Readers and Reviewers: Responses to Fiction in Antebellum America.* Ithaca, New York: Cornell University Press, 1984.

Bokenkotter, Thomas. *A Concise History of the Catholic Church.* Garden City, New York: Doubleday and Co., 1977.

Bonnett, Jeanne Marie, CSJ. "Problems of a Differentiated Curriculum for Women." *Catholic Education Review* (May 1932): 273-281; (June 1932): 359-366.

——. "The Education of Christian Character." *Catholic Education Review* (June 1933): 345-357.

——. "The Religious Development of Women at the College of St. Catherine." *Journal of Religious Instruction* (June 1933): 868-885.

——. "General Report of the College of St. Catherine to the Phi Beta Kappa Committee on Qualifications." Unpublished Manuscript, St. Catherine University Archives, 1935.

Buzicky, Charles. "Mother Antonia's Impossible Dream: The College of St. Catherine." *Scan* (Fall 1973): 5-12.

Carnegie Commission on Higher Education. The *Open Door Colleges: Policies for Community Colleges.* New York: McGraw Hill, 1970.

Carroll, Jane Lamm. *Taking Women Seriously for 100 Years.* St. Paul, Minnesota: College of St. Catherine, 2005.

——. "The College of St. Catherine: Taking Women Seriously for 100 Years." Unpublished Manuscript, St. Catherine University Archives, 2005.

Chase, Mary Ellen. *A Goodly Fellowship.* New York: MacMillan and Co., 1940.

Coburn, Carol K., and Martha Smith. *Spirited Lives: How Nuns Shaped Catholic Culture and American Life, 1836-1920.* Chapel Hill, North Carolina: University of North Carolina Press, 1999.

Collins, Patricia Hill. *Black Feminist Thought: Knowledge, Consciousness, and the Politics of Empowerment.* Second Edition. New York: Routledge, 2000.

Conway, Jill Ker. *A Woman's Education.* New York: Borzoi Books, 2001.

Curran, Charles E. *Catholic Social Teaching: A Historical, Theological, and Ethical Analysis*. Washington, D.C.: Georgetown University Press, 2002.

DeBerri, Edward P., and James E. Hug. *Catholic Social Teaching: Our Best Kept Secret*. Washington, D.C.: Centers of Concern, 2003.

Evans, Sara. *Personal Politics: The Roots of the Women's Liberation Movement in the Civil Rights and New Left*. New York: Vintage, 1980.

Evans, Sara, and Harry C. Boyte. *Free Spaces: The Sources of Democratic Change in America*. New York: Harper and Row, 1986.

Flannery, Austin P., editor. *Documents of Vatican II*. Grand Rapids, Michigan: Eerdman Publishing Co., 1975.

Folwell, William Watts. *A History of Minnesota.*Volume IV. St. Paul, Minnesota: Minnesota Historical Society, 1926.

Geiger, Susan. "Women's Life Histories: Method and Content." *Signs, Journal of Women and Culture in Society* 11 (2) (1986): 334-351.

———. "What's So Feminist About Women's Oral History?" *Journal of Women's History* 2 (1) (1990): 169-182.

Gere, Anne Ruggles. *Intimate Practices: Literacy and Cultural Work in U.S. Women's Clubs, 1880-1920*. Urbana, Illinios: University of Illinois Press, 1997.

Hesse-Biber, S. N., and M. L. Yaiser, eds. *Feminist Perspectives on Social Research*. New York: Oxford University Press, 2004.

Horowitz, Helen L. *Campus Life: Undergraduate Cultures from the End of the 18th Century to the Present*. New York: Knopf, 1987.

Hurley, Angela, CSJ. *On Good Ground: The Sisters of St. Joseph of Carondelet*. Minneapolis, Minnesota: University of Minnesota Press, 1957.

Ireland, Reverend John. *The Church and Modern Society*. St. Paul, Minnesota: The Pioneer Press, 1904.

Kennelly, Karen, CSJ. "The Dynamic Sister Antonia and the College of St. Catherine." *Ramsey County History* (Fall/Winter 1978), 3-18.

———. "An Immigrant Drama: The College of St. Catherine and Phi Beta Kappa." *U.S. Catholic Historian* 28 (3) (Summer 2010): 43-63.

Lonergan, Bernard, SJ. *Method in Theology*. New York: Seabury, 1972.

Lorde, Audre. *Sister Outsider: Essays and Speeches*. Trumansburg: Crossing Press, 1984.

Massero, Thomas, SJ, and Thomas Shannon, eds. *American Catholic Social Teaching*. Collegeville, Minnesota: The Liturgical Press, 2002.

Mich, Marvin L. *Catholic Social Teaching and Movements*. Mystic, Connecticut: Twenty-third Publications, 1998.

National Council of Catholic Bishops. *Economic Justice For All: Pastoral Letter on Catholic Social Teaching*. Washington, D.C.: U.S. Catholic Conference, 1986.

Newcomer, M. *A Century of Higher Education for American Women*. New York: Harper and Brothers, 1959.

Norton, Mary Beth, and Ruth Alexander, eds. *Major Problems in American Women's History*. Third Edition. New York: Houghton Mifflin, 2003.

Peck, Helen Margaret, CSJ. "The Growth and Expansion of the College of St. Catherine to the End of the Presidency of Mother Antonia McHugh." Unpublished Manuscript, St. Catherine University Archives, 1982.

———. "An Academic History of the College of St. Catherine." Unpublished Manuscript, St. Catherine University Archives, 1982.

Ruether, Rosemary, and Eleanor McLaughlin. *Women of Spirit: Female Leadership in the Jewish and Christian Traditions.* New York: Simon and Schuster, 1979.

Ryan, Rosalie, CSJ, and John Christine Wolkerstorfer, CSJ. *More Than a Dream: 85 Years at the College of St. Catherine.* St. Paul, Minnesota: College of St. Catherine, 1992.

Sampson, Ann Thomasine, CSJ. *Care With a Prayer.* Minneapolis, Minnesota: St. Mary's Hospital, 1987.

———. *Seeds on Good Ground.* St. Paul, Minnesota: Sisters of St. Joseph of Carondelet, St. Paul Province, 2000.

Schier, Tracy, and Cynthia Russett, eds. *Catholic Women's Colleges in America.* Baltimore: John Hopkins University Press, 2002.

Sisters of St. Joseph of Carondelet, St. Louis Province. *The Sisters of St. Joseph of Carondelet.* St. Louis, Missouri: B. Herder Book Company, 1966.

Sisters of St. Joseph of Carondelet, St. Paul Province. *Eyes Open on a World.* St. Cloud, Minnesota: North Star Press, 2001.

Sisters of the Immaculate Heart of Mary. *Building Sisterhood: A Feminist History of the Sisters, Servants of the Immaculate Heart of Mary.* Detroit, Michigan: Sisters of the Immaculate Heart of Mary, 1997.

Tidball, M. Elizabeth, Daryl Smith, Charles Tidball, and Lisa Wolf-Wendel, eds. *Taking Women Seriously: Lessons and Legacies for Educating the Majority.* Phoenix: American Council on Education and the Oryx Press, 1999.

Toomey, Teresa, CSJ. "The Best and Highest of Its Kind." *Scan* (Spring, 1958): 10-20.

Tracy, David. *The Analogical Imagination: Christian Theology and the Culture of Pluralism.* New York: Crossroad Press, 1981.

Woloch, Nancy. *Women and the American Experience.* Boston: McGraw Hill, 2000.

Index

About the Contributors

Julie Balamut, former bookstore manager at the College of St. Catherine, received her B.S. and M.A. from the College of St. Catherine. She started working in the St. Catherine Bookstore the day she arrived on campus her freshman year. It was this student employment assignment that began a 32-year career in the bookstore industry.

Jane Lamm Carroll, associate professor of history and women's studies at St. Catherine University, received her B.A. from the College of St. Catherine and her Ph.D. from the University of Minnesota. She teaches courses in history and women's studies. Her research interests focus on the relationships between Native American women and Anglo-American men in 19th-century Minnesota.

Joanne Cavallaro, professor of English and women studies, received her B.A. from the University of California, Berkeley, her M.A. from San Francisco State University, and her Ph.D. from the University of Minnesota. She is currently chair of the English department at St. Catherine University, where she teaches courses in English and women's studies. She focuses her scholarly work on the intersection of language and power; her research interests include gender perspectives on politeness, indirectness, and language.

Deborah Churchill, assistant professor, liberal arts and sciences, St. Catherine University, received her A.A. from St. Mary's Junior College and B.A. and M.A. from the University of Minnesota. She has a background in nursing and educational psychology. She is interested in issues of access to higher education for students with a variety of backgrounds, including those with interrupted educational histories and challenges related to disability, language, motivation, finances, and other issues. Her focus is on developing curriculum, pedagogy, and intervention strategies to overcome these barriers.

Russell Connors (1949–2011) became professor of theology at St. Catherine University after receiving his B.A. from Borromeo Seminary College, his M.Div. from St. Mary Seminary, Graduate School of Theology, and his S.T.L., S.T.D. from Pontifical Lateran University, Academia Alfonsiana, Rome. His background was in Christian ethics, with special interests in conscience, moral discernment, and, more recently, the relation between aesthetic experience and moral experience.

Joyce K. Dahlberg, retired volunteer pastoral minister, received her B.A. from Hamline University and her M.A. and Pastoral Ministry Certificate from the College of St. Catherine. She has spent many years working in communications, including 25 years as a consultant. She is deeply influenced by Celtic spirituality and is currently writing a religious work.

Sharon Doherty, professor of women's studies and Director of the Abigail Quigley McCarthy Center for Women at St. Catherine University, received her B.A. from the University of Minnesota, Morris, and her M.A. and Ph.D. from the University of Minnesota, Twin Cities. Her research and teaching interests include race/class/gender and community, women's coalitions across differences, and transformations in higher education.

Cecilia Konchar Farr, professor of English and women's studies, received her B.A. from Slippery Rock University of Pennsylvania, her M.A. from Brigham Young University, and her Ph.D. from Michigan State University. She teaches, studies, and writes about modernism, American literature, feminist theory, reception theory, and the novel in contemporary U.S. culture. Her study of Oprah's Book Club, *Reading Oprah: How Oprah's Book Club Changed the Way America Reads*, was published by SUNY in 2004, followed by a collection, *The Oprah Affect: Critical Essays on Oprah's Book Club*, with co-editor Jaime Harker in 2008.

John Fleming, associate professor of occupational science and occupational therapy, received his B.A. from the University of Iowa and his M.O.T. from Western Michigan University. He has more than 25 years' experience in occupational therapy education and a clinical background in geriatrics and acute-care therapy. His research interests include the meaning and significance of occupation in story and historical contexts and cognitive therapies.

Lynne Gildensoph, professor of biology and women's studies, received her B.A. and M.A. from Rutgers University and Ph.D. from the University of Illinois, Urbana. She teaches a wide range of courses in biology and women's studies, from Foundations of Women's Studies to general biology and plant physiology to biology of women. She is the coauthor of a textbook, *Women's Biology and Health: A New Perspective*, a feminist look at women's health issues.

Sister Catherine Litecky, CSJ, professor emerita, received her B.A. from the College of St. Catherine, her M.S. from the University of Minnesota, and her M.A. from St. John's University. She began as a faculty member at the College of St. Catherine in 1950. Her long service to the College included serving as registrar, teaching biochemistry, and being one of the pioneer members of the Theology Department, where she taught for over 20 years.

Mary Lou Logsdon received her B.A. and M.A. from the College of St. Catherine. She practices spiritual direction in St Paul, Minnesota. She works with people exploring discernment questions, engaging with church and work concerns, healing from childhood abuse, or seeking an adult relationship with God.

Catherine Lupori, professor emerita, received her B.A. from the College of St. Benedict and her M.A. from the University of Minnesota. She has been fortunate in being able to combine her research interests in literature and women's education with her professional life. During her 40-some years as an educator, she followed her research interests in literature as a member of English departments in two women's colleges. Her conviction about the value of women's education prompted research interests in that area, culminating during the last years of her professional life with being Director of the Abigail Quigley McCarthy Center for Women.

Joan Mitchell, CSJ, publisher, Good Ground Press, received her B.A from the College of St. Catherine and her Ph.D. from Luther Seminary. She is a theologian and author of *Beyond Fear and Silence: A Feminist Reading of Mark*. Sister Joan has dedicated her life to the study and teaching of scripture and has published religious education materials for more than 30 years. She was elected to the leadership team of the Sisters of St. Joseph of Carondelet, St. Paul Province, in 2004. She is currently teaching scripture, leading parish retreats around the country, and writing.

Mary Alice Muellerleile received her B.A. from the College of St. Catherine, her J.D. from William Mitchell College of Law in St. Paul, Minnesota, and her Ph.D. from the University of Chicago. She taught English at the College of St. Catherine and was the founding director of the Weekend College Program. She went on to serve as the Vice President of Academic Affairs at Clarke College in Dubuque, Iowa; President of Holy Names College in Oakland, California; and Special Assistant to the President of Heritage University in Toppenish, Washington. She is currently a higher-education consultant. The novels of Jane Austen remain her research interest.

Thelma Obah, Director of O'Neill Center for Academic Development at St. Catherine University, received her B.A. and M.A. from the University of London and her Ph.D. from the University of Nigeria, Nsukka. She has spent more than 25 years teaching students in the classroom or working with them in Reading Clinics and Writing Centers on the fundamentals of academic literacy–reading comprehension, writing composition, and critical thinking and reasoning. She has taught in Jamaica, Canada, Nigeria, and the U.S. Her research interests include cross-cultural comprehension, text processing, and ESL writing.

Virginia Steinhagen, senior lecturer in German at the University of Minnesota, received her B.A. from the College of St. Catherine and her Ph.D. from the University of Minnesota. Her main interests are in pedagogy and in issues of multiculturalism and integration in Germany.

Thomas West, professor of theology at St. Catherine University, received his B.A. from the University of Minnesota, his M.A. from Marquette University, and his Ph.D. from the Graduate Theological Union, Berkeley. His early interest in Marxism and religion led to his book on the German Neo-Marxist Ernst Bloch. Since then, his research has been primarily concerned with the correlation between the human search for meaning and Christian faith, resulting in his book *Jesus and the Quest for Meaning*.